PAULA OLIVEIRA   GILNEU VIVAN

THE NEW FRONTIERS OF

SUPERVISION

The history of the **banking supervision model evolution in the Central Bank of Brazil** and its importance for the **assessment of financial stability**

(t.)

ISBN: 978-65-84821-67-5

Original title: *As Novas Fronteiras da Supervisão*

COVER AND ILLUSTRATION:
Arthur Camanho

Ccover photo:
Thaís Mallon

FINAL ARTWORK:
Victor Tagore

INTERVIEW LOGISTICS:
Ricardo Jiménez
Victor Salazar

TRANSCRIPTIONS:
Clara Medeiros Rizel Santana
Iassanã Seixas do Amaral Pereira Soares
Patrícia Seixas de Oliveira
Weslley João Marques de Oliveira

TEXT REVISION:
Clara Medeiros Rizel Santana
Weslley João Marques de Oliveira

SIG Qd. 8, Lt. 2356, Térreo, Brasília/DF
Fone: (61) 3032-5755 — (61) 98440-1100
contato@tagoreeditora.com.br
www.tagoreeditora.com.br

"The extensive databases and analytic capacity of the BCB are impressive.

At the time of the FSAP, the assessors were not aware of any other supervisory authority with such capability."

(IMF/FSAP - Brazil: Financial System Stability Assessment – November 2018)

To my sisters Patrícia and Iassanã and my husband Weslley, for their unconditional support for all my crazy ideas.

To our children and grandchildren, so that they enjoy living their own adventures.

Paula

To Ms Lourdes, for her example, to Sandra, for sharing the journey and to Pedro and João, for listening to my stories.

Gilneu

Table of Contents

BCB 13

CEMLA 16

ASBA 24

IREE 27

FOREWORD 30

INTRODUCTION 34

CHAPTER 1

Evolution of the supervisory process in the 20th century

1.1 INTRODUCTION 42

1.2 THE IMPACT OF CURRENCY STABILIZATION ON THE NATIONAL FINANCIAL SYSTEM – SFN (*SISTEMA FINANCEIRO NACIONAL*).. 46

1.3 STRUCTURE AND FUNCTIONING OF SUPERVISION 53

1.4 CONSOLIDATED GLOBAL INSPECTION - THE SUPERVISION X-RAY APPROACH.. 58

1.5 FIRST STEPS TOWARDS THE SUPERVISORY MODEL MODERNIZATION 62

1.6 THE USE OF GRANULAR DATA 68

Microdata from Credit Operations:..................................69

Microdata from Financial Market Operations (securities and

derivatives): 70

Payment System Data 74

1.7 ON-SITE AND OFF-SITE SUPERVISION...............76

CHAPTER 2

The Evolution of the Brazilian Supervisory Model

2.1 THE BCBS RECOMMENDATIONS FOR AN EFFECTIVE ONGOING SUPERVISORY APPROACH 82

2.2 THE IMPLEMENTATION OF THE ONGOING BANKING SUPERVISORY MODEL IN BRAZIL.........................85

2.3 MICRO-GROUNDED MACRO MONITORING PROCESS.......94

2.4 THE STRATEGIC AREA: PLANNING SUPERVISION 96

2.5 THE SUPERVISORY MODEL 103

2.6 STAFF CAPACITATION 106

2.7 THE TRANSPARENCY OF SUPERVISORY PROCEDURES ...109

CHAPTER 3

Micro Prudential Monitoring

3.1 THE OFF-SITE SUPERVISION IMPLEMENTATION..............114

Off-site activities based on financial statements' data:.............117

Off-site activities based on credit register data:......................119

Off-site activities based on trade repositories' data:.................124

Off-site activities based on payment system data: 132

3.2 MONITORING & SUPERVISION MODEL – A NEW MICRO PRUDENTIAL APPROACH.................................135

3.3 MONITORED ISSUES FRAMEWORK: A MAJOR STEP

TOWARDS INTEGRATING THE SUPERVISORY MODEL..... 140

CHAPTER 4

Information Management

4.1 TRAJECTORY OF INFORMATION MANAGEMENT AT THE BCB.. 148

4.2 FINES, A BAD STRATEGY TO ENSURE DATA QUALITY..... 157

4.3 APPROACHING DATA TO THE USERS 160

4.4 MULTIDIMENTIONAL TEAMS.. 161

4.5 LAW ON ACCESS TO PUBLIC INFORMATION - LAI (*LEI DE ACESSO À INFORMAÇÃO*) AND THE MANAGEMENT OF DEMANDS FOR INFORMATION 162

4.6 THE INCORPORATION OF DATA QUALITY IN THE MONITORED ISSUES FRAMEWORK................................ 168

CHAPTER 5

Supervision

5.1 THE IMPLEMENTATION OF A SUPERVISORY MODEL ON A CONTINUOUS BASIS... 174

5.2 SPECIALIZED TEAMS 179

5.3 SUPERVISION OF NON-BANKING FINANCIAL INSTITUTIONS 184

5.4 SUPERVISION OF MISCONDUCT 193

CHAPTER 6

Macro Prudential Monitoring

6.1 THE GLOBAL FINANCIAL CRISIS 202

6.2 THE PECULIAR APPROACH OF THE BRAZILIAN MACRO PRUDENTIAL MONITORING FRAMEWORK 208

6.3. THE EVOLUTION OF MACRO MONITORING PROCESSES 213

Credit risk macro monitoring: 216

Monitoring of derivatives, securities and funding market: 217

Monitoring of foreign exchange market: 218

Macro monitoring approach to financial statements information: ... 219

Systemic risk monitoring: 219

Step-in risk monitoring: 221

Alignment of working processes: 223

6.4 FINANCIAL STABILITY REPORT – REF (*RELATÓRIO DE ESTABILIDADE FINANCEIRA*) 231

6.5 FINANCIAL STABILITY COMMITTEE - COMEF (*COMITÊ DE ESTABILIDADE FINANCEIRA*) 235

CHAPTER 7

Suptech in Process

7.1 EXPANDING DATA COLLECTION BEYOND SUPERVISED ENTITIES 249

7.2 THE USE OF MACHINE LEARNING TECHNIQUES IN SUPERVISION AND ITS CHALLENGES 252

7.3 FINTECHS & SUPTECHS 257

7.4 CHALLENGES OF A GLOBAL ENVIRONMENT 260

7.5 CYBER RISK AND THE NATIONAL SIMULATION EXERCISE
   ON CYBER-SECURITY 266

EPILOGUE.. 270

AFTERWORD 274

THE INTERVIEWEES.. 279

APPENDIX 323

1. THE BRAZILIAN NATIONAL FINANCIAL SYSTEM FRAMEWORK
   323

3. BCB SUPERVISION FRAMEWORK 327

4. BCB'S ROLE TO ENSURE FINANCIAL STABILITY 332

GLOSSARY 334

BCB

This book describes the evolution of the supervisory model of financial institutions of the Banco Central do Brasil (BCB), from the 1990's structure focused on auditing the balance sheet of banks to the development of a macro and micro prudential supervision model with intensive use of microdata and technology solutions. My experience in the private sector, interacting with different supervisory bodies in Brazil and abroad, and then as the BCB Governor made clear the importance of a solid and efficient supervisory framework to ensure the stability of the financial system.

Over time, the process of structuring, redesigning and improving BCB's supervisory framework required the construction of a vast set of databases, the assembly of a data crossing and analysis structure, the teams' capacitation on the most varied techniques to transform data into information, and an in-depth analysis of the functioning of the various supervised business models. As a result, we have achieved a robust supervision model with great speed of adaptation and responses to events, even those not expected.

The importance of our supervision framework became evident, for example, when we developed the measures to mitigate the consequences of the Covid-19 pandemic. Among the various measures taken, the Guaranteed Financial Letter (LFG), collateralized by credit operations from the issuing bank's portfolio, was designed to provide liquidity assistance to financial institutions. The structure built by the supervision over time played a fundamental role not only to the measure's planning, by defining the characteristics of the credit operations that would be accepted as collateral, but also to its operationalization, by validating each credit operation from the collateral pool, before BCB took the bank's LFGs to grant liquidity.

The stress tests performed by BCB to measure the impacts of Covid-19 on the National Financial System (SFN) is another example of our macro prudential supervision capacity. In early May 2020, less than two months after the entry into force of the isolation measures in Brazil, our Financial Stability Report (REF) published the first estimates of the impacts that the pandemic could cause to the SFN. The BCB was one of the first central banks to make public estimates of the pandemic's impact at that time.

In the micro prudential perspective as well, we regularly monitor the estimates of expected losses individualized by institution and by credit modalities since 2021. This information will only be required from the financial system from 2025, according to the adoption of IRFS9 in Brazil.

The book presents testimonials from users and developers of processes and methodologies that serve as the basis for the analyses currently presented to the BCB Collegiate Board. Their narratives allow the reader to understand the great potential of the supervisory framework and the dynamics of its evolution over time.

I am sure that this framework will be fundamental to address the challenges that supervision will face. Some will come from the very technological progress that the financial system undergoes. In this environment, BCB has adopted a broad agenda of innovations. We have already implemented the PIX, innovations in currency, and we continue to move forward with Open Finance and the development of Real Digital, which will be the Brazilian CBDC. All these innovations will continue to bring more and more transformations to society and to the Brazilian Financial System, requiring that the BCB supervision continues to evolve to keep up with the changes.

At the global level, new advances in regulation and supervision are being demanded. The recent episodes of bankruptcy and distrust of banking institutions in the US and Europe have shown that in times of greater stress in this new technological environment, deposit redemptions are enhanced by the greater dissemination of information through social media and by the low cost at which people, with the use of technology, can transfer resources between institutions. It is critical that regulatory and supervisory frameworks take these new risks into account. In addition, there are risks that will increasingly require attention from supervision and the financial system as a whole, such as the climate risk and cyber risk. We have come a long way on this issue, but there is still much more to be done.

These are important challenges, but from all that I have seen, I believe that good steps have already been taken in the direction of overcoming them. And this book is an excellent record of those advances.

Roberto Campos Neto
Governor of the Banco Central do Brasil

CEMLA

Over the past 50 years, financial systems have evolved dramatically and, by extension, the supervision of financial systems as well. Some of the most salient mega trends that have transformed the financial sector are the rapid globalization, the growing complexity of the financial system, and the tremendous progress in information and communications technology. While all these developments have undoubtedly contributed to increase wealth and economic growth, the overarching task of supervisors is to understand and contain the risks they involve.

The globalization of financial markets and the subsequent increase in global supervisory arrangements has certainly shaped the advances in financial supervision in the last decades. Since the end of the Bretton Woods System, financial markets have integrated globally. Financial institutions expanded beyond national borders and became global players adapting to an overall globalizing world. Currency markets have grown, providing the gateways of international capital flows to local economies. Indeed, financial markets are so connected and mostly open today that investors operate on a global scale, which constitutes a Global Financial Cycle[1]. Keeping up with the globalization of financial markets and financial institutions is an ongoing challenge for supervisory authorities that are confined within the boundaries

---

1. See Rey and Miranda-Agrippino (2022).

of their jurisdictions. International coordination and cooperation of supervisory authorities worldwide are key to design an internationally harmonized regulatory framework and to address the complex political economy of financial institutions operating globally and being subjected to supervision across multiple jurisdictions, which, as in the case of banking resolution, often have conflicting interests.

It is against this backdrop that bilateral cooperation agreements between supervisory authorities have constantly increased over the last decades[2]. Supranational institutions, including the Center for Latin American Monetary Studies (CEMLA), were founded with the role to provide a platform for coordination and exchange of knowledge and to promote this cooperation. These initiatives had repercussions on the work and organisation of national supervisors. For instance, national supervisors had to find their place in the process of designing and adapting international rules in accordance with their domestic conditions. Especially, supervisory authorities in emerging markets had a steep learning curve on how to protect the domestic financial system from excessive volatility while allowing the benefits from foreign investment to be reaped[3].

But globalization has also gone hand in hand with a growing complexity in financial systems, mainly due to a proliferation with new instruments and institutions. This growing complexity is another major challenge that needs constant attention from financial supervisors. Since the 1990s, innovation sparked the creation of new financial products allowing for more and refined risk sharing. Derivative markets boomed and financial institutions' off-balance sheet exposures built up. While commercial banks have traditionally been the largest players in many financial markets, new intermediaries such as money market funds have gained

---

2. See Beck, Silva-Buston, and Wagner (2023).

3. See, for example, the evolution of the problem of "Original Sin" (Hausmann and Pani-zza; 2006) to "Original Sin Redux" (Bertaut, Bruno, and Shin; 2022).

importance. Most recently, financial stress has found its origin in non-bank financial intermediaries (NBFI)[4].

Financial institutions became more interconnected through risk-sharing agreements and reciprocal liquidity provision. Since many of these new financial contracts were initially settled over-the-counter (OTC), i.e., in bilateral arrangements that were not reported, authorities faced an everlasting process of updating and adapting the regulatory framework in order to ensure they would have the authority to monitor these markets and institutions. Moreover, supervisors developed new tools and methodologies so that they could assess the complex structures and exposures within increasingly interconnected financial systems.

Most of these developments reflect a third key challenge for supervisors, represented by the way technological progress transformed the society, including the economy and the financial system. Many of the aforementioned phenomena were only possible because of advances in data science, communications technology, and market infrastructures. The digitalization of financial market infrastructures has immensely accelerated the speed at which financial transactions are executed. Nowadays, contracts can be settled almost instantly and traders can exploit arbitrage opportunities that arise only within nano-seconds. While in the past, technologies were mainly facilitators of traditional finance, recent innovations pose more acute threats to it.

Financial contracts based on the blockchain technology and artificial intelligence have the potential to replace financial institutions or even the monetary system as we know it. Staying on top of innovations with high disruptive potential, puts an enormous pressure on supervisors to evaluate the risks correctly. Supervision, therefore, not only monitors the system in real time, but also needs to understand how it might evolve in the future. Technology itself has become an important input in by providing supervisors with prognostic tools and analysis. As technology has developed from

---

4. See Chapter 2 in the Global Financial Stability Report (IMF; 2023).

personal computers to big data, the supervisors' job has become increasingly analytical.

Amidst this environment of continuous change, the Great Financial Crisis unfolded and demonstrated new dimensions of risks underlying a globalized, complex, and technology-fuelled financial system. This crisis was a moment of catharsis for supervisory authorities. While supervision always operated under one unifying doctrine, namely to safeguard the functioning of financial markets and ensuring the resilience of financial institutions, it has undergone one marked paradigm change in the past decades: from microprudential supervision to macroprudential supervision.

The initial focus of supervisory attention was on individual financial institutions or markets. This mindset was driven by a bottom-up perspective. However, the Great Financial Crisis unraveled many shortcomings in this thinking and shifted the focus to systemic risk in its many facets: contagion, common exposures, systemically important institutions, and interconnectedness. Assessing and mitigating systemic risk required new types of methodologies to be incorporated in supervisors' policy toolkits. For example, network models can map complex contract relationships between market participants, thereby offering an understanding of interconnectedness of institutions and helping to identify those institutions that are critical for market functioning. Moreover, since the 2007-2009 crisis, macroprudential supervisors introduced and refined the use of stress tests in order to assess capital needs and potential contagion risks in hypothetical recession scenarios. These new tools illustrate the growing complexity of supervisors' functions and the need to permanently re-think supervisory approaches.

Overall, the shift towards a macroprudential perspective extended supervisory authority as well as the supervisory toolbox. Yet, it has not diminished the necessity for microprudential assessments since supervisors are still expected to detect common failings, mismanagement, and plain violation of law in individual firms by keeping a tight scrutiny of their everyday businesses.

Nevertheless, one of the greatest challenges for supervisory authorities remains to discern and understand fundamental shifts in the financial architecture at the time they arise. Only then, would they be able to devise the suitable means to counteract potential future risks to financial stability.

In a world increasingly reliant on large sources of micro-data, the aforementioned challenges for supervisory agencies necessarily depend on the development of comprehensive information systems including granular data, even beyond supervised financial institutions themselves.

Data is the key resource that enables supervisors to understand what is happening in financial markets and financial institutions. Most supervisory processes are data-driven, i.e., the supervisory authorities collect, store, access, and analyse data about financial markets and institutions. A timely access to data is crucial to inform judgements and justify policy decisions aimed at safeguarding the resilience of financial systems. Therefore, data is a cornerstone for fulfilling supervisory tasks. While IT innovations have facilitated supervisory activity, they have also made supervisory scrutiny more effective. The quality of supervision improves when more sophisticated methods and more granular data become available. The supervision of single institutions has evolved from an inspection of balance sheets and sporadic on-site talks with loan officers to detailed and comprehensive reporting on loan characteristics, even reaching the inspection of banks' internal risk models.

The ample references to information systems in this book illustrate the growing importance of microdata and give multiple examples of its use. In a context in which central banks rely on complex supervisory instruments that require being properly targeted, the use of granular data is key to achieve central banks' mandates and to obtain solid evidence-based feedback on central banks' supervisory actions. The development of sophisticated early warning systems at the Banco Central do Brasil referenced in the book and based on the intensive use of novel data sources is a good example of the strong link between a solid information system and a well-functioning and effective supervisory model.

An interesting case for the extension of central banks' information systems and for the incorporation of big data techniques is represented by the need for monitoring increasingly digitized financial markets. Financial markets' digitalization has left relevant economic activities and information channels outside the regulatory perimeter that allows public institutions to collect data. Moreover, the very nature of digitalization means that firms and individuals are producing themselves unprecedented amounts of data that remain stored online in the servers of firms with which they interact.

Against this backdrop, it is not surprising to see mounting evidence suggesting that the degree of interconnection between digital and traditional bank-based financial markets is creating relevant financial stability risks that require being assessed[5]. As a reaction to the need of adjusting to this new scenario and its associated data gaps, we are witnessing a rapid spread of novel statistical applications at central banks. The experience of the Banco Central do Brasil illustrated in the book is therefore of paramount importance for policymakers interested in understanding how solid information systems can be adapted to feed a supervisory model.

Relevant data gaps affect supervisory objectives in areas that are beyond challenges associated with markets' digitalization. A prominent example that the book emphasizes relates to data gaps affecting the assessment of climate-related financial risks. As the authors point out, these risks can be considered as borderless risks. This definition implies that they require a universe of novel data infrastructure that is not available in traditional data sources accessible to supervisors. Moreover, borderless risks can be also understood as those that can only be mitigated by a plethora of coordinated policy actions, certainly beyond the scope of supervisory mandates themselves.

---

5. See IMF (2022).

It is in the field of climate-related risks where supervisory authorities face their largest and more complex ongoing challenge. Current data gaps impair their ability to measure and trace financial sector's exposure to climate-related risks, affecting supervisors' capacity to implement new regulations that can moderate physical risks and boost countries' resilience to climate shocks. Certainly, these data gaps also affect supervisors' ability to evaluate their own policy actions and to promote an evidence-based approach to tackle the consequences of climate change and environmental degradation for financial systems. The book contributes to shed light on these pressing challenges by discussing how data collection efforts that go beyond supervised entities have contributed to bridge those gaps in Brazil.

While bridging data gaps by means of an intense use of non-traditional data sources offers multiple opportunities for central banks seeking to enrich their statistical frameworks, policymakers should be aware that these approaches also come together with demanding challenges. These include difficulties in creating an appropriate IT infrastructure and attracting highly-trained staff capable of enriching a supervisory model with new statistical models. Data protection and legal issues are also key to be considered, as the data storage in private firms can impose limits to large-scale data collection. Certainly, these concerns should promote a critical approach to discussions around the use of non-traditional data sources to bridge the data gaps that supervisory authorities face.

Banco Central do Brasil is among the most respected financial institutions in the Latin American region and the book, as an account of the evolution of its supervisory model, represents a key contribution to Latin America. The book provides a historic overview about the evolution of micro and macro prudential supervision in Brazil from the 1990s to today. This epoch spans several stress episodes, bank failures, and the experience from the Great Financial Crisis and Covid-19 crisis. Thus, it represents an unprecedented account of how an institution evolved and changed in order to cope with the challenges presented to supervisors in the last 30 years.

Building on the experience the authors have gathered in Brazil, the book highlights the growing and important role of technology and data for the implementation of an effective supervision of financial institutions. Supervisors can draw numerous lessons from the Brazilian experience, including the need to leverage their work on the latest technologies, such as big data and artificial intelligence. It is important for financial authorities to stay ahead of the curve and use the opportunities of technologies for supervisory purposes, commonly known as Suptech. They can not only facilitate the supervision process but also inspire new avenues of analyses.

Policymakers will find in this book a unique vantage point to learn from the experience of the Banco Central do Brasil in facing topical challenges. The authors' first-hand experience in developing innovative solutions and governance approaches to enhance the bank's supervisory strength gives the reader an excellent opportunity to understand the complexities involved in modern financial supervision and the challenges ahead, with implications for supervisors both in advanced and emerging market economies.

Manuel Ramos Francia
General Director of the Center for Latin American Monetary Studies (CEMLA)[6]

---

6. References

Beck, T., Silva-Buston, C. and W. Wagner (2023). The economics of supranational bank supervision, in: Journal of Financial and Quantitative Analysis, 58(1), pp. 324–351.

Bertaut, C., Bruno, V. and H. S. Shin (2022). Original sin redux. Mimeo, Bank of International Settlements.

Hausmann, R. and U. Panizza (2006). The Pain of Original Sin, in: Other People's Money: Debt denomination and financial instability in emerging market economies, ed. by Eichengreen, B. and Hausmann, R., Chicago: University of Chicago Press, pp. 13–47.

International Monetary Fund (2022). Global Financial Stability Report: Implications of the War in Ukraine. Washington, DC, April.

Rey, H. and S. Miranda-Agrippino (2022). Chapter 1 - The Global Financial Cycle, in: Handbook of International Economics Volume 6, ed. Gopinath, G., Helpman, E. and K. Rogoff, pp. 1–43.

ASBA

Financial institutions play a crucial role in any nation's economy. Their ability to provide essential financial services to individuals and businesses is crucial for economic growth and stability. However, their intrinsic characteristics and complex nature demands diligent regulation and supervision to ensure the stability of the financial system and safeguard against potential risks.

The globalization and interconnectedness of financial markets need the establishment of supranational institutions to coordinate and improve regulatory and supervisory practices. Organizations such as the Basel Committee on Banking Supervision have been instrumental in developing and promoting regulatory frameworks that enhance the resilience of financial institutions worldwide. These institutions emphasize the importance of coordination, recognizing that effective supervision requires a unified approach and the sharing of best practices among regulators and supervisors.

Within the Americas, the Association of Supervisors of Banks of the Americas (ASBA) was established to strengthen banking regulation and supervision in the region by training supervisors, fostering their cooperation and dialogue, and promoting the implementation of practices aligned with internationally recognized standards. ASBA has facilitated a continuous dialogue among its members, enabling them to improve their supervisory practices and navigate the ever-changing landscape of financial systems and banking regulation. The remarkable transformation of banking supervision in Brazil provides an excellent example to supervisors in the Americas of how supervisory institutions could use more granular data to address the challenges that all bank supervisors face.

In the case of Brazil, as well as in many other countries in the region, the banking supervision model primarily focused on monitoring banks' balance sheets and their compliance with capital and liquidity adequacy requirements. While this approach provided insights into the overall health of the banking sector, it lacked the granularity necessary to identify and address emerging risks in a timely manner.

Recognizing the need for more comprehensive and proactive supervision, the Central Bank of Brazil embarked on a transformative journey, embracing the power of microdata. By leveraging advanced technologies and data analytics, the Central Bank of Brazil now possesses the ability to analyze vast amounts of granular data from financial institutions enabling supervisors to detect early warning signals, identify potential vulnerabilities, and take preemptive measures to mitigate risks.

This book serves as a comprehensive exploration of the paradigm shift in Brazil's banking supervision model, emphasizing the pivotal role played by microdata. It delves into the theoretical foundations of banking supervision, the evolution of international regulatory frameworks, and the practical implementation of microdata-based supervision in Brazil. Through interviews with key stakeholders, and analysis of the impact of these transformations, this book sheds light on the journey undertaken by the Central Bank of Brazil and offers valuable insights for policymakers, regulators, and supervisors worldwide.

As readers embark on this journey through the pages that follow, the reader will gain a deeper understanding of how the use of microdata has revolutionized the field of banking supervision in Brazil. The stories within these chapters highlight the remarkable strides made in leveraging technology and data, the challenges encountered, the lessons learned, and the enduring importance of coordination, cooperation, and knowledge sharing among regulators and supervisors. Ultimately, this book aims to inspire and empower those responsible for financial stability and regulatory oversight to embrace the transformative potential of microdata in their jurisdictions, forging a path toward a more resilient and secure financial system for the benefit of all.

Pascual O'Dogherty
Secretary General of the Association of Supervisors of Banks of the Americas (ASBA)

IREE

The assertion that the Financial System is part of the Economic Order, as the responsible for promoting a balanced development of the country and for serving the interests of the community is not in vain.

When conceiving arts. 170 and 192 of the 1988 Brazilian Constitution[7], the legislators were clear about the relevance of banks, financial institutions and other regulated agents in the promotion of economic activity, business, full employment, the reduction of social and regional inequalities, and consumer protection, among other imperative principles and values for the democratic environment and life in society. Credit, payment services, deposits, and investments are just a few elements of this equation.

For this and other reasons, they conferred, in article 164, constitutional stature to the Central Bank and designated it a State institution destined to, among many other attributions, exercise the surveillance of the Financial System and the supervision of the entities that are part of it. Its competence scope, however, was gradually being expanded, supported by the increasing technical capacity of the Autarchy's staff. Today, it also reaches the infrastructures of the financial market, consortium administrators, payment institutions, and now even virtual asset service providers.

---

7. The new Constitution of the Federative Republic of Brazil was enacted on October 5, 1988. (https://www.stf.jus.br/arquivo/cms/legislacaoConstituicao/anexo/brazil_federal_constitution.pdf)

The so-called Supervision of the Financial System is one of the BCB's most relevant functions, essential to monitor the dynamics of a market permeated by risks of varied natures, to guide regulated institutions, identify weaknesses, determine corrective measures and intervene more drastically, if and when necessary, always with the aim of preserving the liquidity, solvency and soundness of institutions and the market itself. Supervision is, therefore, one of the main instruments to ensure the stability and efficiency of the Financial System, one of the objectives or 'mandates' of the now autonomous Central Bank.

For all those reasons, it is with great honor and satisfaction that IREE, the Institute for the Reform of State-Business Relations[8], supports and presents this book, which narrates the history of BCB's supervision, the evolution of its approach, its tools and its results. The book highlights the importance of Monitoring as a method of Supervision and the intensive use of microdata for an increasingly comprehensive assessment of the Financial System and of each regulated institution, as well, according to its profile, size and risks involved.

This book was written by public servants, who contributed to the supervision model evolution and helped to build many of the solutions used today by the Central Bank and other regulators. In addition, the text is filled with testimonies from other agents who effectively built the history of this relevant public function and went through intense challenges, such as domestic banking crises, the international financial crisis of 2007-2008 and the Covid-19 pandemic.

We, therefore, have in hands an authentic interpretation of the Financial System Supervision and, more than that, an accountability of all the efforts and advances made in recent decades, which have raised Brazil to the level of global reference in the matter, as

---

8. IREE is an independent organization whose mission is to promote democratic and pluralistic debate to improve the interaction between the public and private sectors in Brazil (www.iree.org.br).

proven by the most recent assessments performed by international organizations[9], testifying that we are prepared for the future.

This is also a conceptual, explanatory, exemplifying book, which made the effort to highlight principles, criteria, metrics and objectives. It is a work, therefore, that brings together the public and the private, which allows regulated institutions, economic agents, professionals and academics to understand how Supervision works and to seek maximum convergence, contributing to the formation of a well capitalized and sound ecosystem.

We congratulate Paula Oliveira and Gilneu Vivan for the initiative, for their dedicated research and for their contribution to the debate and to the history. Thus, we wish you all a great reading!

Walfrido Warde, Henrique Machado e Marcel Mascarenhas
President and directors of IREE, all lawyers

---

9. The FSB Peer Review of 2017 and the IMF/FSAP - Brazil: Financial System Stability Assessment, of – November 2018, exemplify the recognition of the high technical capacity of the BCB supervision. See the full report at https://www.fsb.org/wp-content/uploads/Brazil-peer-review-report.pdf (FSB) and https://www.imf.org/external/pubs/ft/scr/2012/cr12206.pdf (FSAP).

Foreword

When Paula invited me to tell the story of the development of Brazilian supervision, I wondered if we really had a story to tell. When you're deeply involved in a process, it's sometimes hard to realize how much and how they change over time.

At the end of the 1990s, Brazil went through a banking crisis that hit the largest public and private banks of the time. At that time, it had become clear the need to review how supervision operated. After deep changes, in 2009 Brazilian banking supervision had already been pointed out as one of the most efficient in the world. A lot had happened, changing not only the way our supervision operated, but the perception about the quality of its work. Yes, we had a story to tell.

As we progressed in the design of the book, reporting the facts from the perspective of an observer, it was possible to verify the dimensions of that evolution. Certainly, it has not developed in the direction, speed, or depth that each of us would like, as the path was a collective construction. It was a dynamic process, that step by step incorporated the contributions of many people, sometimes conflicting ones, to reach a new balance, and so on over time.

Personally, I have had the privilege of following all the evolution closely. Although I had worked at the BCB since 1994, I moved to Brasilia[10] in 1999, in order to collaborate with the construction of one of the work fronts that initiated the transformation of supervision.

The first major step in the review of our working processes was the change of focus. Instead of confronting the accounting documentation, an assessment process should be focused on the risk, on the viability of the institutions. To this end, we have developed new working methodologies and reorganized the supervision structure, dividing the teams between on-site and off-site, which was considered as a good practice by international organizations.

Although the division has allowed each team to develop itself towards its goal, it has also created a gray zone that resulted in various frictions between them. Sometimes, the conflicts provoked by the overlapping of tasks and responsibilities blurred the teams' and the managers' performances.

Among the developments, off-site teams started to use the large databases available for supervision in the working processes. Not only the accounting information, but detailed information of transactions with securities and derivatives, a data source not common in other jurisdictions. In Brazil, since last century the supervised institutions were required to keep detailed information of their operations with securities and derivatives in the registration and custody centers. It was also during this period that BCB initiated the construction of a credit operations information center.

As time went by, we could observe the off-site evolution to the use of data analysis as a supervisory tool and the development of an on-site supervision process increasingly focused on the risk and the viability of financial institutions. The synergy observed between these processes and the growing demands associated with financial stability in a macro prudential perspective has created the conditions for the evolution of the supervisory approach from the

---

10. Brasília is the capital of Brasil and where the BCB headquarter is located.

classic on-site & off-site structure to a monitoring and supervision model.

The new framework has not only mitigated ancient conflicts among on-site & off-site teams but has allowed for the development of an integrated micro and macro prudential monitoring process as well. Micro and macro processes interacted to understand events and consequences. At the supervision side, in turn, the focus on the risk and feasibility analysis allowed the supervisor an ongoing understanding of each financial institution's business model.

The evolution of the supervision model, however, did not follow a linear growth. Instead, there were long discussions, debates, and several back and forths to eliminate overlapping processes. Obviously, life is not always a bed of roses. To achieve long-term goals, it was necessary to face the challenges of the short deadlines, like the disagreements, the distractions, the needs for cultural change, the conjunctural problems, the lack of resources, the lack of staff... In fact, not all problems have been overcome, and they certainly have affected and conditioned the solutions found.

To achieve writing this book, we have carried out long research that involved not only the reading of several reports and publications, but almost 70 interviews. BCB governors, supervisory deputy-governors, representatives of the financial market, and colleagues who occupied different positions in all departments of supervision throughout this period have kindly shared their memories and experiences with us.

Thus, this book is not a 'case study', it is a 'case report', as we gave voice to various actors who have contributed to make the 'case' become 'history'. Throughout the chapters, citations from the interviewees allow the reader to experience the events, the challenges, the conflicts, the procrastinations, and the solutions we all have lived along those years: the steps taken, the comings and goings, and how the path was being built.

This is not a book about 'how to do supervision' or 'what should or should not be done'. Obviously, that's the background, but the core message regards the evolution of the working process, i.e., how the interactions, conflicts and technological evolution have conditioned the solutions found.

Finally, like our history, this work was also a collective construction. Without the precious collaboration of Clara, Weslley, Iassanã and Patrícia, our trajectory would have been much harder. They helped us to turn the nearly 80 hours of interviews into more than 500 pages of reports, to revise the various versions, and to raise data to illustrate the history. Obviously, the responsibility for all errors and omissions is entirely ours.

Gilneu Francisco Astolfi Vivan
Head of the Financial System Monitoring Department - Banco Central do Brasil

Introduction

The stabilization of the economy achieved with the Real Plan[11] in 1994 brought structural challenges for Brazilian banks. The loss of revenue due to the end of inflation evidenced management problems of their business models, which culminated in the collapse of large institutions, such as Banco Nacional and Banco Econômico.

At that time, the BCB supervision model was still focused on auditing the banks' balance sheets, which did not allow the identification in a timely manner of existing problems. However, an unusual event made supervisors awaken to modernity. And they went far beyond!

At first, supervision was split into a classic on-site and off-site model, although with a peculiarity: to structure the off-site activities, the teams went beyond the information reported by supervised institutions and started to collect daily data from financial operations carried out in the market and recorded in the trade repositories.

Years later, the on-site & off-site supervision model evolved to the Monitoring and Supervision (M&S) model, where monitoring routines focused on specific issues and reported to the supervisor any concern or irregularity, while the supervisor kept the on-site

---

11. The Real Plan was one of the most important economic stabilization plans in Brazil's history. Its purpose was to regulate inflation rates. See more information on Real Plan in Chapter 1.

tasks and the responsibility of assessing each financial institution, individually.

For monitoring, the change of focus, allied to the use of microdata, has favored the development of more comprehensive and intrusive monitoring tools, and has also settled the basis to the birth of the macro prudential monitoring processes.

In 2008, the great financial crisis definitely placed the macro prudential perspective on the financial stability agenda. As macro monitoring was 'micro grounded', i.e., structured in the same sources of micro monitoring processes, it could develop more accurate and timely models for the analysis of vulnerabilities, and for the assessment of contagion effects among the financial system and the economic sector, as well.

For supervision, the new model allowed the structuring of units responsible for the implementation of a continuous supervision process and proportional to the systemic relevance of the institutions, extending the supervisor's attention to all financial segments and to customer issues, such as activities to assess the combat money laundering and terrorist financing in the financial market.

Along the years, Improvements to the M&S model have followed advances in technology, and data access went beyond the scope of supervision. Investments in data science training and a new solution of big data permitted the development of tools with the use of machine learning technologies, giving a leap in efficiency and productivity to the supervision and the monitoring of micro and macro prudential processes, as well as consolidating the Brazilian model as a SupTech.

Certainly, the challenges, conflicts, restrictions and constraints that led the BCB to achieve the current supervisory model were not exclusive to Brazilian supervision. The purpose of writing its story, in addition to the value as a historic record, is to inspire readers who seek solutions to challenges similar to those faced by the BCB in its trajectory, whether they are in national or international organizations directly involved on activities of central bank, financial supervision or financial market, or acting in the area of regulation or supervision in general.

Chapter 1 presents the trajectory of the BCB supervision along the twentieth century. It describes how the banking crisis resulting from the stabilization of the Brazilian currency in the mid-1990s provoked the replacement of an approach focused on the auditing of financial statements for a supervision model focused on risks. The chapter highlights the first steps towards the modernization of the supervision model: an intrusive and comprehensive approach to perform on-site inspections, the Consolidated Global Inspection (IGC), and the use of microdata since the early stages of the off-site supervision processes.

Chapter 2 explains the rationale behind the transformation of the classic on-site and off-site supervision model into the current Monitoring & Supervision model (M&S), as well as the reasons for the symbiosis between micro and macro prudential monitoring in Brazil. The chapter also highlights the importance of a strategic infrastructure to support an integrated and effective model of supervision.

Chapter 3 provides details on the scope of micro prudential monitoring activities, as it describes its main microdata-intensive processes and tools. It also explains why the structuring of the micro prudential monitoring process in the form of Monitored Issues allowed a leap in the evolution of the Brazilian supervision model.

Information management in the BCB is the theme of Chapter 4. In this chapter, the book's scope is extended beyond the boundaries of the supervision perimeter to highlight the importance of an adequate model for information management in an organization. In the case of the BCB, the supervisory area has played a key role in the creation of the current model, which was awarded internationally in 2018. The chapter also highlights the importance of data quality processes being designed as supervisory activities in Brazil and, regarding transparency issues, it highlights how the enactment of the Law on Access to Public Information (LAI) in Brazil has affected the prudential monitoring processes.

Chapter 5 describes the trajectory of the 'Supervision' activities of the M&S model (the former on-site supervision) and the development of the supervision process on a continuous basis. It also presents the allocation of supervision activities into three different departments, as a strategy to optimize its workforce not only proportionally to the systemic importance of the supervised entities (banking vs. non-banking institutions), but to adequately address issues related to compliance, consumer, fraud, money laundering and combating the financing of terrorism, as well. The innovations implemented for the supervision of non-bank financial institutions and credit unions in large-scale are also a prominent topic in this chapter.

Chapter 6 details the activities of the macro prudential monitoring model and its importance in the management of financial stability in Brazil: the peculiar Brazilian macro prudential monitoring model, micro-based on supervisory databases and tools, allows a more intrusive and accurate performance in the identification and measurement of vulnerabilities of the financial system. The chapter describes the involvement of the supervisory area in the trajectory for the structuring of a financial stability framework at the BCB, as well as its participation in relevant pillars of the process, such as the Financial Stability Report (REF) and the Financial Stability Committee (Comef). The chapter also presents the testimony of then-Governor Henrique Meirelles regarding BCB's strategies and actions to mitigate the effects of the great financial crisis of 2007-2008.

Finally, the challenges for the use of machine learning for supervisory purposes, as well as the new risks to the financial system arising from externalities that affect the planet as a whole, such as climate risk and cyber risk, are addressed in Chapter 7. The chapter also discusses how the expansion of data collection beyond the boundaries of supervised entities has enabled the cross-referencing of data and the expansion of micro and macro prudential analyses' capacity.

For those readers not familiar with the Brazilian financial system environment or the BCB Framework, it is recommended to consult the Appendix before starting to read the book. It presents some general information about the National Financial System composition, its main participants, and respective roles. It also comprehends information on the BCB organization framework, the scope of financial entities under its umbrella and a few basic explanations on the supervision infrastructure and responsibilities. That information will certainly help the reader to better understand the book's context.

The book was developed based on the testimony of people who experienced entirely or partially the transformation process of Brazilian supervision. The authors have counted with the support of CEMLA to conduct almost 80 hours of interviews with representatives of the BCB and the Brazilian financial market, as well. The initial proposal of interviewing about 15 people in three months was gradually evolving, as each interviewee suggested new names for the interviews. As a result, at the end of 15 months, a total of 66 testimonies from governors (Arminio Fraga, Henrique Meirelles, Alexandre Tombini and Ilan Goldfajn), deputy governors and consultants for the supervisory board, Comef secretaries, heads of departments, deputy heads, heads of division, advisors, coordinators and analysts of the supervision, regulation and IT areas, as well as representatives of banking entities and financial market infrastructures, allowed the construction of this book in a wealth of details, curiosities and emotions never recorded in themes of this nature.

The testimonies of the interviewees along the whole text allow the reader to share the joys, anxieties, uncertainties and hopes experienced by them in each challenge faced and goal achieved. The narrative provides an easy, exciting and accessible reading experience for all, which invites the reader to extrapolate the metaphor of the supervisory environment, to apply its message in diverse spheres of his/her professional and personal life.

Enjoy reading the book!

CHAPTER 1

Evolution of the supervisory process in the 20th century

"The big turn was the stabilization of the economy!"

(Cláudio Mauch)

This chapter presents the trajectory of the BCB supervision model along the twentieth century. It describes how the banking crisis resulting from the stabilization of the Brazilian currency in the mid-1990s provoked the replacement of an approach focused on the auditing of financial statements for a model focused on risks. The chapter highlights the first steps towards modernization: the implementation of an intrusive and comprehensive approach to perform on-site inspections, the Consolidated Global Inspection (IGC), and the use of microdata since the early stages of the off-site supervision processes.

1.1 INTRODUCTION

In Brazil, the functions of monetary authority and banking supervision were initially performed by Banco do Brasil. Only in 1945, President Getúlio Vargas[12] established the first Brazilian monetary authority, the Superintendence of Currency and Credit - Sumoc (*Superintendência da Moeda e do Crédito*)[13]. At the time, it was understood that an intermediate stage was necessary before the creation of a central bank[14], a fact that was only achieved on March 15, 1965[15].

> "Sumoc played a decisive role in the Brazilian economy for almost twenty years, until the reform of the Financial System in 1964. The economic situation was challenging, marked by the complexity of the post-war period, in which the international flow of resources prioritized the reconstruction of the affected countries. In this context, Sumoc was driven by the objective of making the Brazilian economic system more stable and better structured, facilitating internal and external financial relations.
>
> By the end of its existence, Sumoc had fulfilled its mission well. The staff was technically prepared to run an institution with many of the typical activities of a central bank. Law No. 4,595/1964 transformed Sumoc into the Central Bank of Brazil." (Sumoc history, Banco Central do Brasil[16])

---

12. Getúlio Dornelles Vargas was the president of Brazil, from 1930 to 1945 and from 1951 to 1954.

13. Sumoc was created by Decree-Law No. 7,293, of February 2, 1945. It was directly subordinated to the Minister of Finance.

14. Octavio Gouvêa de Bulhões proposed the creation of Sumoc in 1939.

15. The initial staff of the BCB was formed by employees from the extinct Sumoc and Banco do Brasil. Only in 1973, the BCB promoted its first tender, hiring more than 1,000 people. Along the years, BCB continued to improve its workforce, mainly in the supervision area, with specific tenders for auditors in 1977 and 1978.

16. https://www.bcb.gov.br/acessoinformacao/sumoc.

Figure: Current normative and supervisory structure of the National Financial System (SFN)

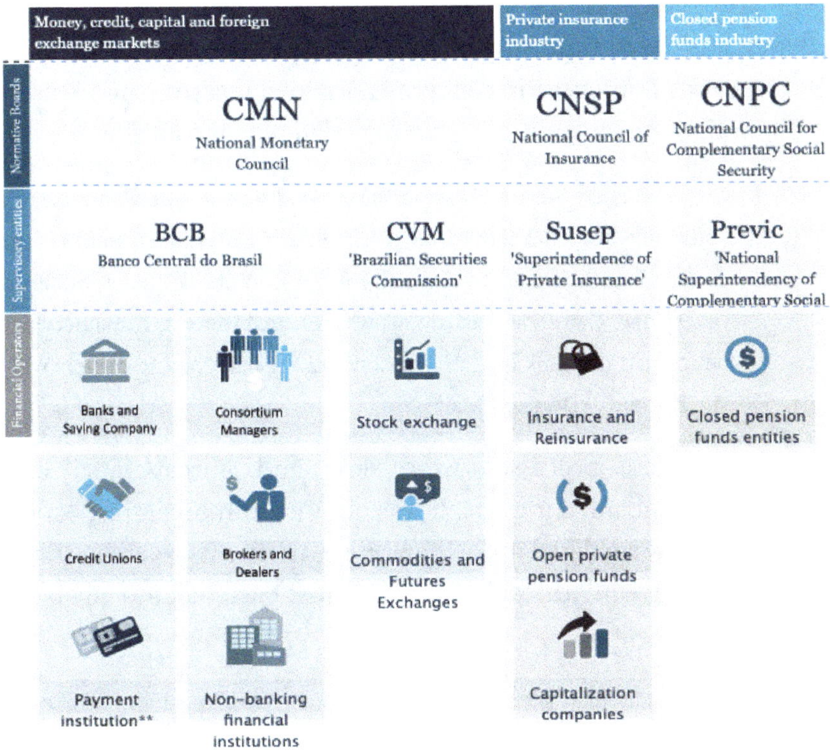

Money, credit, capital and foreign exchange markets			Private insurance industry	Closed pension funds industry
Normative Boards				
CMN National Monetary Council			**CNSP** National Council of Insurance	**CNPC** National Council for Complementary Social Security
Supervisory entities				
BCB Banco Central do Brasil	**CVM** 'Brazilian Securities Commission'		**Susep** 'Superintendence of Private Insurance'	**Previc** 'National Superintendency of Complementary Social
Financial Operators				
Banks and Saving Company · Consortium Managers	Stock exchange		Insurance and Reinsurance	Closed pension funds entities
Credit Unions · Brokers and Dealers	Commodities and Futures Exchanges		Open private pension funds	
Payment institution** · Non–banking financial institutions			Capitalization companies	

* There may be shared regulatory competence with the CVM, depending on its activities.
** The payment institutions are not within the SFN, but are regulated and supervised by the CMN and the Banco Central do Brasil.

Source: Banco Central do Brasil - https://www.bcb.gov.br/en/financialstability/nationalfinancialsystem

A supervisory activity had been present in the structure of the Brazilian monetary authority since before the existence of the Banco Central do Brasil (BCB); however, the Supervisory Board - Difis (*Diretoria de Supervisão*) was only created as a unit at the Board of Governors on March 16, 1985[17]. Previously, capital market supervision and banking supervision were carried out by different areas within the BCB framework. In terms of supervisory approach, however, both adopted the same police-like procedures, focused on

---

17. The following link summarizes the main organizational changes in the BCB's Board of Governors framework along the time: https://www.BC.gov.br/content/config/Documents/sintese_mud_estrutura_en.pdf.

the investigation of possible irregularities committed by supervised institutions.

The supervisor's performance as 'custos legis'[18] was perpetuated over time. In the mid-1980s, even after 20 years of BCB creation, supervision concerns remained reactive and focused on investigating irregularities, mainly related to accounting issues.

> "There were lockers on the ground floor of the Central Bank buildings for communication with supervised entities. Banks used to send a messenger to the Central Bank to check correspondence every day. There was no dialogue with the institutions. The supervisor informed the bank his/her decision and the bank had to comply with it. The end." (Donizeti Maia)

The work processes were slow and bureaucratic, and sometimes concluded too late. It was not uncommon an inspection letter[19] being formalized more than one year after its reference date, charging for irregularities that, for the most part, had already been overcome.

> "It may seem absurd today, but it was common to close a supervision proceeding with a standard order like: 'Due to the time elapsed without manifestation, we are closing the present case', or 'In view of a new inspection carried out in [date], we propose the closing of this case.'" (Osvaldo Watanabe)

The 1990s came with a strong expansion of the universe of institutions under the BCB's supervision. The extinction of the Credit Union National Bank - BNCC[20] (*Banco Nacional de Crédito Cooperativo*) by President Collor[21] provoked greater attention to the supervision of credit unions, which at the time included about 500

---

18. Surveyor of the law.
19. An inspection letter was the concluding document of an inspection work. It contained the supervisor's main findings, as well as eventual penalties applied to the institution.
20. The BNCC was established in 1951 with the aim of ensuring assistance and financial support to credit.
21. Fernando Affonso Collor de Mello was president of Brazil from 1990 to 1992.

institutions. In 1991, the supervision of consortia[22] was transferred from the Internal Revenue Service to BCB[23], which represented an increase of about 500 institutions in the supervised entities universe. Years earlier, the supervision of rural credit operations had already been transferred to the supervisory area. In addition, there were many problems in other types of institutions, such as finance companies[24], brokers and dealers.[25.]

Supervisory staff was composed of 840 employees, with the responsibility of supervising different types of institutions and subjects. In this way, it reached the great Brazilian banking crisis of 1995[26] with about 80% of its staff allocated in activities other than bank supervision.

---

22. Consortium is the meeting of natural and legal persons in groups, with pre-defined-duration and number of quotas, with the purpose of providing resources to its members, in an isonomic way, to acquire goods or services, through self-financing. The consortium administrator is the legal entity service provider with main social purpose aimed at the administration of consortium groups, constituted in the form of a limited company or corporation. (https://www.bcb.gov.br/content/cidadaniafinanceira/documentos_cidadania/Cartilha_Migrantes_Refugiados/cartilha_BC_INGLES.pdf)

23. On December 20th, 1971, Law No. 5,768 assigned the attributions of consortia authorization, supervision and regulation to the Ministry of Finance (Internal Revenue Service Secretariat). On March 1st, 1991, Article 33 of Law No. 8,177 transferred such responsibilities to the BCB.

24. The Credit, Finance and Investment Companies (SCFIs) – also known as finance companies – are private non-banking financial institutions that provide funding for the acquisition of goods, services and working capital. Several SCFIs operate as financial arm of commercial or industrial corporations – such as department stores and vehicle assemblers – and concentrate their operations on the financing of their own products. (https://www.bcb.gov.br/en/financialstability/creditfinance)

25. Securities brokers (CTVM) and securities dealers (DTVM) operate in the financial and capital markets and in the foreign exchange market mediating the trading of securities among investors and policyholders. The Joint Decision (BCB and CVM) 17/2009 authorized dealers to operate directly in the environments and trading systems of the organized stock exchange markets, which eliminated the main difference between brokers and dealers, who today can carry out virtually the same operations.

26. In 1994, the monetary stability achieved in Brazil imposed the challenge of restructuring the regulatory base of the financial system, then characterized by significant participation of state banks, inflationary gains, lack of diversity of financial instruments, deficiency in risk controls and limited competitiveness. Challenges were even greater because of serious liquidity problems and the detection of accounting fraud in large Brazilian banks between 1995 and 1996, which generated a serious banking crisis. (https://www.bcb.gov.br/conteudo/home-ptbr/TextosApresentacoes/Apresentação%20Universidade%20de%20Lisboa%20Final-Limpa%20(2).pdf)

1.2 THE IMPACT OF CURRENCY STABILIZATION ON THE NATIONAL FINANCIAL SYSTEM – SFN (*SISTEMA FINANCEIRO NACIONAL*)

For many years, Brazillians lived in a hyperinflationary environment. During the 1980s and early 1990s, several government initiatives popularly known as 'economic plans' were implemented as an attempt to solve the problem. The first one was the Cruzado Plan, in February 1986, whose main measures involved price and wage freezing, as well as cutting three zeros in the currency, which changed its denomination from 'Cruzeiro' to 'Cruzado'. Despite efforts, the plan was ineffective in curbing inflation, and in the same year, the government launched Cruzado Plan II, reinforcing restrictive measures, although still with no lasting results.

The runaway devaluations of the currency continued, always combated by economic plans: Bresser[27] (1987), Verão[28] (1989) and Collor[29] (1990), the most traumatic for the population because it came accompanied by the confiscation of savings. Each new attempt to reduce inflation was accompanied by 'the cut of zeros', price freezes, wage triggers, indexers and confiscation.

---

27. Price and wage freeze for 90 days.
28. Price and wage freeze, as well as the creation of a new currency, the Cruzado Novo (NCz$).
29. Replacement of the NCz$ by the Cruzeiro (Cr$), confiscation and freezing for 18 months of savings and amounts invested in excess of NCz$50,000 (USD 1,592.00).

Figure: Brazilian Currencies in the Inflationary Period (1986 - 1994)

Juscelino Kubitschek Cz$ 100,00

Cecília Meireles NCz$ 100,00

Cecília Meireles Cr$ 100,00

Feb-86
Cruzado Plan
Cruzado (Cz$)
Cz$ 1,00 = Cr$ 1.000,00

Jan-89
Summer Plan
Cruzado Novo (NCz$)
NCz$ 1,00 = Cz$ 1.000,00

Mar-90
New Brazil Plan (Collor Plan)
Cruzeiro (Cr$)
Cr$ 1,00 = NCz$ 1,00

Anísio Teixeira CR$ 1.000,00

Aug-93
Itamar Plan
Cruzeiro Real (CR$)
CR$ 1,00 = Cr$ 1.000,00

Jul-94
Real Plan
Real (R$)
R$ 1,00 = CR$ 2.750,00

Source:Banco Central do Brasil • https://www.bcb.gov.br/cedulasemoedas/cedulasemitidas

Despite the various attempts, unfortunately, each of these plans had loopholes: a rule was created, and exceptions followed. Most of the time, though, the exception ended up becoming greater than the rule. As a result, the price freezing provoked excess liquidity and then inflation skyrocketed again.

On June 1st, 1994, the Real Plan brought the long-awaited economic stability to the country. After a decade of hyperinflation, where the currency had 6 different names and suffered a cumulative cut of 12 zeros, Brazilians were finally able to stop making supermarket purchases for the entire month on the payday. And to crown the supreme happiness of the nation, Brazil won the World Cup for the fourth time in the following month, after 24 years of the previous title! Those were good times...

Figure: Brazilian Inflation During the Economic Plans' Period

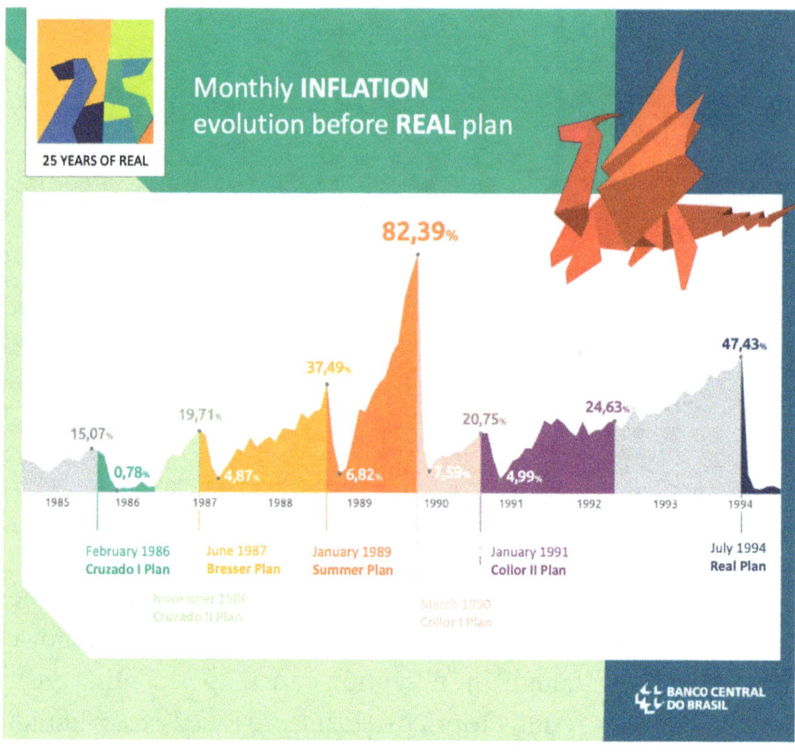

Source: Banco Central do Brasil. https://www.bcb.gov.br/detalhenoticia/355/noticia

"It was very complicated to explain the Brazilian currency to foreigners. In 1996, I spent 1 month studying German in a small village in the south of Germany. On the last day of class, each student had to give a 10-minute presentation about their country. The class was basically made up of young US Americans, with the exception of a French lady, a young man from Poland and myself. I was quite simple in my presentation, as my vocabulary was very restricted. At the end of my speech, the Polish guy raised his arm and asked: 'Brazil has recently come out of a long period of hyperinflation and has stabilized the currency. How did you do that?'

Everyone turned their eyes to me. I was in shock. He wanted me to explain the Real Plan in GERMAN?????? When my soul came back to my body, I started by reporting the succession of economic plans and the various cuts in currency values. When saying that 3 zeros were cut from the currency, an US young lady shouted in disbelief: 'You mean if I had 1000 dollars in the bank, the next day I would only have 1 dollar?', to which I replied: 'Well, our currency is not exactly the dollar, but yes, that's it'. The uproar was instantaneous. It was useless to clarify that something that used to cost $1 in a short time was worth $1000. They didn't have that concept and couldn't believe that something like this was possible in such a short period. Everyone was talking at the same time, quite annoyed. The Polish guy gave up on having any dialogue amid all that confusion and left. What a relief!" (Paula Oliveira)

The main revenue of banks during the inflationary period was through floating[30]. The government, for example, did not pay fees for banking services, but would keep the money collected from taxes in demand deposits account for 15 to 20 days, which would be equivalent to a fee of 30% of the deposited amount, according to the overnight rate practiced at that time. The currency stabilization provoked by the Real Plan eliminated this sort of income, which led banks to seek for profits in more classic sources such as service fees and credit operations. However, an adequate credit risk management culture had not yet been developed.

In fact, inflation had covered up serious management and performance problems in both private and public banks[31]. The stability of the currency gave transparency to the figures, aggravating the situation. In addition, state banks also struggled with strong political pressure[32], which often led them to legal and regulatory non-compliance.

---

30. Floating is the remuneration that the bank received overnight for the money collected but not passed on to the customer for a period, as contracted.

31. Public banks have also been heavily affected by delinquency problems on a significant portion of their credit portfolios.

32. For example, regulation established that the opening of branches should be authorized by the BCB. However, even if a certain state bank had its request denied, the governor would open the branches promised to his voters. Of a more serious nature, Law 7.492/ 1986 had declared it a crime for a bank to lend to its controllers. However, to fulfill campaign promises, the governor would create a public building company to carry out constructions (like a road or a hospital, for example) funded by loans granted from the state

> "In March 1995, banks had the highest historic level of non-performing loans recognized on the balance sheet!" (Cláudio Mauch)

Banco Econômico was the first large bank to whom BCB decreed intervention[33] (1995). Then, Banco Nacional[34] and Banco Bamerindus[35] went through similar process. In a short period, three of the seven largest private banks underwent bankruptcy.

> "For some time, Banco Nacional had been recognizing revenue from non-existent credit operations, Banco Econômico was facing shortfalls in provisions and issues related to operations in tax havens, and Bamerindus had an investment in a cellulose company that was a financial drain. These three banks were bankrupt." (Sidney Marques)

> "Unrecognized credit losses were the main problem. Banks rolled over operations with a high risk of delinquency and did not make provisions according to the level of risk they represented. The company went bankrupt, became insolvent, did not pay, and the bank continued to rollover the loans. In the end, the bank's equity had been consumed by bad loans." (Henrique Meirelles)

In response, the government implemented two programs, the Program to Stimulate the Restructuring and Strengthening of the National Financial System - PROER (*Programa de Estímulo à Reestruturação e ao Fortalecimento do Sistema Financeiro Nacional*)[36] and the Program to Reduce the Presence of the Public Sector in Financial Activities - PROES (*Programa de Incentivo à Redução da Presença do Setor Público na Atividade Financeira*)[37],

---

bank to the company. Normally, the company didn't honor these loans.

33. An intervention occurs when the BCB suspends the mandate of the failing bank's directors and members of any body created by the bank's statutes, and nominates an intervener to replace them, with the aim of avoiding its extrajudicial resolution.

34. Banco Nacional was taken over by Unibanco in 1995.

35. Banco Bamerindus was partially acquired by HSBC in 1997.

36. PROER consisted of a 'good bank & bad bank' solution for private banks, via BCB. The 'good' part was sold to interested banks and the 'bad' part went into liquidation. In this design, buyers took over assets and liabilities and the branch network.

37. PROES consisted of lines of financing from the federal government to the states, so that they could adopt the following alternatives in relation to their financial institutions: extinction, privatization, transformation into a development agency, acquisition of control

aiming for a market solution for private banks in difficulties and the reduction of the activities of state public banks, respectively. A program for restructuring and strengthening Federal Government Banks was also implemented, focusing on strengthening the two largest public banks, Banco do Brasil and CAIXA[38].

> "PROER avoided what would be the biggest banking crisis in Latin America and perhaps in the world, without the use of public money. Everything was accompanied by a change in regulation and in the supervisory approach." (Cláudio Mauch)

Figure: Mergers and Acquisitions under PROER

PROER	Acquiring Bank	
Acquired Bank	Domestic Bank	Foreign Bank
Large Bank	3	1
Medium and Small Bank	4	0
Total	7	1

Source:Banco Central do Brasil/Geraldo Villar Sampaio Maia, Nota Técnica n.38 'Bank Restructuring in Brazil: The PROER Case' https://www.bcb.gov.br/content/publicacoes/notastecnicas/2003nt38ReestrutBancBrasilp.pdf

> "The financial support strategy that made PROER viable was designed on the night of the Real Plan's launch. After the ceremony, Alkimar Moura[39] and I proposed to Governor Malan[40] Circulars and Resolutions' drafts increasing the banks' reserve requirements with a liquidity shortage effect similar to the Collor Plan's, but without affecting anyone's rights. Although it wasn't designed for that, it ended up being PROER's funding source." (Cláudio Mauch)

---

by the federal government or restructuring.

38. The SFN restructuring process followed the logic of crisis resolution, i.e., a decreasing sequence of risks to the financial stability: first, private banks, starting by the systemic ones; second, the state banks and, lastly, the federal banks. During this process, several non-systemic private banks went into liquidation too.

39. BCB Deputy Governor for Monetary Policy from 1994 to 1997.

40. Pedro Malan was the BCB Governor from September/1993 to December/1994.

Figure: Destination of Financial Institutions in the Scope of PROES

Financial Iinstitutions in the Scope of PROES

Category	Value
Privatised by the State Government	24
Privatised by the Federal Government	17
Transformed into a Development Agency	16
Terminated	14
Sanitized	7

Source: Banco Central do Brasil/Cleofas Salviano Júnior, 'State Banks: from Critical Problems to PROES' https://www.bcb.gov.br/htms/public/BancosEstaduais/livro_bancos_estaduais.pdf

"It is important to note that PROES was not intended to clean up only state banks, but also state government debts. In order to join the program, the states committed themselves to stop issuing securities debt, which has closed a drain hole of public resources." (Sidney Marques)

The economic stability promoted by the Real Plan provoked the interest of foreign banks to come to Brazil. Coincidentally, BCB was looking for buyers for the troubled state banks, as a strategy for solving the structural problems of the financial system. Thus, foreign banks came to Brazil through the acquisition of state banks in privatization auctions.

"The arrival of foreign banks in Brazil was a great opportunity. They disputed banks that needed to be liquidated. We saved half of the resources designed for PROES' implementation." (Cláudio Mauch)

The crisis provoked a relevant change in the SFN geographic distribution. There was a huge concentration of the financial market in São Paulo, as the largest private banks, mainly Bradesco and Itaú, were the major buyers. States that used to own several public banks were left with none or only one.

Figure: Geographic Distribution* of Banking Institutions and Conglomerates in 1994 and 2004 (number of institutions and % Total Assets)

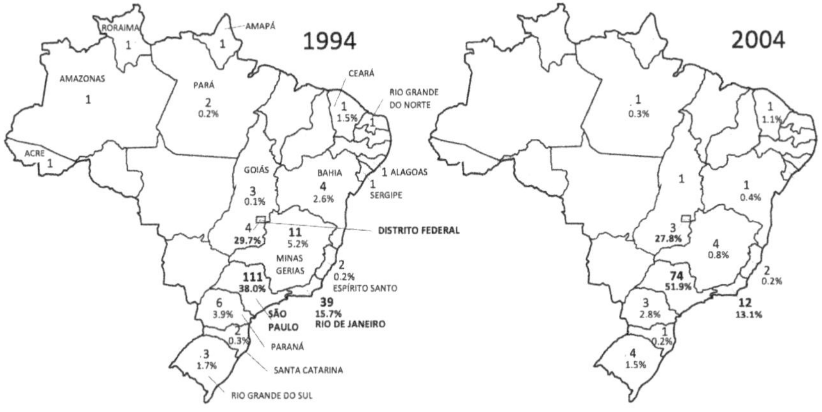

Total Assets below 0,05% are not represented in the figure.

(*) Geographic location of the bank's/conglomerate's head offices

Source:Banco Central do Brasil - IF.Data https://www3.bcb.gov.br/ifdata/

1.3 STRUCTURE AND FUNCTIONING OF SUPERVISION

In the early 1990s, the BCB's geographical distribution consisted of a head office in Brasília and 10 Regional Branches spread across the country[41]. The supervisory teams were located in those branches and were responsible for supervising the banks whose head offices belonged to their supervisory perimeter.

---

41. In 1999, the 10 Regional Branches gave way to 9 Regional Administrative and Technical Management offices (the Regional Branch in Brasília was extinguished), physically located in the extinct Regional Branches' buildings. BCB headquarters remained in Brasília. The Regional Offices were responsible to manage the circulation of banknotes and coins, study the regional financial environment supervise financial institutions and provide more direct assistance to citizens.

Figure: BCB Regional Framework in 1990

DEBEL - Regional Office in Belém (capital of the state of Pará)

DEBHO - Regional Office in Belo Horizonte (capital of the state of Minas Gerais)

DEBRA - Regional Office in Brasília (capital of Brazil)

DECUR - Regional Office in Curitiba (capital of the state of Paraná)

DEFOR - Regional Office in Fortaleza (capital of the state of Ceará)

DEPAL - Regional Office in Porto Alegre (capital of the state of Rio Grande do Sul)

DEREC - Regional Office in Recife (capital of the state of Pernambuco)

DERJA - Regional Office in Rio de Janeiro (capital of the state of Rio de Janeiro)

DESAL - Regional Office in Salvador (capital of the state of Bahia)

DESPA - Regional Office in São Paulo (capital of the state of São Paulo)

Source:Banco Central do Brasil

Each Regional Manager was responsible for the BCB's activities carried out in his/her branch, including supervisory tasks, and reported directly to the BCB Governor. Although the regional supervisory teams were formally subordinated to the Supervision Department - Defis (*Departamento de Fiscalização*) headquartered in Brasília, operationally, the command of the supervisory process was in the hands of the Regional Managers, which conducted the work according to his/her own priorities and methodologies.

Inspection activities were planned and conducted by the regional supervisory teams. They were autonomous in deciding what to do and when to do it. The lack of a centralized management resulted in inefficiency, as it did not allow for agenda prioritization nor the standardization of routines and procedures among supervisory teams.

> "The supervisor decided his/her activities, by his/her feeling, taking into account the history of the institutions and the time since the last inspection. Then, the agenda was submitted to Defis head office for approval." (Harold Espinola)

In some cases, one single team was responsible for all institutions belonging to the same peer, such as the consortium supervisory team or for a specific product, like the team responsible for supervising the rural credit portfolio of all institutions, for example.

> "We used to check the collateral of rural credit operations 'in loco'. Once, we went to a place called 'Cruel do Jussara'. We chose which credit operation we wanted to verify: 'I want to go to this customer's property'. Then, we were taken by car to his farm, and we really checked the plantation fields. This was how we assessed whether the credit operation existed for its purpose and whether the harvest was sufficient to pay back the bank.
>
> Our work was executed by sampling. We would accompany someone picking up cotton flowers in a cotton plantation, for example, to then estimate the production: 'if in X square meters there is Y cotton produced, 1 hectare, it would be 10000Y/X '.
>
> It was also necessary to verify whether the client had really complied with all the requirements and steps prescribed in the credit operation contract. After all, BCB was the manager of public resources destined for rural credit in Brazil. Thus, it was our obligation to verify whether the Treasury was not being harmed." (Álvaro Freitas)

Supervision acted as a compliance checker, which made it very bureaucratic and ineffective. Traditional auditing methods were applied to inspect credit operations, such as questioning the institution's twenty largest debtors and verifying whether they were paying on time, whether the operations were properly provisioned or not. Banks were also asked to provide an analytical report on their non-performing loans portfolio and on some specific portfolios. The inspector who had an inquiring, inquisitive spirit could learn a lot about the institution's business model, but this attitude was an individual skill of a few supervisors, not a general practice.

> "During inspections, data collection was carried out on spreadsheets hand-drawn on graph paper, where credits in liquidation or of worse quality were highlighted in red pen. The spreadsheets were folded like engineering and architectural blueprints. The reports were written manually and then, at the BCB, they were typed, printed and attached to the spreadsheets. Electronic working papers were created around 1997-1998." (Ismária Miranda)

In addition to the on-site inspection activities, the supervisors assessed the banks' financial statements (reported to BCB), investigated eventual complaints from the public, and verified the banks' compliance with operational limits and reserve requirements[42].

In order to support the off-site activities, an accounting indicators system, the Indcon (Sistema de Indicadores Contábeis), provided automatically a set of economic-financial indicators, based on data of financial statements reported to BCB[43]. Indicon had been conceived using the most advanced technological resources available in the late 1980s. Even so, in practice, it had little flexibility for the user and was of difficult maintenance for the BCB's IT team.

---

42. Banks are required to maintain a minimum balance in Reserves Account equivalent to the minimum reserve requirement established by the BCB.

43. Accounting information is reported to the BCB in a standardized template named Accounting Plan for Institutions of the National Financial System (Cosif). See more details at https://www.BC.gov.br/estabilidadefinanceira/cosif.

In addition, there was still no adequate quality control process for the reporting documents, and the frequent data gaps and errors affected the credibility of the information produced. These factors, together with the lack of experience in interpreting the indicators, undermined eventual interest on the tool. The truth is that the great majority of supervisors didn't use it.

On-site inspections were modular, i.e., focused on specific issues: credit operations, ALM[44], foreign exchange operations, etc. The inspection reports had to summarize the entire supervision procedure as well as the irregularities detected, properly enumerated by the regulations of the BCB and the National Monetary Council - CMN (*Conselho Monetário Nacional*). However, the process did not allow for a holistic view of the institution. Even so, he/she was required to prepare a summary report called 'Supervisor's Comments', based on these various segmented reports, and upload it periodically in the Supervision Management System.

In case of any sign of deviation in management, operational controls or accounting documents, the supervisor would classify the institution as 'In Evidence', which gave rise to a step-by-steollow-up. There was, however, no severity scale to measure the problems. Thus, an evidence could mean anything from a mere regulatory noncompliance up to serious issues, such as the risk of continuity of the institution.

The Administrative Proceeding – PA (Processo Administrativo) was the supervisor' instrument to apply penalties to institutions where irregularities were identified. However, those procedures were usually opened without considering the materiality or relevance of irregularities, as well as the adequate evidence or regulatory capitulation to support its assessment.

At the time, BCB's technological infrastructure consisted primarily of a mainframe and its network of terminals. All data processing was performed by the mainframe and each user accessed the information necessary to carry out his/her tasks via

---

44. Assets and Liabilities Management.

terminal. In the early 1990s, the use of personal computers was still precarious and not broadly accessible to BCB staff. There was a pool of 2 or 3 computers to be shared by the personnel on each floor of the building. Teams used computers mostly to the elaboration of reports, even so, in a very incipient way.

> "Handling information was very difficult. We needed to know how to program in Natural to download Cosif information in a .txt format." (Marcelo Fernandes)

After the bankrupcy of large banks in the mid-1990s, it was no longer possible to work that way. The first step towards change was taken in 1998, with the centralization of supervision management. From then on, regardless the geographic location, everyone from the supervision staff responded directly to Defis, which, in turn, took over the planning of the Semiannual Inspection Program - PSFPrograma Semestral de Fiscalização) at the national level, allocating human resources to activities according with its priorities.

1.4 CONSOLIDATED GLOBAL INSPECTION - THE SUPERVISION X-RAY APPROACH

> "Forget the past and let's clean up the Brazilian Financial System!" (Sidney Marques)
>
> "The IGC is the cornerstone of everything." (Paulo Sérgio Neves)

The 1990s bank crisis proved that the supervision model was inefficient in the identification and measurement of existing problems. Many institutions well evaluated by supervisors were, in fact, in very critical situation. Supervisors needed to carry out an in-depth inspection and diagnosis of each institution, individually, should they properly want to take adequate measures towards the recovery of the financial system's soundness.

The Consolidated Global Inspection - IGC (Inspeção Global Consolidada) emerged as a methodology able to provide a consolidated view of a financial conglomerate and understand its strategy. It basically consisted of bringing together a large contingent of inspectors to carry out, at once, a complete assessment of all activities practiced by the conglomerate.

> "Banrisul had a branch in the United States with 4 employees. Once, 7 inspectors from the OCC arrived to inspect the bank. There weren't even chairs to accommodate all those people. They did an in-depth inspection of all details. From this experience, we came up with the idea of making IGCs." (Alvir Hoffmann)

IGC was a paradigm shift for Brazilian supervision. The benchmark was to gather a consolidated panorama, with the most accurate calculation of assets and liabilities, in order to verify the real equity and financial situation of a conglomerate on a given date.

The first prototype of IGC was carried out in 1997, at Banco Boa Vista, in Rio de Janeiro, and soon it became the new BCB's supervisory model. This comprehensive and intrusive methodology, called "The Mauch's SWAT"[45] by the journalists, had completely changed the supervisory approach for banking conglomerates' assessment.

> "We stayed at Banco Boa Vista for 20 days. There were 20 inspectors from all areas. Finally, we concluded that all credit portfolios consisted of rolled over operations, with little expectation of payment. How we reached that conclusion was so impressive that the Deputy Governor for Supervision sent a second team there three months later to check our work. And they concluded that we were right." (Vânio Aguiar)

> "There were 40 to 45 people inside the bank, wanting to know everything about the institution! And they didn't want to work with

---

45. Cláudio Mauch was the Deputy Governor for Supervision at the time of the IGC model implementation.

the bank's reports, but with direct access to their databases, extracting the information they wanted." (Cláudio Mauch)

"One of the preconditions I imposed to President Fernando Henrique[46] to accept the chair of BCB Governor was to have freedom to supervise public banks. Shortly after, we had 100 people inside Banco do Brasil (BB), in the first IGC in a public bank." (Armínio Fraga)

Planning an IGC consisted of choosing the banking conglomerate, defining the number of inspectors, coordinators, supervisors and identifying who would be qualified to do the work. For these purposes, it was necessary to carry out an extensive survey on the capacities and potential of the technical staff. The competence of each one had to be identified, to enable an appropriate allocation in IGC processes.

Inspectors were allocated according to the National Inspection Plan. In this way, they were no longer restricted to their regional borders. They could be assigned to do on-site work anywhere in the country.

"Each one was allocated according to his/her expertise. Those who knew about credit worked with credit, and so on: foreign exchange, ALM, offshore activities, etc. All teams reported their findings to the bank's supervisor, who coordinated the consolidated global inspection of the entire conglomerate." (Vânio Aguiar)

"The IGC teams physically 'moved' to the bank. The inspected bank had to provide an office space to the inspectors, so that they could work close to the bank's business areas." (Harold Espinola)

The IGC model forced the inspector to make a judgment regarding his/her findings about the institution. This new approach provoked a large theoretical and operational evolution in the entire technical staff. They started to improve, standardize and

---

46. Fernando Henrique Cardoso was the President of Brazil from 1995 to 2002 and Armínio Fraga was the BCB Governor from 1999 to 2002.

disseminateprocedures[47], such as validation of assets, identification of contingent liabilities, verification of financial statements' data quality, consolidation of branches and subsidiaries overseas, among others.

> "We wanted to know everything about the conglomerate. We used to go to all the companies in the group to verify everything they had. A bank president once asked us when we would return, because the inspection had identified issues that even he, the owner, wasn't aware of." (Donizeti Maia)

Most of the analyses were carried out by people who did not belong to the bank's supervisory team. These inspectors formed teams specialized in certain topics, such as credit risk, ALM, IT, internal controls etc. Each 'specialist team' produced a diagnosis report and prepared a letter of inspection, pointing out the irregularities within their area of expertise. The conglomerate's supervisor was responsible for the elaboration of the IGC's concluding report, which would consolidate all the analyses received from the various specialist teams, and to sign and deliver the letter of inspection, with the capitulation of all irregularities identified by each specialized team, to the bank.

> "The specialized teams were very important, given that the complexity of the issues was not low and the inspectors were young and still gaining experience." (Irany Santana)
>
> "The ALM specialist team participated every day at the bank's ALM opening meeting. Usually, the Chief Economist attended those briefings. We requested information directly from the Trade Repositories and cross-checked it with the one provided by the bank. We participated in strategic meetings. As we were there for many months, there was no way for the bank to hide information from us.

---

47. Staff located in the regional offices went to São Paulo for a more complex inspection and learned a lot in practice. Likewise, supervisors and inspectors went to the regional offices to compose local working groups and could share their experience and expertise with them.

As a result, we produced a very comprehensive report, around 600 pages." (Harold Espinola)

The IGCs were very important within the historic context, as supervision needed to understand in depth what a complex bank was and how it operated. From this practice, it was possible for the BCB to restructure the financial system. However, despite providing an extremely detailed panorama, comprehending all areas of the financial institution, it was not a sustainable model. Besides consuming a lot of resources, it resulted in a photograph of a certain date[48]; it was not possible to apply the principle of ongoing supervision, nor to assess the impacts of trends and the evolution of the financial system on the examined institution.

"The IGC was one of the largest laboratories and one of the most efficient ways of training inspectors in banking supervision. The best talents from all over Brazil were mixed, covering all expertise types. There was a fabulous integration among teams, and many talents were discovered across the whole country. In an IGC, everyone had the opportunity to learn in practice how to work in an integrated framework." (Osvaldo Watanabe)

1.5 FIRST STEPS TOWARDS THE SUPERVISORY MODEL MODERNIZATION

"At the turn of the century, there was an effervescence within supervision, a fertile field for developing ideas." (Andreia Lais Vargas)

When Law 4,595 created the National Monetary Council and the Central Bank in 1964, it gave them powers and autonomy to decide, among other things, on the structure, organization and functioning of the national financial system[49]. This legal framework

---

48. Data was analyzed with a certain time lag from the reference date. It was not timely information.

49. Art. 4 of Law 4,595 of December 31, 1964 establishes the CMN's powers and Art. 9 determines that BCB is responsible for complying with the rules issued by the CMN. (http://www.planalto.gov.br/ccivil_03/leis/l4595.htm)

granted regulatory agility to those bodies, so that any necessary change or improvement could be done, without the need for approval at the Congress.

In the late 1990s, many BCB employees retired. The teams were missing senior inspectors, which were basically being replaced by new staff[50]. In fact, this phenomenon contributed a lot to the modernization of supervision, as several very skilled newcomers quickly began to occupy leadership positions, due to the vacancy opened by retirees. The real trigger for change, however, came from an unexpected event, when the BCB was forced to carry out inspections in banks' branches abroad.

In July 1995, supervisors from the US Federal Reserve (Fed) contacted BCB supervision, asking for information regarding the financial situation of Bank Econômico. The response was brief: 'in normal operation'. A few weeks later, BCB decreed intervention[51] in that bank.

The implementation of this special regime and the suspicion of possible problems in state public banks led Fed to take restrictive measures against Brazilian banks in the US[52]. At that time, there were 16 branches from Brazilian banks in New York and from the Fed's perspective, they were not being properly inspected by BCB. In response, BCB designated 2 inspectors to do the job. It was the first time that BCB supervisors left Brazil for supervisory activities. This event opened doors for greater interaction with the Fed, including the participation of Brazilian supervisors in its training activities.

---

50. In 1998, 160 new employees were assigned to reinforce the supervision teams in São Paulo.

51. Intervention is a measure adopted to prevent the worsening of the institution's patrimonial risk situation or to put an end to any irregular practices. The BCB appoints the intervenor, who assumes direct management of the institution, suspending its normal activities and the directors' mandates.

52. The Fed imposed a heavy punishment on Brazilian banks with operations in the United States. The punishment consisted of a mandatory deposit at FED equivalent to 120% of the amounts raised in US territory (including funds raised for transfer to the banks' headquarters in Brazil).

> "Inspecting Brazilian banks' branches abroad was a very important experience, because it provoked our first contacts with supervisors from the Fed (Board and New York), the New York State Banking Department, the OCC[53], which permitted us to start some interaction with them." (Tereza Grossi)

At the time, BCB had launched a program in partnership with the World Bank for the improvement of the Brazilian supervisory model. The program provided consultants from the World Bank and the International Monetary Fund (IMF) to the design of a new supervisory model, as well as financial support for training and equipment acquisition. The program allowed supervisors to participate in various training courses abroad and BCB to purchase the first laptop computers for supervisors[54].

The laptops were equipped with a data auditing software[55], which allowed for a deeper and more efficient analysis of information and for the automation of working processes. Thus, inspectors were able to assess the institution's complete portfolios, regardless of their size.

> "In my second inspection work, I took a laptop with me. My supervisor arrived at the institution, looked at what I was doing and said, in a joking tone: 'Ms Ismária, you came here to inspect, not to play on a computer!'" (Ismária Miranda)

> "When we started using laptops in inspections, we also had to carry a small portable printer to issue information requests to the bank. Any requirement had to be formalized in paper. We couldn't send a requisition electronically; it was necessary to print and sign it." (Álvaro Freitas)

The trigger to the modernization of the supervisory model, however, was the BCB's participation in a training in Basel, though

---

53. US Office of the Comptroller of the Currency.
54. Initially, laptops were used practically as notebooks. As they were not connected to the BCB network, it was necessary to use floppy disks to pass information from one device to another.
55. The software used was ACL Analytics (Audit Command Language Analytics).

not the training itself. During the event, participants commented about a training program promoted by Toronto Centre[56], where several case studies of banking supervision activities were presented. Given the course's proposal, it was evident to BCB the need to provide this training to supervisors on a large scale. However, to reach a significant number of employees, the training should be carried out in Brazil, which was not the entity's practice. Nevertheless, after intense negotiations[57], this was done.

> "The instructors from Toronto Centre were supervisors who had experienced systemic crises. The opportunity of interacting with them opened our supervisors' minds in terms of thinking and rethinking the way of doing things. This training changed even the way we made the most complicated decisions." (Tereza Grossi)
>
> "Many times, the minister of the economy or a top-level senior advisor presented him/herself the case, telling us how the financial crisis was managed in his/her country." (Osvaldo Watanabe)

This training was a milestone. Since then, a Permanent Training Program - PPC (Programa Permanente de Capacitação) was established for all staff. Training, courses and internships became a priority and were carried out frequently. When gaps in capacitation were identified, a training framework was created and implemented to fulfill it, covering both technical and managerial aspects. It was mandatory for the teams to have the capacity to identify and assess all the risks to which financial institutions were exposed.

Modern banking supervision was rising in Brazil. A series of infrastructures began to be developed, such as the Credit Risk

---

56. The Toronto Center is a Canadian entity with the objective of delivering capacity-building programs in the areas of banking, insurance, securities, pensions, microfinance, and microinsurance supervise. Its team of instructors is made up of consultants and instructors from the most diverse countries. (https://www.torontocentre.org)

57. Negotiations with the World Bank and the Toronto Center were necessary to conduct the training outside of Canada. Finally, all the people who were conducting the course in Toronto went to Brasília to give the training to more than 30 participants, including department heads and supervisors.

Register, the automatization of working papers[58], the Supervision Manual, the Unicad Project[59] and the use of data from trade depositories in off-site processes.

The existing inefficiencies in the PA process were resolved with the creation of the Administrative Proceeding Committee - Copad[60] (Comitê de Processo Administrativo) in July/2000, whose purpose was to review and evaluate the proceedings opened by the supervisors from all regions, seeking standardization of procedures, as well as a gradation of severity on the application of penalties. Discussions within Copad were intense and rich, which contributed greatly to iimprove the proceedings' quality. Before being submitted to the analysis of merits, PAs had first to be approved by Copad.

> "We were gradually establishing objective rules and the improvement in the quality and timeliness of proceedings was evident. There was an increasing number of convictions and a sharp drop in cases of PAs closed due to lack of proof of the irregularities pointed out." (Osvaldo Watanabe)

In terms of advances in regulation, two major milestones deserve highlight: CMN Resolution 2,682/1999, which classified credit operations according with their risk level[61], and CMN Resolution 2,554/1998, which established criteria for internal

---

58. There were specific working papers covering each assessed technical issue, like credit, FX operations, ALM, accounting statements, and working papers with coordination purpose: 'Prog' (scope and definition of the work), 'Coint' (internal controls), Irre (irregularities found) and 'Conclu' (synthesized the work and the 'diagnosis' of the institution in the work carried out).

59. Unicad - Information on Entities of Interest of the Central Bank - is a system developed to integrate the various existing FI registry databases into a single, complete, comprehensive, and secure system. Before Unicad, each user created his/her own source of FI registry, which often provoked mismatches among information produced from different areas or teams.

60. Copad was composed by the supervisory team managers, the head of the Supervision Department - Defis (Departamento de Fiscalização) and a BCB's legal advisor. Its regulation determined that the committee should meet once a month, with a minimum quorum of 2/3 of its members.

61. Resolution 2,682, of 12/21/1999, provides for criteria for credit operations classification and rules for setting up provisions accordingly. The previous regulation, Resolution 1,748, of 08/30/1990, classified credit operations simply as 'delayed' or 'non-delayed'.

controls, based on the document 'Framework for Internal Control Systems in Banking Organizations', issued in September/1998 by the Basel Committee for Banking Supervision (BCBS)[62]. Those two regulations were the roots of the Brazilian supervision's new approach, focused on risk.

> "The 'trick of the trade' of Resolution 2682 was that although banks could classify the credit operation as they wanted, there was a floor, function of the delay in payment, and if the operation were restructured, its classification could only be changed if the client complied with the new payment schedule and demonstrated an improvement on his/her risk level. Besides, BCB had powers to reclassify any operation. That's why the rule is still in force." (Alvir Hoffmann)

The 'icing on the cake' of the Toronto Centre's training, however, was teaching supervisors how to exercise supervisory power using the legal instruments at their disposal. Initially, there was some resistance to the change of approach, but the renewal of staff provoked by the massive retirement wave in the 1990s helped to speed up the process. Young inspectors wanted to hold meetings with the bank's Board, learn about its dynamics, and participate in the ALM Committee meetings, instead of being limited to interact only with the institution's Accountant Chief.

> "It is important to have a sound legal instrument to support supervisory actions. It allows us for important actions that could not be done without it. Law 9,447/97[63], for example, permitted the establishment of the 'Term of Attendance', which gives powers to supervisors call the bank's entire executive board, the board of

---

62. See https://www.bis.org/publ/bcbs40.htm to access the document.
63. Law No. 9,447, of 03/14/1997, art. 5th states: "... the Banco Central do Brasil ... may determine the following measures: I - capitalization of the company, with the contribution of resources necessary for its recovery, in an amount fixed by it; II - transfer of control; III - corporate reorganization, including incorporation, merger or spin-off. Single paragraph. If the measures referred to in this article were not implemented, within the period established by the Banco Central do Brasil, the applicable special resolution regime shall be decreed."

directors, the fiscal council and the independent auditors to say: 'your bank has a problem, either you improve the capital level, or sell it, or find a way to fix it." (Vânio Aguiar)

"We once identified serious problems in an inspection, which needed to be brought to the bank's Board of Directors. There was no such culture at the time, but we held a meeting with them. The Chairman took our inspection letter and said that we could be confident that they would address the recommendations with the highest priority. Later, he confided to us that if we hadn't warned them and they hadn't taken the measures, they would face serious operational problems from 2009 onwards. More than a decade after this event, Basel published the Principles for Enhancing Corporate Governance[64], recommending supervisors to dialogue with senior management. At that time, I thought, 'How come other countries don't do that?' And then I realized they didn't!" (Paulo Sergio Neves)

1.6 THE USE OF GRANULAR DATA

"In Brazil, financial market infrastructures contribute significantly to data collection and quality. In general, as a legal requirement, the validity of financial contracts depends on their registration with a TR[65]. It is worth noting that all transaction types in Brazil that are reported to TRs identify the final investor." (FSB – Peer Review of Brazil – April/2017[66])

---

64. "BCBS Principles for Enhancing Corporate Governance' was published in October/2010. The current version 'BCBS Guidelines - Corporate Governance Principles for Banks' dates from July/2015.
65. Trade Repository.
66. See the full report at https://www.fsb.org/wp-content/uploads/Brazil-peer-review-report.pdf.

Figure: Types of financial transactions reported to a TR or TR-like entity in the Americas

*Fixed income securities issued by financial institutions

Source: FSB Regional Consultative Group for the Americas Report - October 2015

http://www.fsb.org/2015/10/reporting-financial-transactions-to-trade-repositories-in-the-americas/

A series of different events contributed to the structure of Brazilian supervision process based on the intensive use of granular data, collected not only from the institutions themselves, but from independent sources, such as trade repositories and clearing houses, as well.

Microdata from Credit Operations:

During the IGC work, supervisors identified many inaccuracies in the calculation of credit operations' provisioning, which often resulted in significant adjustments to provisions. However, the identification of such problems was only possible through on-site inspections, where operations were checked by sampling. Thus, over time, there was a high probability that credit operations would become under-provisioned again, even if they had already been the object of on-site work.

The Banco Nacional fraud event[67] was the trigger for the BCB to create an infrastructure to receive granular information on credit operations on a regular basis. International experiences of credit information centers were taken as reference, in order to design the first version of the Credit Risk Register (CRC), which came into operation in 1997. It was a major innovation at the time[68].

Since its inception, financial institutions had access to data reported to the CRC, as its architecture was also designed as a credit bureau for the financial system. Even so, in the beginning, institutions considered the provision of credit information to the CRC more as a burden than a bonus, maybe because data available to them was still very limited and not useful for credit risk management purposes.

> "Before joining the BCB, I worked in a commercial bank in Brasília. At that time, we had an 'informal' Credit Risk Register: managers of several local banks used to sit in a bar and exchange information about bad-paying customers.." (Jorge Paulino)

Microdata from Financial Market Operations (securities and derivatives):

During the IGC work, supervisors realized that the information provided to the BCB by financial institutions had many quality problems, which raised questions about how much BCB could rely on declaratory information and make decisions based on it. During the financial system's recovery programs PROER and PROES, this issue became even more evident. Thus, supervisors decided to collect data directly from the source of information,

---

67. Banco Nacional created more than 600 ghost accounts to carry out fake loans., which were classified by the bank as performing loans, counterbalancing the balance sheet. In order not to be discovered, the bank's data processing system inhibited the printing of these fake loans, when providing the list of the bank's credit operations to BCB, for inspection work.

68. CRC information was reported at the customer and credit modality level. Micro data at the credit operation level was introduced later.

i. e., where the financial transactions were registered, and better understand how they were negotiated and priced.

The financial instruments' registration and custody market is well developed in Brazil, covering all major public and private securities, equities, and derivatives. In fact, an electronic system to control debt ownership and negotiation of government securities was developed in the late 1980s, due to the need to control public debt, the Selic[69]. At the same time, the same concept was expanded to the private securities' market (Cetip) and, afterwards, to the derivatives' market (BM&F)[70]. Since then, these systems have continuously improved and multiplied.

An important particularity of Brazilian registry systems is that all of them record the identification of the real players involved in each transaction. The capacity of knowing exactly the counterparties of each operation and, in consequence, the final holder of a security or a derivative contract (even OTC[71] derivatives), permitted BCB to develop even more accurate monitoring processes along time, based on this data.

In the late 1990s, two events contributed to consolidate the immersion of supervision in the world of financial transaction records. The first concerns a Parliamentary Committee of Inquiry - CPI (Comissão Parlamentar de Inquérito), formed in Congress to investigate allegations of corruption[72]. The CPIs requested

---

69. The Special System for Settlement and Custody (Selic) is the central depository for most securities issued by the National Treasury. (https://www.bcb.gov.br/en/financialstability/selicsystem)

70. In 2017, the *Bolsa de Mercadorias e Futuros* (BM&FBovespa) and the *Central de Custódia e de Liquidação Financeira de Títulos Privados* (Cetip) merged and became the *Bolsa Brasil Balcão – B3*. (https://www.b3.com.br/pt_br/)

71. Over the Counter.

72. The event that became popular as the 'Dwarves of the Budget' concerns a group of representatives from the Budget Committee of the National Congress who, in the late 1980s and early 1990s, were involved in fraud with resources from the Federal Budget. The group collected bribes from mayors and construction companies to include amendments to the Budget or to obtain the release of funds. They also benefited from the approval of social subsidies from the ministries to shell companies controlled by them. They were called 'dwarves' due to the fact that the group was composed of seven members and, coincidentally, all of them had short physical stature. The BCB also participated in investigations of fraud involving 'precatorios', which were government debts arising from court

technical support from BCB to identify the mechanism by which those involved carried out money laundering operations in the financial market. Information on the counterparties of derivative transactions registered at the BM&F and of state and municipal government bonds' negotiations was essential to identify those responsible for the embezzlement of public money.

The second event occurred when the government decided to apply a sharp FX rate adjustment in January 1999. BCB was unaware that two banks, Marka and FonteCindam, were excessively exposed to currency derivatives. These banks were following BCB's strategy, which had been supporting the value of the Real, despite its true devaluating conditions. When the currency's support was interrupted, Real suffered a sharp devaluation and those banks became unable to honor the positions assumed. At the time, the only source of off-site information was Indicon, a system based on accounting data. Information was neither timely nor detailed enough for BCB to be aware of that risk in advance.

Figure: FX Rate Real X Dólar – July/1998-June/1999

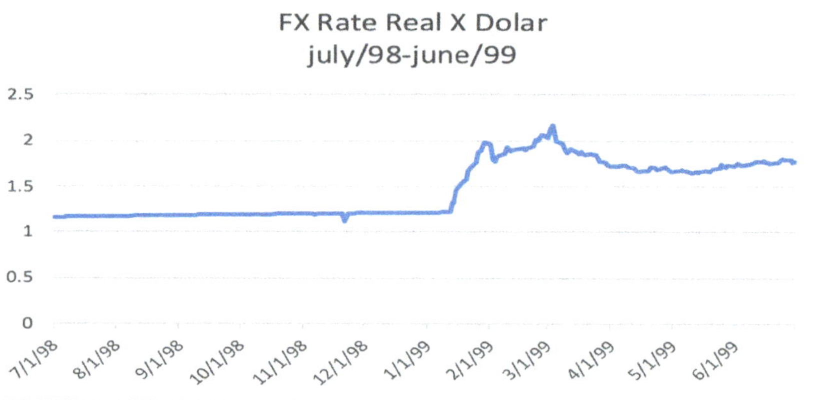

Source: Banco Central do Brasil - https://www.bcb.gov.br/en/currencyconversion

---

decisions, such as compensation for land expropriation. To pay them, states and munici-palities issued bonds that were traded on the financial market. In the 1990s, several frauds were discovered in this process, both in the illegal issuance of securities (often backed by false 'precatórios') and in their negotiation in the financial market, through a chain of operations that allowed large profits to companies that operated the bonds and losses to the issuing government's coffers.

These events were essential for accelerating the improvement of regulatory and supervisory activities. The regular collection of financial markets' information from trade repositories became routine and the obligation to register operations was gradually improved and expanded.

> "The first data we collected on a daily basis at the registry level referred to the federal government securities, registered at Selic, due to the *Precatórios'* CPI[73] works. In sequence, came the information on derivatives, registered at the BM&F. Then, negotiations began with Cetip for the collection of information on interbank deposits and certificates of bank deposits. This process continues to this day, each time adding more information." (Marcelo Fernandes)

In the beginning, the market participants accounted for mandatory registration only in terms of the cost of compliance. Over time, they started to profit the benefits of having a safer financial environment and could better understand the consequences of sound and well supervised financial system[74].

> "No serious banker wants to participate in any business conducted outside the law and regulation. Registration may be costly, but the bankers themselves consider that the cost is compatible with the needs for the well-functioning of the market. Once implemented, the cost is irrelevant, and registries help institutions to keep a proper record of their business." (Sidney Marques)
>
> "Today, banks see this requirement as an opportunity, as it brings more legal certainty to operations, reduces the information gap, and gives smaller banks more conditions to operate in a market that is super-competitive and aggressive." (Everton Goncalves - ABBC[75])

---

73. Inquiry Parliament Commission.
74. It is mandatory to report to the BCB all transactions traded on and registered in CCP (Central Counterparty) and electronic trading platforms; the transactions with OTC derivative, spot FX, fixed income assets; and the credit operations. Besides, reporting to a TR is mandatory in Brazil for most transaction types and for nearly all asset classes.
75. Brazilian Association of Banks.

Payment System Data [76]

In Brazil, transfers of funds between two banks, as well as the settlement of their operations in the various financial markets, are settled at the BCB. The banks' 'Reserves' account works as the hub of the Brazilian Payment System - SPB (*Sistema de Pagamentos Brasileiro*).

Debits in a bank's Reserves used to be settled automatically, by command of the paying bank or a settlement clearing system, regardless of the existence of sufficient funds. There were no restrictions on overdrafts throughout the day. However, banks had to comply with reserve requirements in this same account, which means that a minimum overnight balance should always be maintained. To this purpose, banks exchanged liquidity among themselves in the Federal Government Securities - TPF (*Títulos Públicos Federais*)) market, operated by Selic, whose net deferred settlement in the Reserves account happened at the close of the day.

Should a bank be liquidated by the BCB, the bank immediately lost its authorization to operate in the market and its Reserves account was closed. As such a decision could happen anytime during business hours, it was not uncommon for the Reserves account to be closed with a negative balance. The return of these funds to the public coffers was a long and uncertain journey, as there was no preference for the BCB in the list of creditors of the bankrupted institution.

In 1998, the BCB assigned a team to study in detail the functioning of the Brazilian Payments System and to propose solutions to this problem. During the diagnostic phase, the team mapped all the financial flows carried out in the country that involved the transfer of funds between two or more financial institutions, through Reserves accounts. Due to this intensive investigation

---

76. The Brazilian Payment System - SPB (*Sistema de Pagamentos Brasileiro*) consists of the entities, systems and procedures related to the processing and settlement of fund transfer operations, operations with foreign currency or with financial assets and securities, also generically referred to as Financial Market Infrastructure (FMI). In addition to FMIs, payment arrangements and institutions are also part of the SPB.

work, they obtained a deep understanding of the *modus operandi* of each transaction carried out in the financial market. The trading, settlement and custody systems were studied one by one, which allowed the BCB's team to thoroughly comprehend their processes, and, thus, to discuss with the financial market infrastructures (FMI) the improvements to make processes more robust and able to absorb defaults.

Figure: Main Settlements in Reserves Account prior to April/2002

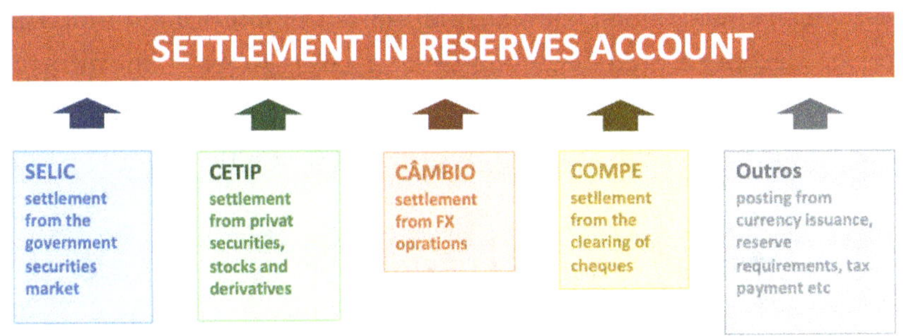

SELIC[77]: Special Settlement and Custody System (*Sistema Especial de Liquidação e de Custódia*)

CETIP[78]: Custody and Settlement Center for Private Securities (*Central de Custódia e Liquidação de Títulos Privados*)

CAMBIO[79]: Settlement of interbank foreign exchange operations

COMPE[80]: Clearing System for Checks and Other Bills (*Sistema de Compensação de Cheques e Outros Papéis*)

Source:Blog Cidadania & Cultura. Fernando Nogueira da Costa.

---

77. SELIC consists of a computerized system managed by the BCB for the registration, custody and settlement ot transactions with government federal securities issued by the National Treasury.

78. CETIP was a publicly traded company that offered registration, central depository, trading and settlement services for assets and securities. Until the implementation of the new SPB in April 2002, settlements in the stocks and derivatives markets registered with the CBLC and BM&F, respectively, were settled in the banks' Reserves by Cetip.

79. The BCB operated the 'leg' of the settlement in national currency related to the purchase and sale of foreign currencies carried out by financial institutions.

80. COMPE is the clearing system for checks and other payment instruments in the financial market. Its activity is managed by Banco do Brasil.

In 1999, one employee from the 'SPB Project' team moved to the supervision area and joined the team responsible for developing the first monitoring processes based on granular data from the trade repositories.

Monitoring the information from the payment system brought the understanding of the operational procedures of each financial operation. When put together with granular data of banks' operations in the securities and derivatives markets , it brought a very clear and detailed view of the market's *modus operandi*. This framework permitted the evolution in large steps of monitoring processes for liquidity and market risks, with the development of increasingly accurate and complex monitoring tools.

1.7 ON-SITE AND OFF-SITE SUPERVISION

Since the turn of the century, there was a strong movement for enhancing BCB's independence and autonomy. Some believed that the supervisory activities inside the BCB could hamper the achievement of those goals. Thus, pros and cons regarding the segregation of supervision from the classic central bank activities were largely debated. In fact, segregation would mitigate eventual conflicts in the conduction of supervisory and monetary policy activities. On the other hand, supervision was a relevant source of information for the BCB to exercise its role as lender of last resort and monetary policy maker. In both scenarios, however, it was absolutely necessary to improve the supervisory framework. With a staff of 633 'old school' employees[81] in June/2000, supervision had an excess of responsibilities and new challenges in its agenda. It was

---

81. The largest contingent of supervisory personnel in the 1990s occurred in Dec/1994, when it counted with 1,202 employees. Supervisory teams reduced gradually over the following years, stabilizing, as of mid-1998, at around 750 employees. In Jun/2000, however, the Defis contingent had again declined to 633, with the retirement of many supervisors. Part of this deficiency was quickly remedied with the entry of 123 new employees that same year.

imperative to take actions to improve rationality, efficiency, and effectiveness.

> "I have studied this subject all my life and have always felt that the central bank as a provider of last resort and monetary policy maker had much more to gain from being close to supervision. There could be some loss in a super purist line of monetary policy, as it may let inflation run because of eventual financial fragility in the system, for example, but I didn't think so. I thought it was recommendable to have segregation between central bank and supervision activities, but at the department level it would be sufficient. In the case of the BCB, at the board level, as well. However, as our board is collegiate, the most important segregation is by department." (Armínio Fraga)

The events that took place in the 1990s had already demonstrated in practice the strong need for the establishment of a more intrusive off-site supervision process. Data needed to be easily available, both as a source of information of regular off-site processes, as well as to permit the assessment of eventual specific issues.

Besides, although BCB's Board resented the lack of consolidated information on the SFN, the macro perspective had never been the focus of supervision. The supervisory framework had been designed to produce its opinion on the soundness of financial institutions one by one, based on on-site activities. Although there were a few off-site supervision teams, which could develop processes to produce consolidated information, their needs ended up never being prioritized, due to the increasing demands from on-site activities.

> "When I became Deputy Governor for Supervision, Aguiar[82] started to create a prototype of off-site supervision at Defis. He could produce some information, but very little. The information was not used in a systematic or consolidated way." (Tereza Grossi)

---

82. Vânio Cesar Pickler Aguiar was the first head of the Department of Indirect Supervision (Desin).

The supervision model of Banco de España, with on-site and off-site activities in segregated departments, was chosen as a benchmark to restructure BCB's supervision. Additionally, off-site supervision was also expected to provide consolidated information on the SFN to the Board.

On July 1st, 2000, Defis was split into two departments: one focused on on-site supervision, and the other, on off-site. The headquarters of on-site supervision was established in São Paulo, where the headquarters of most financial institutions were located, while off-site supervision remained in Brasília, close to the BCB Board, its main client. Thus, BCB off-site supervision was born with micro and macro prudential mandates, although in the beginning 'macro' meant merely the sum of individual information.

> "On a trip to Washington, I asked Alan Greenspan for his views on supervision activities. He told me: 'I see 3 perspectives: there is the traditional one, which will never cease to have its role, basically based on on-site inspection; there is off-site supervision, which seeks to create a flow of information that can be useful without the need to be inside the banks all the time; and, finally, the supervision that the market makes itself, where you can check if the risks' flags really work.'" (Armínio Fraga)

> "I had a conversation with Armínio about the impossibility of doing both things together: 'if you want to know how bank Itaú is doing, we can tell you, but if you want to know how the Financial System is doing, we cannot give you that information. I am sure that by allocating on-site and off-site supervision activities into different departments, we will be able to support you with information that is essential nowadays.' He accepted." (Tereza Grossi)

Over time, the banks' financial statements reported to BCB improved in quality, which permitted the development of useful economic-financial indicators to monitor the soundness of financial institutions. In addition, there were large granular and timely databases available for the development of metrics for the analysis of banks' exposures to credit, liquidity, and market risk, such as the credit operations in the CRC, financial market operations from the trade repositories and the money flow data from the Payment System. Thus, off-site supervision was structured based on these data sources.

For on-site supervision, moving the central management to the BCB's regional branch in São Paulo provoked some unexpected reactions. Supervisory teams used to submit their report to the final decision of the head office in Brasília[83]. Naturally, teams located in São Paulo started to prepare themselves to become the decision and strategy makers for on-site supervision activities of the whole country. However, it was necessary an extra effort to mitigate some resistance from other regional teams to report to a BCB branch, still taken by a few supervisors as 'at the same [regional office] hierarchic level' as they were.

Once the new supervisory framework was formalized, the next step was to organize the teams according to the new geographic distribution, both of financial institutions, provoked by the recent changes in the financial system composition (after PROER and PROES), as well as of supervisory teams, provoked by the segregation of on- and off-site activities.

Regional teams were extinguished, and the personnel mandatorily transferred to Brasília and São Paulo, to reinforce the head offices' teams. Choices to the personnel allocated elsewhere consisted of only two alternatives and both implied in leaving the hometown: either to join the off-site teams in Brasília or to join the on-site teams in São Paulo. No exceptions were granted to avoid undermining the great effort of restructuring supervision. Thus, despite the strong reaction of many people, the changes were carried out as planned, which made the birth of the new supervisory model a very traumatic process to them.

---

83. The former Defis central management was located at the headquarters of the BCB, in Brasília. See more details on BCB's geographic distribution in item '1.3 Structure and functioning of supervision' of this chapter.

"Several people transferred to Brasília in the year-2000 restructuring process made considerable progress in their careers, as they had more professional opportunities in the head offices. Others preferred to return home in the following years, when some specific inspection activities were allocated in the BCB's regional branches." (Sidney Marques)

CHAPTER 2

The Evolution of the Brazilian Supervisory Model

"An effective banking supervisory system should consist of some form of both on-site and off-site supervision."

(Core Principles for Effective Banking Supervision – BCBS/1997 – Principle 16)

"Our model is very different from on-site & off-site supervision; it is Monitoring & Supervision."

(Paulo Sérgio Neves)

This chapter explains the rationale behind the transformation of the classic on-site and off-site supervision model into the current Monitoring & Supervision model (M&S), as well as the reasons for the symbiosis between micro and macro prudential monitoring in Brazil. The chapter also highlights the importance of a strategic infrastructure to support an integrated and effective supervision process.

2.1 THE BCBS RECOMMENDATIONS FOR AN EFFECTIVE ONGOING SUPERVISORY APPROACH

The city of Basel in Switzerland is home of the Bank for International Settlement (BIS), an international organization with the purpose of promoting cooperation between central banks and other agencies in the pursuit of financial stability. At the BIS, the Basel Committee for Banking Supervision (BCBS) is responsible for setting international standards of conduct, improving the quality of banking supervision, and strengthening the soundness and security of the international banking system[84].

In September 1997, BCBS published the 'Core Principles for Effective Supervision'. The document consisted of 25 principles[85], with minimum standards to be observed by regulatory entities and by banking supervisors[86], as well. According to the principles, it was

---

84. BCBS Webpage: https://www.bis.org/BCBS/

85. The 'Basel Core Principles' issued in 1997 comprise twenty-five basic Principles that need to be in place for a supervisory system to be effective. The Principles relate to:
Preconditions for effective banking supervision - Principle 1
Licensing and structure - Principles 2 to 5
Prudential regulations and requirements - Principles 6 to 15
Methods of ongoing banking supervision - Principles 16 to 20
Information requirements - Principle 21
Formal powers of supervisors - Principle 22, and
Cross-border banking - Principles 23 to 25.
Source:Core Principles for Effective Banking Supervision – BCBS/1997.

86. Principles focused on recommendations to conduct supervisory work on an ongoing basis:
Principle 16: An effective banking supervisory system should consist of some form of both on-site and off-site supervision.
Principle 17: Banking supervisors must have regular contact with bank management and a thorough understanding of the institution's operations.
Principle 18: Banking supervisors must have a means of collecting, reviewing and analyzing prudential reports and statistical returns from banks on a solo and consolidated basis.
Principle 19: Banking supervisors must have a means of independent validation of supervisory information either through on-site examinations or use of external auditors.
Principle 20: An essential element of banking supervision is the ability of the supervisors to supervise the banking group on a consolidated basis. Source:Core Principles for Effective Banking

mandatory for supervisors to establish some type of monitoring of the institutions during the intervals between inspections[87], for the timely identification of potential problems. In this way, corrective actions could be taken before the worsening of a problem.

In 2006, the Core Principles were revised, establishing essential and additional criteria for each principle, which created a gradation of relevance to the recommendations. This new version also highlighted the concern with financial stability as part of the supervisor's agenda. The analysis of risks and vulnerabilities that could impact the soundness of supervised institutions started to incorporate the macro perspective.

> "An effective banking supervisory system requires that supervisors develop and maintain a thorough understanding of the operations of individual banks and banking groups, and also of the banking system as a whole, focusing on safety and soundness, and the stability of the banking system." (Principle 19, Supervisory Approach – Core Principles for Effective Banking Supervision. BCBS/2006)

In 2012, BCBS published a new version of the document, where it mainly reinforced the areas where gaps were identified during the Great Financial Crisis of 2007-2009 (GFC). The new version emphasized the need for adequate resources for the supervision of systemically important banks, and for developing prudential macro analysis and strengthening market discipline.

> "An effective system of banking supervision requires the supervisor to develop and maintain a forward-looking assessment of the risk profile of individual banks and banking groups, proportionate to their systemic importance; identify, assess and address risks emanating from banks and the banking system as a whole; have a framework in place for early intervention; and have plans in place, in partnership with other relevant authorities, to take action to resolve

---

Supervision – BCBS/1997.

87. The interval between on-site inspections is a function of several factors, such as the systemic relevance of the institution and its level of risk.

banks in an orderly manner if they become non-viable." (Principle 8, Supervisory Approach – Core Principles for Effective Banking Supervision – BCBS/2012)

Even with the evolution of the document over time, the recommendation for structuring an ongoing supervision process has kept its essence. According to 'Basel', it should be based on a mix of well-planned on-site and off-site activities, with clear and well-defined objectives and responsibilities, to allow the coordinated execution of work and the exchange of information between teams[88].

On-site inspections would mainly be focused on activities where the physical presence of the inspector would be essential, such as the evaluation of governance, where policies, procedures and controls would be verified, as well as monitoring the progress of the institution's actions to meet the recommendations from previous inspections. Another fundamental point would be to verify the quality of information provided to the supervision, as it is the main input for off-site supervision work.

In off-site activities, supervision would be responsible for collecting prudential and accounting information from the supervised institutions and establishing procedures to analyze their economic and financial condition, as well as monitor the main risks to which they are exposed.

In Brazil, as the off-site teams took part of the IGC works[89] and they were used to handle data from trade repositories[90] (where the registry of financial operations was mandatory[91]), they crossed the barriers of information reported by the supervised institutions to develop off-site supervision processes, and collected granular information, normally used by on-site teams to validate the banks' financial statements, directly from the trade repositories.

---

88. According to BCBS, the collection and analysis of information must be activities of both on-site and off-site work, and may also be outsourced to qualified external auditors.
89. See Chapter 1 topic 1.4 Consolidated Global Inspection - the X-ray of the financial institution.
90. See Chapter 1 topic 1.6 The use of granular data.
91. Brazilian regulation required the registration of custody and trading of financial assets and derivative contracts.

The access to granular information from independent sources brought to the off-site supervision the capacity to carry on activities that in a classic supervisory model would be beyond its scope, such as checking the quality of information reported to the supervisor, a typical on-site activity.

Gradually, the off-site supervision started to oversee the financial system in a holistic perspective, identifying the flows among participants and mapping their interconnectedness. All the off-site framework was structured based on micro data of each financial operation. This new approach permitted that the mix of on-site and off-site activities in Brazil could evolve to a model not yet existent.

> "The advances were extraordinary. Activities that had never been done in the supervision process were being performed." (Fabio Lacerda)

> "This was the stepping stone that allowed the subsequent evolution of our on-site & off-site model to the Monitoring & Supervision model." (Paulo Sergio Neves)

2.2 THE IMPLEMENTATION OF THE ONGOING BANKING SUPERVISORY MODEL IN BRAZIL

Despite the great potential for analysis provided by granular data, the implementation of an ongoing supervision model in the BCB was an arduous and complex process, as it required a very strong cultural change. The process started in 2001 had several setbacks over time, which contributed to its continuous improvement.

In the beginning of the 21st century, supervision had just passed through a robust cycle of IGCs in the main banks of the financial system, exclusively based on on-site activities. Empowered by intense training focused on risk and internal controls, supervisors proceeded inspection works with a new approach, more intrusive and inquiring. Armed with laptops and a software to handle data, they could themselves extract information for analysis, directly from the banks' databases. Therefore, they took their working process as adequate and sufficient. In their perspective, there was no need for further off-site work, especially carried out by another department.

On the other hand, the off-site teams worked intensively on the development of tools and reports. In a short time, they started to provide to the on-site teams early warnings regarding concerns on credit and liquidity risks, as well as economic and financial analysis of the supervised entities.

> "In the beginning, off-site supervision work was taken as unnecessary; on-site supervisors considered that supervisory work was already being fully exercised by inspection processes." (Kathleen Krause)

> "When we realized that the off-site could check compliance of the credit portfolio, perform economic-financial analysis, and identify evidence of high liquidity risk, we felt as if we were losing power. Supervisors used to feel themselves as the 'owners of the bank'. That new reality was very traumatic to us." (Ailton Aquino)

Being in separate departments and, consequently, under different commands, did not favor the coordination of an integrated planning for on-site and off-site activities. The production cycle of off-site teams, which consisted of reports on micro and macro analysis and early warnings of identified relevant issues, followed the data frequency of each team (daily, monthly). Thus, there was a huge mismatch with the on-site annual inspection's agenda.

> "The problem did not consist in dividing the work to execute it, but in putting it back together afterwards!" (Anthero Meirelles)

Feedback to the early warning processes was essential for the improvement of still incipient tools. As a result, it was established as mandatory[92] to on-site supervisors, even when the return was

---

92. As of 2008, both off-site warnings and on-site feedback were required to be registered in the Integrated Monitoring System - SIM.

an 'unfounded or irrelevant issue'. In terms of the working process, they were expected to immediately investigate any off-site warning and provide a timely response to that. However, this demand rarely matched the agenda of inspections, annually planned. Thus, instead of useful, these warnings were taken as something that distracted them from their 'real' duties.

Besides, warnings were taken as simple indications. Thus, supervisors used to redo all the investigation work, normally requiring to the bank the same information already reported to the BCB and used as data source of off-site tools.

> "The supervisor was obliged to respond, for example, to a simple alert of a significant variation in a specific balance sheet account. This was bureaucratic and not relevant, just an extra obligation, not linked to his work and inspection plan." (Caio Ferreira)

Regarding the micro and macro analysis, off-site teams were still incipient in the elaboration of reports and the scope of analysis was limited by data availability. Qualitative information was not accessible in a structured format, thus, it could not be an input to off-site tools, which hampered its capacity to help analysts to better understand the numbers inside the banks' context. As a result, off-site reports were taken as superficial and uninformative by on-site supervisors.

The problem, therefore, was not just the alignment of agendas. The definition of off-site products and their use by the on-site teams was also a point of conflict. Off-site teams were autonomous to define metrics and create products. On-site supervisors were not consulted neither whether they wanted or needed a product conceptually destined to 'help' them, nor if they were comfortable with the methodology and calibration of tools developed for its purpose. Besides, while the off-site processes became increasingly robust and automated over time, the number and frequency of warnings to supervisors significantly increased and strongly competed with the on-site work agenda.

The sophistication of the models has also played its role to blur the communication between on-site and off-site teams. Immersed in the environment of their metrics, the off-site supervisors developed their own vocabulary, very technical and based on the terms and parameters of the methodology itself. Without realizing it, they used 'off-site' idioms in their warning reports, which made it difficult for the on-site supervisor to understand the message[93].

Message: We have identified a 38% increase in the 'Deposit Outflow' component of the institution's 'Estimated Liquidity Need', which has negatively impacted its 'Liquidity Ratio' by 10%.

It was the first time in the BCB's history that the systematic use of information produced with collected data was part of the supervisory model. Thus, false-positive warnings occurred more frequently than expected, either due to data quality issues, still incipient modeling, or lack of important information for a more

---

93. The specialized teams of the IGCs, which had the specific knowledge, did not migrate to off-site activities. They remained in the on-site supervision structure as specialized support for the on=site teams, which had a more generalist profile.

complete analysis. Despite the continuous improvements, there was still a long way to go before the calibration and inputs of off-site tools reached a level of excellence.

> "Once, we identified that the liquidity buffer of a large bank had practically disappeared overnight. Due to the size of the bank, even the Deputy Governor for Supervision was warned. The supervisor responsible for the bank came to Brasília to give explanations. We then discovered that the problem was in our model. We did not consider investment fund quotas as liquid assets and the bank had packed its entire portfolio of government securities in funds, where it was the only shareholder. We adjusted the model and learned the lesson: discuss with the bank's supervisor before alarming catastrophic warnings." (Paula Oliveira)

Initiatives to integrate on-site and off-site teams started to rise. In an attempt to familiarize on-site supervisors with off-site products, courses on methodologies and the use of off-site tools were included in the supervisor's training schedule. On-site supervisors also gained free access to off-site tools developed to support the analysis of flags produced by early warning systems. In the other direction, off-site supervisors were encouraged to participate in inspection works focused on topics of their expertise. Those were good opportunities to make on-site and off-site teams work together and allow off-site supervisors to confront their assumptions with reality, to identify points for improving the models and even seek new data sources.

> "The off-site tools, such as the CRC, were very useful and widely used by supervisors in the preparation of an inspection work." (Irany Santana)

These were normal difficulties in a complex process that was still in its infancy. However, there was an imbalance of responsibilities between the on-site and off-site teams, which undermined any attempt of strategy to improve integration: the legal risk of supervision materialized exclusively in the figure of the on-site supervisor. He/she was legally and administratively liable for any action or omission in relation to the bank under his/her supervision. Besides, the consequences of an unfounded off-site warning also mainly affected on-site supervisors, who had their time and staff consumed by unnecessary investigations.

In fact, the investigation of the off-site warning process, as it had been established, put on-site supervisors in a deadlock situation: whether the warning was irrelevant, they were wasting scarce resources; on the other hand, they could be held responsible for omission, whether not investigating a serious problem. Thus, the only way to avoid such a risk was not to receive warnings!

> "The off-site people sent warnings 'round the clock', and the on-site supervisor thought to themselves: 'hey, man! What if I can't handle all this?'" (Álvaro Freitas)

In this scenario, any initiative of integration was fruitless. Raising opportunities for on-site and off-site supervisors to meet and become familiar with each other's activities was very important, but it didn't stop the snowball. The problem was not just a matter of lack of empathy. The problem needed to be solved at the strategic level.

In July/2005, BCB restructured its activities and transferred the whole responsibility for collecting data to the off-site supervision department. At that time, the off-site teams were the biggest users of information collected by the BCB and were constantly questioning data quality, demanding for changes in the templates and for new information. So, it was reasonable to hand over the process to them. However, they received the complete package, that is, not just the data they used, but all the data collected by the BCB.

The transformation from user to information manager caused a significant increase in the off-site department's responsibilities and infrastructure. This range of new attributions took up space on the managers' agenda and contributed to shift the focus away from the search for greater integration with on-site supervision.

Once off-site personnel had taken over the management of information, it was decided to review the balance between power and responsibility, giving back to the on-site supervisor the command of the ongoing supervision process. In 2006, a work agreement clearly defining what off-site supervisors could and could not do was formally signed by the heads of the two areas. The 'Armistice', as the agreement was nicknamed by the off-site teams, limited their activities, and defined the need for prior agreement with the on-site area for changes and evolution of the warning process and tools. The medicine was bitter and difficult to swallow, but it was an important and necessary step for the survival of the supervisory model. The battle seemed to have finally come to an end.

> "Purpose of the Armistice (from an off-site point of view): 'I will not intrude on your work'; 'I won't send you anything you don't want'." (Harold Espinola)

The Armistice was justifiable. Having two opinions from the same hierarchical level[94] about the same financial institution was overwhelming and unproductive. Furthermore, attempts to adapt the off-site warning flow to the on-site work capacity had already been exhausted. Severe, even if unpopular, measures had to be taken. The agreement restored responsibility for the financial institution's assessment to the on-site supervisor and prohibited off-site from issuing any assessment, opinion or referral suggestion in its reports and warnings. These attributions became exclusive to the on-site. The off-site also lost the autonomy to define its metrics and the calibrations of the early warning filters had to be compatible with the analysis capacity of the on-site supervisors. From then on, any off-site step needed to be discussed and agreed beforehand with the on-site personnel.

---

94. On-site and off-site supervision.

As it was agreed, so was it fulfilled. The early warning off-site processes were maintained, but on-site supervisors were free to decide when to investigate a warning. It didn't need to be immediate anymore. It could, for example, be included in the inspection schedule, when considered not urgent. Communication between teams had also evolved. Upon suspicion of a relevant event, before issuing the warning, the off-site supervisor would call the responsible for the institution to discuss the issue. All off-site processes that involved analysis of financial institutions one by one were discontinued. The tools that produced information for these assessments, however, were maintained and put at the disposal of on-site supervisors for consultation.

Finally, working processes started to integrate, but slightly different from the classic on-site & off-site model. The on-site supervisors incorporated the assessment tools usually used by the off-site as a source of information. Meanwhile, off-site monitored all institutions regarding a given issue, signaling to the on-site team when an institution appeared to be presenting more risk than expected. On-site team was responsible for assessing the causes, consequences, and eventual necessary measures to be taken, while the off-site team focused on understanding how risks materialized and the exposure level of each institution to them. The supervisory model was undergoing transformation. The off-site team increasingly assumed a risk monitoring role, while the essence of supervision responsibility remained on the on-site team.

At first glance, these differences might go unnoticed, but they were structural. A classic off-site supervisor develops tools and processes to analyze each institution and provide feedback on it. Monitoring, in turn, focuses on the problem; that is, it is concerned with identifying and signaling who fits into a specific situation. It is up to the supervisor to assess the warning's relevance and pertinence in the context of the institution and decide whether to take action or not.

The understanding of those roles was fundamental for the establishment of boundaries, which drove the BCB's ongoing supervisory model to new trails. In 2006, Brazil finally broke with the classic on-site & off-site and assumed its own model, structured in the form of monitoring and supervision. The title of 'supervisor' was given to the former on-site supervisors, while off-site supervisors became 'monitoring analysts'. The M&S - Monitoring and Supervision model was formally born.

> "We no longer have the segregation of on-site and off-site, our supervision work is integrated." (Belline Santana)

> "By the time of the 2012 FSAP[95], we had already consolidated an integrated understanding on the role of all those involved in supervision tasks. The FSAP assessors required the existence of an information system able to provide indications for on-site supervision work. They wanted to understand how supervisors worked and how monitoring teams cooperated with them. They wanted to see the institution's response and feedback from on-site to off-site supervision. In other words, they wanted to see the whole supervisory cycle. I remember an example: an institution issued a bond with an interest rate considerably higher than the one practiced in the market. In two days, the monitoring had already detected the issuance and the supervisor required explanations from the issuer. That was impressive!" (Donizeti Maia)

> "The BCB's broad powers and well-developed banking supervision are reflected in very high compliance with the Basel Core Principles. The supervisory process is risk-based, robust, and intrusive. It uses a mix of on-site and off-site supervision and well-structured methodologies to identify and assess the most relevant risks of institutions, as well as the quality of internal controls and risk management systems, in order to allocate supervisory resources."
> (IMF/Brazil: Financial System Stability Assessment, July/2012)

---

95. See the entire FSAP report at: https://www.imf.org/external/pubs/ft/scr/2012/cr12206.pdf.

2.3 MICRO-GROUNDED MACRO MONITORING PROCESS

As monitoring activities evolved, teams became increasingly specialized in their respective topics: credit risk, liquidity risk, foreign exchange operations etc. Thus, in addition to understanding and analyzing the risk and the exposure of each institution to it, to report possible problems to the supervisor, they also produced aggregated analyzes of the financial system on their respective topics, to be published in the Financial Stability Report[96] - REF (Relatório de Estabilidade Financeira).

Since the beginning, off-site supervisors, now 'monitoring analysts', had taken the first steps towards a consolidated approach. After all, one of the purposes of the department's creation had been to subsidize the BCB Board with information about the financial system. When the Financial Stability Report emerged in 2002, off-site was named responsible for the elaboration of a chapter on the main risks of the SFN, as well as for editing the whole report. Thus, despite having been structured to perform off-site supervision, the department always had an ugly duckling in its nest: the team responsible for the consolidated view of the SFN[97]. This 'REF-Team' was, in fact, the first component of the BCB's macro prudential monitoring process.

Over time, the REF-Team realized that 'consolidating numbers'[98] was a very poor approach for a macro prudential analysis, as it did not make explicit the links among the various perspectives. In order to understand the financial system as a whole, it was necessary to know each part and how they interacted among themselves. Thus, with the support of the respective specialist areas, the team started to produce macro studies of the

---

96. The Financial Stability Report is a semiannual publication issued by the BCB that presents an overview of recent developments and the outlook on financial stability in Brazil, focusing on the main risks and on the domestic financial system resilience. (Source: https://www.bcb.gov.br/en/publications/financialstabilityreport)
97. For a long time, when monitoring functions were those of the classic off-site model, many people questioned why this work was carried out by the department.
98. The sum of the exposures of all financial institutions in a given risk or position.

various topics monitored by the department, in the search for identifying and understanding the interrelationship among them. Analysts developed skills to monitor the system, as a whole and by peer groups as well, using all the information that the micro area already produced. The macro perspective arose analyzing the available micro data, exploring their interconnections, criticizing, and contributing with other ways of assessing the events. In general, macro-prudential monitoring processes emerge from the economic area of central banks. In Brazil's approach, it represented the supervisor's macro perspective.

The fact that both types of analysis were in the same department allowed the macro monitoring to have easy access to the same level of information as the micro monitoring teams' and both to be anchored in the same reference dates, data sources and methodologies. For this reason, the Brazilian macro prudential monitoring model was built bottom up, supported by supervisors' and monitoring analysts' expertise, who knew in detail each financial institution and were able to extract relevant information from the various databases. Thus, the micro prudential data has also become essential to form the basis for the macro prudential analysis. The expertise to identify what was happening with each entity and how it could impact the whole system became a prerequisite to all macro teams that emerged in the future.

> "We've created the micro-grounded macro prudential monitoring." (João André Calvino)

In contrast to those conflicts regarding the products developed for off-site supervision purposes, macro-prudential monitoring had ample freedom to expand. In fact, there was an increasing demand for information from the Board, largely due to the Global Financial Crisis (GFC)[99]. The Board needed information to manage the crisis and it was in the hands of monitoring teams. Thus, the

---

99. The 2007–2008 financial crisis, or Global Financial Crisis (GFC), was the most serious financial crisis since the Great Depression (1929).

department began to strongly direct its workforce towards this end. Tools based on micro data allowed monitoring analysts to identify risks and vulnerabilities, pointing out those impacted, as well as the magnitude of impact in each institution, with accuracy and timeliness never seen in other models.

Based on this information, the Board could take measures more focused on the problem, which were designed with the support of the monitoring teams, aiming to focus on the target and to avoid as many undesired effects as possible. Besides, the micro monitoring tools were able to monitor the measures' effectiveness almost in real time, which allowed for fast adjustments, whenever necessary. Conclusion: the department that initially had macro monitoring as a byproduct, had found its role in it.

> "One of the fundamental pillars for the development of BCB's monitoring capacity was the freedom given to teams to investigate, create, develop and continuously improve the performance of tools and processes." (Ricardo Almeida)

2.4 THE STRATEGIC AREA: PLANNING SUPERVISION

In 2005, the Supervisory Area consisted of 5 departments[100]. Each department was autonomous in defining its goals and priorities, planning capacitation, and implementing projects to improve its activities. The decentralized management of all those activities worked against the efforts to integrate the supervision model. A neutral forum to discuss supervision in a strategic and integrated manner was missing in this framework. The solution came in the form of a reorganization of functions and responsibilities among the departments, so that administrative and strategic activities were concentrated into a single department.

---

100. Decec – Department of Foreign Capital and Exchange; Decif – Department for Combating Illicits in Foreign Exchange and Financial Opereations; Defin – Department of the Management of Financial System Information; Desin – Department of Off-site Supervision; and Desup – Department of Supervision of Banks and Banking Conglomerates.

Figure: Ongoing Supervision Model - 2004

Source:Information reported in interviews

To start, the new department developed a system for registering and monitoring all activities carried out by supervision, the Integrated Security Assets' Management System – Sigas (*Sistema Integrado de Gestão de Ativos de Segurança*)[101], as well as centralized the capacitation and project management of the entire supervision area. In the beginning, its activities were still at an operational level, but just the fact that they were concentrated in a single component permitted the other departments to focus on their core activities.

Once Sigas was implemented, the process for the elaboration of the supervision annual planning was segregated into two steps: strategic and operational. At first, a collegiate committee composed by the Deputy Governor for Supervision and the heads of department defined the supervision's priorities and guidelines. In the next step, departments should elaborate the planning of their respective activities for the upcoming period, in line with the established priorities.

A committee composed of 1 deputy head of each supervision department, the Supervisory Advisory Committee – Cofis (Comitê de Consultoria da Fiscalização), was created to discuss supervision from a strategic perspective. Initially, Cofis was responsible for mapping all supervisory working processes, identifying their

---

101. At the end of the year, each department should register in Sigas its planning of activities in detail for the following year and, along the year, input its execution, as the planned activities were being carried out.

redundancies and gaps, and proposing the necessary adjustments to the supervisory model.

On the technical level, the 'Strategic' department started to coordinate thematic committees[102], formed by representatives of the operational areas of the various departments. These committees were intended to encourage discussions and seek harmonization for issues that impacted the day-to-day of the monitoring and supervision teams, such as concepts, metrics, working processes and external demands that required a positioning of the supervision area.

> "In complex institutions, the creation of committees is important to joint decision-making. People feel responsible for the decisions and are more committed to implement them." (Anthero Meirelles)

There was, however, a gap in the functioning of the technical committees that needed to be resolved: the lack of legitimacy for decision-making. The participants of these committees were specialists in the topics covered, but they lacked autonomy to be the final word of the department they represented. Thus, department managers did not always agree with the decisions taken by the technical committees, which generated noise in the process and discredited the usefulness of these committees.

To solve the problem, in 2020 the technical committees were replaced by Interdepartmental Technical Networks - RTEC[103] (Rede Técnica Interdepartamental), which incorporated two innovations to the old model: the first concerned the environment for discussions, which became virtual (e-mail), giving much more agility to the process. Second, and most importantly, each RTEC had

---

102. CTCON – Technical Committee for accounting issues; CTCRE – Technical Committee for credit risk issues; CTLIM - Technical Committee for liquidity and market risks issues.
103. As with the old committees, each network is specific to a certain theme. There is a generic network, which covers a variety of topics, which are not yet recurrent enough to justify a specific network. Almost everything goes through the networks: public consultations, reviews of accounting standards, discussions on open banking issues, cyber risk, socio-environmental risk, climatic risk etc.

a single representative (focal point) and a responsible deputy head per department. Regardless of which analyst produced the content within the component, the position taken to be discussed in the technical network represented the department's view (as it should be approved by the deputy head) and not the analyst's. In addition, RTECs had no mandate to decide what was not consensual. In these cases, the issue should be raised to Cofis, to reach a final position of the supervision area.

> "With the RTECs, we brought more governance to the committees that existed before and more commitment with the result." (Carine Bastos)

Figure: RTECs

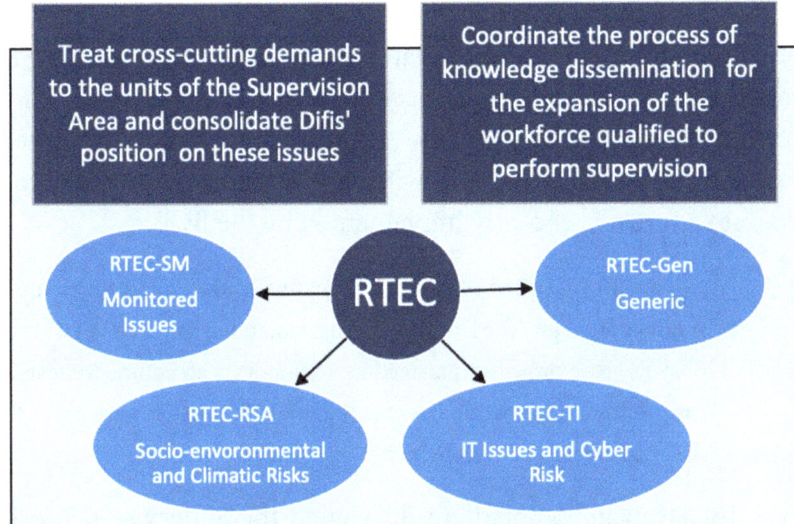

Source:Information reported in interviews

> "The logic of the Monitored Issues[104] technical network, the RTEC-SM (Rede Técnica das Situações Monitoradas), is to increase supervision integration. Every new SM or relevant change is submitted to this network, for discussion among all supervision

---

104. Monitored Issue – SM (Situação Monitorada) is a monitoring process where pre-defined issues that would represent concerns to supervision are verified. More details on the Monitoring Issues process are described in Chapter 3.

departments and Decon[105]. For example: when we created an SM to monitor the institution's net exposure in gold, we used the RTEC-SM to consult the departments and Desuc[106] warned that this type of operation is prohibited for the peer group of brokers, requiring different monitoring metrics for them." (Cleysson Vieira)

The innovative spirit of the teams combined with advances in technology were a fertile ground for constant evolution in tools and work processes. Besides, BCB counted with a special line of financial resources to support strategic projects[107]. Thus, the main evolutions that occurred in the supervision area were materialized through strategic projects. These resources were essential for supervision to reach its level of excellence. On the other hand, the approval and execution of projects demanded great efforts in planning, monitoring and accountability.

Initially, a team was created to conduct the operational management of the various projects carried out by the supervision area. In 2016, the leap to the strategic dimension in project management was materialized, with the adoption of the Corporate Program approach, recently implemented by the BCB.

"A project is a temporary effort undertaken to create a unique product or result. The Corporate Program, in turn, consists of a group of synergistic projects, managed by a temporary structure, to develop capabilities and generate benefits that make it possible to achieve the desired future." (BCB website[108])

The strategic department developed the Supervision Model Program (S-UP), which brought synergy to the projects from various areas of expertise, aligning them towards the same vision of future: 'to act proactively and in a timely manner in the identification

---

105. Department of Conduct Supervision.
106. Credit Unions and Non-Banking Financial Institutions Supervision Department.
107. Strategic projects needed to be in line with the BCB mission and be approved by the BCB's Corporate Projects Committee, composed of BCB Deputy Governors.
108. https://www.BC.gov.br/acessoinformacao/projprogcorporativos.

and solution of situations that could compromise the soundness or regular functioning of the financial system or its institutions'.

"The S-UP Program helped supervision to make its big breakthrough." (Belline Santana)

Figure: S-UP Program

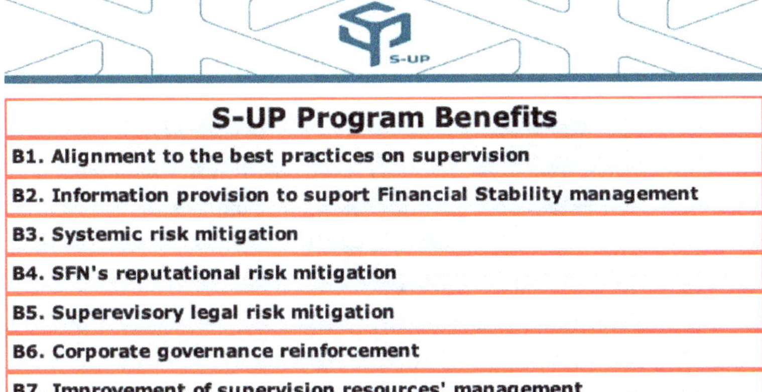

Source:Banco Central do Brasil – Difis' Activities Report – 2017 and 2018

Even after the implementation of the integrated and strategic approach in all areas of supervision management, the strategic department still acted as a coordinator for the integration of supervision processes. Their teams' expertise was focused on the administrative area, but, in practice, they did not add value in technical discussions. The incorporation of the on-site specialized teams in 2018, previously allocated in the banking supervision department, came to solve this gap. The arrival of these teams was an important evolution, as it allowed the department to have an active voice in the discussions.

'Under new management', the specialized teams expanded their scope[109] not only regarding the supervised institutions, previously restricted to banking institutions, but also in terms of attributions. Besides providing technical support to banking and, from then on, non-banking supervisors, they started to act as a

109. While allocated in the banking supervision department, they participated in inspections and carried out 'horizontal work', i.e., the verification of a certain problem in several banking financial institutions. See more details on the trajectory of specialized teams in Chapter 5 - 5.2 Specialized Teams.

technical and management middle ground in interdepartmental discussions, mainly on topics that were still arid, such as cyber risk and socio-environmental risk. In addition, they opened room for dialogue towards the standardization of supervisory procedures, for example, to avoid the adoption of more rigorous measures in a small cooperative than in a large bank, or vice versa.

2.5 THE SUPERVISORY MODEL

> "Taking into account our financial system's characteristics and the size of our country, the current supervisory model with the segregation between monitoring and [on-site] supervision, the last one covering banking and non-banking institutions in separate units, became natural, logical and irrefutable!" (Adalberto Felinto)

BCB supervisory model has evolved over time, making use of its peculiar condition: having a vast set of granular information and developing technology and expertise to make use of this information. The capacity of data analysis learned during the IGCs has evolved into a sound monitoring process, as it expanded to other areas, such as information compliance processes, where, for example, information reported by institutions were compared with data collected from trade repositories. Monitoring also developed the ability to detect fraud and various types of irregularities, such as violations of the Anti-Money Laundering and Combating the Financing of Terrorism (AML/CFT) rules.

At the same time, supervisors counted on a significant number of information reported in standardized templates[110], which allow them to contextualize their opinion about the supervised entities.

---

110. Supervised institutions are required to provide BCB with sufficient information for the execution of supervisory activities. Among others, information regarding their Internal Capital Adequacy Assessment Process (ICAAP) and the following reports deserve to be highlighted: liquidity risk report, market risk report, report on the compliance with operational requirements, report on the effectiveness of internal controls, report on monitoring of AML/CFT action plans and the control report internal audits prepared regarding the assessment of independent auditors.

Thus, the supervisor's direct interaction with the institutions could focus mainly on the assessment of managerial aspects, such as strategies, budget, risks management, internal controls, governance, and the performance of audits.

The existing infrastructure of tools, processes and information permits BCB to carry out ongoing supervision focused on risks effectively and with less consumption of resources.

Figure: The Monitoring & Supervision Model[111]

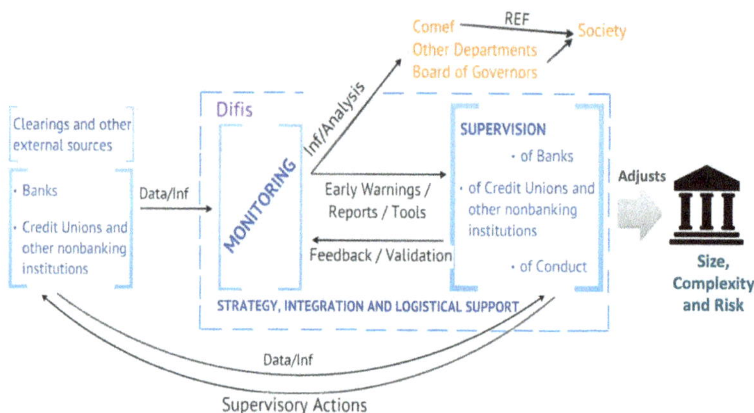

Note: the Supervision of Conduct is subordinated to the Deputy Governor for institutional relations, citizenship and conduct supervision (Direc)

Source:Banco Central do Brasil - https://www.bcb.gov.br/conteudo/home-ptbr/TextosApresentacoes/Apresentacao_Anthero_Meirelles_CPI_HSBC.pdf

"Financial institutions have great respect for Central Bank supervision. The relationship between them has always been very good and they manage to resolve supervisory issues based on dialogue, as long as the compliance with rules is observed. In addition, institutions are used to implement supervisory recommendations to improve their practices and processes." (Sidney Marques)

---

111. The BCB periodically assesses the need for improvements in the Supervisory Model, not only to address eventual weaknesses, but also to anticipate the challenges that will arise. This proactive approach is critical to model risk mitigation.

The BCB supervision model was developed over an extended period of turmoil. The internal conflicts experienced to 'put the house in order' came against a backdrop of successive crises: at the turn of the century, supervision had barely recovered itself from the great banking crisis of the 1990s, when its reputation was shaken with the case of the Marka and FonteCindam banks[112]. Besides the impacts of the GFC in the second half of 2000s, the discovery of frauds in the securitization market contributed to the extension of the crisis effects in the small and medium-size banks until the middle of the following decade. The brief period of calm was soon interrupted by a new global crisis resulting from the COVID-19 pandemic, which hit the financial system in 2019 and has repercussions to this day. This succession of crises, both systemic and idiosyncratic[113], required urgent adjustments to the model, like repairing an aircraft during the flight. There were tense moments, but at the same time, very fertile for the improvement of the model, because adjustments needed to be tested and corrected immediately.

Practice has shown that in times of stress, the roles of monitoring and supervision may assume different proportions, depending on the type of crisis: if idiosyncratic, the main source of information is the supervisor inside the problem bank, reporting in real time to BCB's Board its evolution. Monitoring keeps the background, searching for eventual contagion effects in similar institutions, due to reputational risks. In a systemic crisis, the role of monitoring is more comprehensive, as the entire market needs to be monitored. In that case, monitoring plays a central role in the reports to the Board; gives technical support to the design of macro-prudential measures, as well as of eventual regulatory adjustments to mitigate risks; monitors the impact of the measures taken; and informs supervisors where to intensify supervisory on-site works. There is an intense exchange of feedback between monitoring and supervision teams, with supervision promptly investigating monitoring alerts, taking actions

---

112. See details about these events in Chapter 1.

113. A systemic crisis affects much or all of the financial system. In an idiosyncratic crisis, problems in 1 relevant financial institution may impact other financial institutions.

when necessary, and reporting additional information to the Board, whenever an off-site information gap exists.

> "During the pandemic[114], supervisors sent a monthly questionnaire to several banks with questions regarding credit appetite, comparison of supply and demand of credit with the pre-crisis period, expectations for the coming periods, etc. This type of information is not regularly reported to SCR[115], since it consists only of credit granted, that is, the result of the interactions between supply and demand for credit. Thus, it would not be possible to infer how they were behaving individually." (Cleysson Vieira)

2.6 STAFF CAPACITATION

Since the creation of the BCB, it has established a specific program for the supervisors' capacitation: the Training Course for Inspector – Cinsp (*Curso de Formação de Inspetores*). In 1976, when the BCB structured its career plan by specializations, supervision became held by auditors. Thus, Cinsp was discontinued, as auditors already had the necessary requirements to perform the supervisory activities at the time.

In the end of the 1980s, BCB returned to a single career framework for its entire staff of analysts, which gave rise to the need to train inspectors again. The first Cinsp of the new era was held in the mid-1990s and consisted of a 3-months immersion on capacitation activities.

BCB's area responsible for staff's capacitation is hierarchically subordinated to the Deputy Governor for Administration. However, when the strategic department was created in the supervision area, it comprehended a team dedicated to the planning and monitoring of training activities focused on supervision issues[116].

---

114. During the period of the COVID-19 pandemic, supervision intensified its work to map possible impacts on the Financial System resulting from the slowdown in the economy.
115. SCR is the current Credit Risk Bureau conducted by the BCB. It has replaced the Credit Risk Register (CRC). See more details in Chapter 3.
116. This team works in cooperation with UniBC, BCB's corporate component responsible

In 2012, this team coordinated Cinsp's restructuration, organizing it into three modules: 'Basic', comprising the knowledge necessary for all supervision employees - this module maintained the original concept of Cinsp, with a 360-hours training package, including practical on-site inspection activities; 'Complementary', aiming at the specialization of inspectors in a given area – this module is carried out in the form of specific courses, offered periodically; and 'Updating', addressing topics on the cutting edge, in national and international contexts, this module is offered in the form of lectures open to all BCB employees.

> "Every year, supervision employees must register their training demands for the following year[117]. As the courses are offered, the selection of participants is made based on the staff's demands and the level of importance of the training to the activities performed by them." (Harold Espinola)

Figure: Training Course for Inspector - Cinsp

Source:Banco Central do Brasil

---

for staff capacitation, for the planning and monitoring activities related to supervision.
117. Training demands are registered at the Siscap System, the tool used to manage the training of employees in the supervision area.

In 2014, BCB implemented a management tool called the 'Value Chain', which maps the added value of each workflow, that is, how the result of one activity is an input for the other, until the final product is delivered to end customers. Based on this methodology, each BCB Unit had to map its working processes[118], with details of activities and routines for the execution of each process, as well as to identify the Knowledge, Skills and Attitudes - KSA necessary for each activity. The methodology allowed supervision to boost the strategic vision also in the training area, by aligning the offer of Cinsp's annual training to any gaps in demand of KSA identified in the employees' profiles.

Figure: BCB's Value Chain

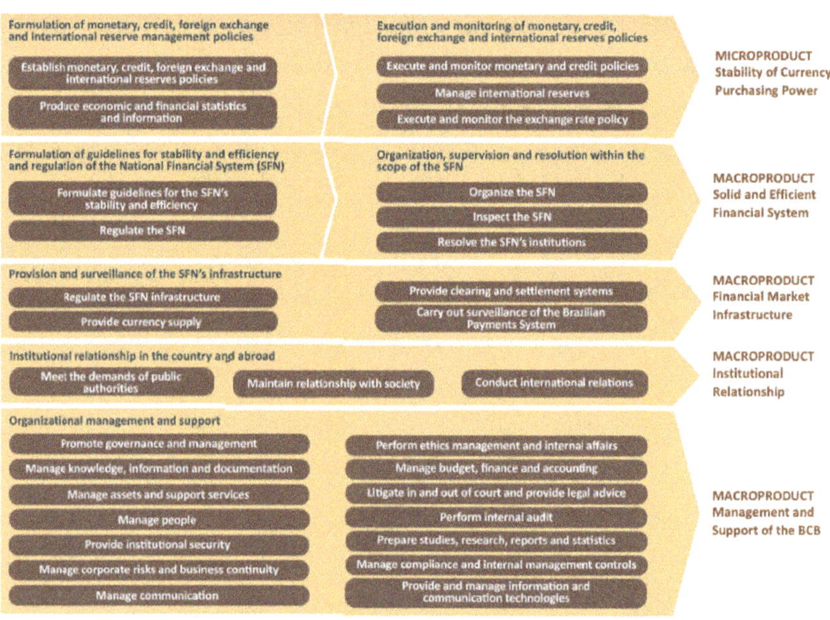

Source:Banco Central do Brasil - - https://www.bcb.gov.br/en/about/valuechainMPR

---

118. The cost of each process is estimated by the System for the Monitoring of Costs and Management Information - SCIG (*Sistema de Custos e Informações Gerenciais*), where all employees must register monthly the time allocated to each process or project in which they participate. By means of this tool, BCB is able to estimate the cost, as well as quantify the human resources actually spent in each performed activity.

"We know, in a structured and formalized way, What must be done in the Units (Value Chain), Where and Who must do it (ADM[119]), How it must be done (MSU[120]), How Much It costs (SCIG) and Which knowledge, skills and attitudes (KSA) are required to perform each work process." (Sergio Tavares)

In addition to the impacts on capacitation planning, the implementation of the Value Chain also contributed to the improvement of the supervision annual planning process. Since the 2014 PAS[121], supervision actions have been established considering the adequacy of the activities carried out in each department to the workflows mapped therein for supervision.

Figure: Elaboration Process of the Supervision Annual Plan

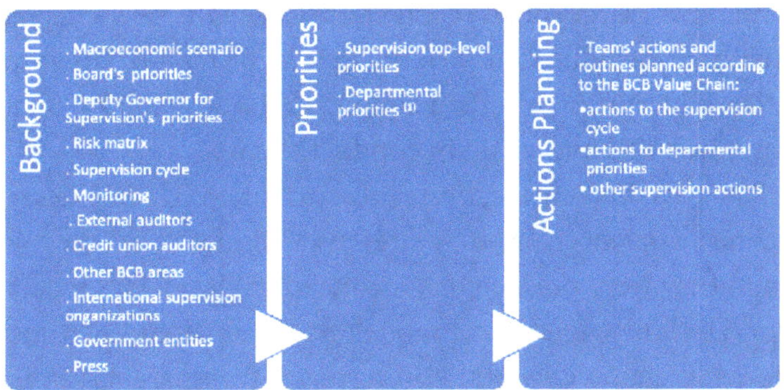

(1) The priorities for supervision of conduct are approved by the Deputy Governor for institutional relations, citizenship and conduct supervision (Direc)

Source:Banco Central do Brasil - Supervision Manual - MSU - https://www3.bcb.gov.br/gmn/visualizacao/listarDocumentosManualPublico.do?method=listarDocumentosManualPublico&idManual=1

2.7 THE TRANSPARENCY OF SUPERVISORY PROCEDURES

The project for the modernization of Brazilian supervision, initiated in 1999, was the trigger for successive improvements of the

---

119. Administrative Organization Manual.
120. Supervision Manual.
121. Supervision Annual Plan - PAS (*Planejamento Anual da Supervisão*).

BCB supervision model. The first step, which not only contributed to standardizing how supervision was carried out among the various BCB regional offices, but also to foster the debate on what should or should not be done, was the replacement of the old Procedures and Routines Manual (MPR) by the Supervision Manual[122] - MSU (*Manual da Supervisão*) in the early 2000s.

> "How could we say whether the supervisor was right or wrong, or if the procedure was right or wrong, if there was no formalized parameter?" (Donizeti Maia)

In its first version, MSU described step by step each inspection and assessment procedure within the new supervisory model, focused on risks and controls. Over time, the various developments in the supervision model brought new chapters to the manual, including micro and macro prudential monitoring activities, supervision of credit unions and non-banking financial institutions, and supervision of conduct, as well.

Since its implementation, the part of MSU that described the scope of supervision activities was disclosed to the public, although they were presented at a conceptual level. Despite having incorporated the supervision model evolution along the time, the 'public' MSU has evolved little in terms of transparency along the time.

Meanwhile, international discussions towards the establishment of minimum standards for the performance of internationally active financial institutions were evolving at a rapid pace. Recommendations of good practices, both for the supervised entities and for the supervisors themselves, were growing in detail.

> "The supervisor issues standards related to, in particular, credit risk, market risk, liquidity risk, interest rate risk in the banking book

---

122. The IGC was the prevailing supervisory model at the turn of the century and many of the procedures described in the MSU are based on experiences gained in on-site works at that time.

and operational risk."(BCBS Core Principles for Effective Banking Supervision Sept/2012 – Core Principle 15, Essential Criterion 11)

More and more, central banks and supervision bodies were being pushed to clarify to supervised entities what was expected from them. However, a regulatory framework aimed at establishing objective and sometimes quantitative requirements, as well as penalties for non-compliance, was not the appropriate instrument for this type of communication. A less imposing and more open channel was needed to discuss in detail technical or principled issues. Thus, they began to publish technical guidance, clarification notes, Q&A[123], principles, best practice recommendations, and other documents, to fill this gap between formal regulation and the regulator's intention[124].

> "…Banco de España may prepare and publish technical guides addressed to supervised entities and groups, indicating the criteria, practices, methodologies or procedures, which it considers appropriate for the compliance with the supervision regulations." (Spain - article 54 of the Law 10/2014)
>
> "The manual gives insight into the elements of sound liquidity risk management on which DNB[125] will base its assessment of whether an institution is compliant with the supervisory standards regarding the management of liquidity risk… This manual explains what is expected of banks, clearing institutions and investment firms (institutions) in the context of ILAAP[126]". (The Netherlands - Principles for the internal liquidity adequacy assessment process (ILAAP))

---

123. Questions and Answers (Q&A) is a document that gathers the most frequent questions asked by those involved in a given topic and their respective answers.

124. In Germany, BaFin (Bundesanstalt für Finanzdienstleistungsaufsicht) publishes on its website 'Interpretive Decisions', where it provides clarification to market participants so that they may "consistently apply the regulations" (https://www.bafin.de/EN/RechtRegelungen/Auslegungsentscheidungen/ae_node_en.html). In December 2015, for example, 12 interpretive decisions were published to explain the correct calculation of Pillar I capital requirements under Solvency II rules.

125. De Nederlandsche Bank.

126. Internal Liquidity Adequacy Assessment Process.

> "…provide supervisory guidance in considerable detail regarding the Board's current policies and procedures for supervising the financial affairs of these banking organizations and will also discuss their respective statutes, regulations, interpretations, and orders that pertain to BHC[127] supervision." (USA – Banking Holding Company Supervision Manual)

In Brazil, the only document with this purpose – the public version of the MSU – was far from satisfactorily meeting the expectations of international recommendations. The document that would best reflect the supervisor's expectations was the manual of the ongoing banking supervision tool – SRC[128] (*Supervisão de Riscos e Controles*), as it presented in detail the criteria used in the assessment of institutions, as well as the supervisor's expectations regarding the banks' risk management and control environment. Thus, in 2016, this manual was made public, under the title of Guide of Supervisory Practices - GPS (*Guia de Práticas da Supervisão*)[129].

> "Putting the standard requirement in a more accessible language is a problem all over the world. In Brazil, we found some resistance to the idea of disclosing the GPS, after all, we would tell the banks how we supervised them. On the other hand, if the banks did everything that was placed in the GPS, it would be tremendous. And the banks asked for it. They said it was much easier to know what the Central Bank wanted from them." (Nelio Magina)

The document was well received by the supervised entities, as it facilitated their communication with supervisors and really served its purpose of recommending good practices, especially for smaller entities. In the following years, recommendations from other supervision areas were gradually integrating the GPS[130].

---

127. Bank Holding Company.
128. See more details regarding the SRC in Chapter 5.
129. GPS comprises almost the entire SRC manual. Only the templates for quantitative assessment of the institutions (score) are not published.
130. MSU and GPS can be found at: https://www3.BC.gov.br/gmn/visualização/listarDocumentosManualPúblico.do?method=listarDocumentosManualPúblico&idManual=1.

CHAPTER 3

Micro Prudential Monitoring

"The monitoring area is in an ongoing crisis, because rethinking, rebuilding, reinventing, redoing is all the time."

(Ailton Aquino)

"I need more and more monitoring outputs to focus my resources where the risk is."

(Andreia Laís)

This chapter provides details on the scope of micro prudential monitoring activities, as it describes its main microdata-intensive processes and tools. It also explains why the structuring of the micro prudential monitoring framework in the form of Monitored Issues has provoked a leap in the evolution of the Brazilian supervision model.

3.1 THE OFF-SITE SUPERVISION IMPLEMENTATION

Off-site teams were created with the objective of reporting to on-site supervisors the potential problems identified. There were three large sets of data available to supervision when the off-site processes were created at the turn of the century: the financial statements, reported by the financial institutions mostly on a monthly basis; detailed information on credit operations informed to the CRC[131]; and information on financial market operations[132] registered in the trade repositories and reported to BCB on a daily basis.

Initially, each off-site team was responsible for one type of analysis, and consequently, for one data source. CRC information, however, had a peculiar characteristic. While the other data sources were destined to BCB's internal use, CRC worked also as a credit information bureau, where data providers could consult the consolidated exposure of their clients throughout the SFN. Thus, besides the off-site supervision activities, the credit risk team was also responsible for the bureau's management.

A short while before, BCB employees' working tools had shifted from mainframe terminals to personal computers. Until then, the IT area had, in practice, the monopoly of developing working tools to the whole central bank: the business area specified its information needs, and the IT area developed a system to provide them. This model was suitable for a structure where the only access to information was through mainframe terminals. But, once personal computers were made available to users, it was no longer possible to restrain the demand for access to raw data, nor to inhibit individual initiatives for the development of data processing tools.

---

131. CRC was replaced by the SCR (Sistema de Informações de Créditos) in 2001.
132. Operations with public and private securities, interbank deposit operations and derivative contracts.

A long cultural change process was needed until BCB achieved the current information management model[133]. At the beginning of the 21st century, business areas were starting to realize they could develop their own tools and the relationship with the IT area began to be questioned. Off-site supervision played a leading role in this evolutionary process.

> "We started developing tools that people could really use. This gave us power to demand for more adequate data processing tools and direct access to databases. When we were allowed to use SQL[134] and replicate corporate data[135], we started to create important databases in our department, which allowed us to evolve really fast. The leap in quality of information produced was huge: it opened room for cross-checking information routines, producing reports and information in an aggregate perspective of the financial system... From then on, off-site activities flowed smoothly." (Helton Maciel)

The demand for IT-expertise in off-site teams was huge. They needed to develop and constantly improve tools for data analysis, which required skilled labor. In addition, many of the Board's demands required database manipulation, as there was no ready-made information in the existing tools.

> "We had information on banks' equity at the financial conglomerate level and also at the individual level. To match them, we needed to eliminate intra group operations. I developed a tool called ' Shareholding Composition' to cross-check this data. It was not a simple job. It was really complicated, I confess, but nobody told me that other people had already tried to do it and didn't succeed. So, I did it!" (Nizam Pfeilsticker)

---

133. The evolution of the BCB's information management model is presented in Chapter 4.

134. Structured Query Language, is a query language for relational databases.

135. Corporate data is managed by the BCB's IT area, as well as corporate systems and tools are developed and maintained by them. Similarly, those developed and managed by users are called 'departamental' databases, tools and systems.

The use of adequate softwares for data manipulation, such as the SQL Server, was an important milestone for the development of monitoring tools, as it allowed for the formation of departmental databases exclusively managed by the off-site teams.

The three areas, which at the beginning of the century struggled with the limitations of Access and Excel to transform data into information, were making great strides. However, evolution depended on individual initiatives. There was no structured planning for the development of tools. Besides, the processes were not integrated, which favored the replication of databases. A typical case was the FI[136] Register database: each area maintained its own register, with different criteria for its composition and updating process. In consequence, it eventually provoked the selection of different lists of institutions to a same peer group or financial conglomerate.

> "There were lots of mergers, acquisitions and extinct banks along the time and no historical record of them. All we had was the current composition of the financial system. So, I took on the task of setting up the historical register and everyone started using my database. Over time, even other departments outside the supervision area became users. That was the most reliable FI Registry of the Central Bank." (André Caccavo)

Feeling pressured to develop products and establish new work processes, each team created its own group of tool developers. At one point, attempts were made to gather these people into a single team, but it didn't work. The new arrangement brought back the problems the supervision area had with the corporate IT team: developers and users being apart resulted in demands not met satisfactorily. Gradually, teams took back the development of their own tools, but the IT-Experts team was not dismissed, on the contrary, it assumed the role of IT consultant for the off-site teams, as well as the manager of the department's IT framework.

---

136. Financial Institution.

The IT-Experts team's mission was somewhat challenging. They needed to negotiate with everyone involved, to establish a framework that would eliminate overlaps and harmonize processes within the same technological standard. The imposition of any standard, software or tool would inhibit more advanced initiatives. Thus, the strategy adopted consisted into highlighting the pros of each successful initiative and, little by little, gaining allies to the standardization process.

Off-site activities based on financial statements' data:

The team in charge of assessing the financial statements database developed a model for the economic-financial assessment of banking institutions and conglomerates, based on risk and performance indicators, similar to the former Indicon[137] and on the experience of other regulators, such as the Uniform Bank Performance Report (UBPR) of the Federal Financial Institutions Examination Council (FFIEC)[138]. The assessment process followed the CAMELS[139] model.

> "We adjusted the financial statements by reclassifying and balancing balance sheet accounts to create the economic-financial indicators. A few years later, we joked that Basel was compliant with us, because Basel II proposed adjustments in balance sheet data. We came to the conclusion that we were doing a very correct job, because a similar methodology was being adopted internationally." (Álvaro Freitas)

---

137. See Chapter 1 - 1.3 Structure and operation of supervision.

138. The Federal Financial Institutions Examination Council (FFIEC) is an interagency council that brings together the main financial supervisory agencies in the United States, with the objective of prescribing uniform principles, standards and report forms for the examination of financial institutions.

139. CAMELS rating is a supervisory rating system originally developed in the U.S. to classify a bank's overall condition. The ratings are assigned based on a ratio analysis of the financial statements, combined with on-site examinations made by a designated supervisory regulator. The components of a bank's condition that are assessed: (C)apital adequacy; (A)ssets; (M)anagement Capability; (E)arnings; (L)iquidity (also called asset liability management); and (S)ensitivity (sensitivity to market risk, especially interest rate risk). Ratings are from 1 (best) to 5 (worst) in each of the above categories.

> "We established the rating scores based on the best methodology
> we could achieve at that moment and we gradually evolved along the
> time, adjusting the deficiencies of each process, as they were being
> identified." (Marcelo Fernandes)

Another activity developed by that team was an 'early warning' system that identified variations in the values of accounting items or in indicators calculated based on the financial statements, for each institution. When a significant variation between two reporting dates was identified, it was reported to on-site supervisors who, in turn, asked the bank for explanations. In the beginning, most variations were due to data quality issues. Thus, this process contributed a lot to improve the quality of balance sheet information, as it indirectly forced FIs to improve their information management processes. On the other hand, in the supervisor's perspective there was too much wear and tear, as these quality-related issues put inspection's work out of focus.

> "Once, we identified a very large variation and called the bank
> for an explanation. Very embarrassed, they reported that, by mistake,
> they had informed the customer's fiscal number instead of the
> operation's amount. This event showed the market that data reported
> to the Central Bank was really being used." (Reynaldo Furlani)

In general, early warning systems consisted of metrics where a set of variables were established, as well as normal ranges associated with each of them. Upon the arrival of new data, the variables were calculated and compared with the corresponding ranges. Those that exceeded the limits were listed for the analysis of an off-site supervisor, who decided whether or not to report it to the on-site supervisor, as a concern. Thus, off-site teams needed tools to provide easy access to the information needed to support their analysis and decisions.

Initially, the tools were for the exclusive use of off-site teams, with the purpose of enabling the investigation of the causes and relevance of suspicious events. However, as they displayed information in an organized and very accessible way, they also became useful to on-site teams, both as a working tool for planning inspections, as well as a source of information for the ongoing supervision process.

The tool developed for the assessment of significant variations in the financial statements gave rise to the 'Analisador' [Analyser], a very versatile tool, capable of organizing information from a sequence of several monthly balance sheets from the same institution[140], to facilitate the assessment of its evolution[141]. Currently, besides the accounting information, it also comprehends registry data, cash flow statement information, recent news from the media, the list of entities belonging to the financial conglomerate and financial information of its peer group, among other information.

> "'Analisador' is our most popular tool. It is available to the entire supervision area and to other BCB departments as well."
> (Andrei Vanderlei)

Off-site activities based on credit register data:

Credit risk off-site supervision activities initially consisted of reporting to the on-site supervisor the relevant changes observed in the credit operations portfolio profile, regarding the default level or credit operations type, for example, as well as significant divergences between the information of a given institution, when compared with its peers or the financial system, such as the provision level or the risk rating assigned to a given debtor. To this end, the team developed reports and tools based on the CRC.

The off-site credit risk tools and reports were very popular among on-site supervisors. As the team was mainly composed by

---

140. For a given time period and FI, 'Analisador' displays standardized reports with the series of balance sheets and income statements, both in adjusted and original formats. Over time, more information has been included, such as credit and market risk data, FI shares, the financial conglomerate composition etc.

141. The team has also developed a tool called 'Comparador' [Comparator], where information from different financial institutions could be compared, enabling the comparison of a FI situation with its peer groups' behavior or the whole financial system's, as well.

former IGC's credit risk specialists, they have also developed several tools aiming at inspection works[142].

> "The tool 'Amostra Dirigida' [Directed Sample] was widely used by on-site supervisors. It allowed the user to select and calibrate his/her own parameters (that would represent evidence of concerns) and generated samples of debtors who met those parameters." (Rogério Rabelo)

In 2002, the CRC evolved into the Credit Information System - SCR (*Sistema de Informações de Crédito*) with a significant increase in the scope of information. New data enabled the assessment of the historical performance of each operation and the whole portfolio, and the development of tools to measure the quality of credit operations. On the data providers side, they started to realize the importance of having access to their client's exposure throughout the SFN, and the use of SCR data on their internal credit risk models increased gradually. Currently, SCR is the main source of information used by financial institutions for credit risk management[143].

> "'BCB Risk' is how banks refer to the client's credit risk level reported in the SCR. Nowadays, this information is vital, there's no way to live without it." (Paulo Cavalheiro)

SCR has evolved substantially over the years. The CRC's initial floor of R$ 50,000 (USD 26,000) to identify the operation's debtor was gradually being reduced, as technological resources were evolving or the assessment of operations of lower value was

---

142. SCR information was displayed in the format of tables, widely used by the on-site supervisor: portfolio values, losses, transition matrix, the larger operations, the larger NPLs, exclusive customer (customers that do not have credit operations in another FI) unique customer (90% of the customer's credits are in this FI) etc.

143. In SCR2 version, SCR participants were able to consult the credit exposures of all their customers by credit modality, performing and non-performing amounts, maturity range, portfolio value, limit, credit to be granted, debentures, commercial notes, and other credit instruments. In SCR3 version, information on guarantees and origin of resources (BNDES, bank's own), were included in the bureau and all information formerly provided in SCR2 version at the client's level is available at the credit operation level.

being required. In 2016, the floor for debtor identification reached its minimum level: R$ 200 (USD 62).

> "Changes in the SCR often provoke a huge implementation effort by financial institutions. The best technical solution and the implementation period are always discussed and agreed among the Central Bank and SCR participants. It is a joint construction." (Rogério Rabelo)

Figure: Historic Evolution of the SCR

Project	CRC	SCR 1			SCR2				SCR3		
Year	1997	1999	2000	2002	2009	2012	2016	2019	2020	2023	2024
Operation Identification Floor (R$/USD)	50,000/ 44,785		20,000/ 10,280		5,000/ 2,872	1,000/ 489	200/ 61	200/ 50			
Number of Customers (million)	0.5	1.3			24	66	103	120			
Number of Operations (million)	0.6	1.6			90	406	618	742			
Total Identified Amount (R$/USD million)	594/ 532	550/ 308			1,286/ 738	2,326/ 1,138	3,109/ 954	3,434/ 852			
Total Non Identified Amount (R$/USD million)					128/ 73	28/ 14	1.7 /0.53	0.71/ 0.18			

Source:Banco Central do Brasil

In 1999, the supervision area contributed to the elaboration of the CMN Resolution 2682/1999, which established the Brazilian rule for credit provision. The regulation defined a risk classification score based on the operation's lag of delay in payment, and established a provision range to each classification level. This rule favored great advances for the supervision of credit risk, as the SCR micro data provided the information needed to the off-site assessment of the FI's provision level, without the need for on-site inspections.

Over time, important tools were developed to assess the quality of an FI's credit portfolio: among other tools, the 'Matriz de Migração' [Transition Matrix] indicates how much of the portfolio had changed its operations' risk classification within a certain time period[144]; the 'Inadimplência Coorte' [Delinquency Cohort[145]], from the credit operations contracted in a given month/year, identifies the volume of default related to those operations, over time; and the calculation of the probability of default (PD) and the loss given default (LGD) allows for the calculation of expected losses. Supported by all those tools, the team is able to identify signs of deterioration in the credit portfolio of a particular financial institution, a group of institutions, and even the entire SFN.

Figure: Transition Matrix

Risk level transition matrix

	Risk level	AA	A	B	C	D	E	F	G	H	Write-offs	Decreases[1]	Total	Credit operations outstanding Jun-16
Jun-16	AA	**64.5**	12.0	5.8	2.0	0.6	0.2	0.1	0.2	0.1	-	14.4	**38.2**	1,204,600
	A	19.5	**42.0**	12.9	4.2	2.4	0.8	0.5	0.6	0.5	0.2	16.0	**20.0**	912,773
	B	8.9	15.0	**35.8**	12.8	5.5	1.9	1.0	1.3	0.8	0.9	16.0	**15.9**	502,260
	C	4.4	7.6	14.2	**28.9**	16.2	3.9	2.3	2.8	1.7	4.0	13.9	**6.5**	204,507
	D	2.3	5.2	7.5	12.6	**28.7**	8.2	3.8	4.5	2.6	10.4	14.1	**4.4**	137,049
	E	0.8	3.0	2.6	3.8	8.4	**12.9**	16.8	8.6	7.2	21.9	13.9	**2.0**	61,924
	F	0.5	1.9	1.3	2.9	4.0	5.7	**12.8**	10.9	5.1	38.5	16.6	**1.2**	38,658
	G	0.3	1.0	0.8	0.9	1.5	1.8	3.6	**15.6**	6.5	53.2	14.8	**1.4**	43,884
	H	0.2	0.7	0.6	0.6	0.7	0.6	0.6	2.6	**21.8**	58.1	13.4	**1.4**	44,787
Total		**32.2**	**20.1**	**13.0**	**6.6**	**4.4**	**1.6**	**1.2**	**1.4**	**1.1**	**3.4**	**15.1**		
BRL million		1,013,012	633,065	499,721	206,721	137,696	50,261	38,304	43,254	35,694	107,175	475,396		3,150,442[2]

1/ Represented by the liquidations of operations and concessions of credit.
2/ This data includes only identified credit operations whose debtors own over R$1,000.

Source:Financial Stability Report - October/2017 https://www.bcb.gov.br/en/publications/financialstabilityreport/201710

---

144. The rows and columns of the Transition Matrix are composed of the credit risk classification score defined by Resolution 2682/1999: AA, A, B, C, D, E and H. The value indicated in each cell of the table represents the percentage of the portfolio that migrated from the classification corresponding to its row to the classification corresponding to its column, after the time period defined by the analyst has elapsed.

145. A Cohort is the group of all credit operations informed in the SCR with the same contractual date (month/year). The BCB publishes quarterly information on the delinquency cohort's historical evolution on its website. (https://www.bcb.gov.br/estabilidadefinanceira/inadimplencia_coorte).

Figure: Delinquency Cohort (>= 90 days)

$$COHORT\ Indicator = \frac{non\ performing\ credit\ operations\ beyon\ 90\ days}{total\ COHORT\ operations}$$

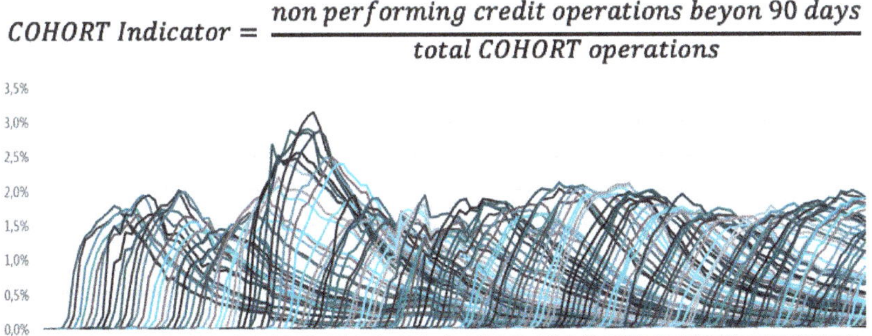

Vertical axis: % non-performing operations (beyond 90 days)

Horizontal axis: reference date of credit operation granting

Curves = COHORTs

Source:Banco Central do Brasil – Graphic Examples of Delinquency Cohort https://www.bcb.gov.br/content/estabilidadefinanceira/scr/inadimplencia_coorte/Exemplos_Graficos.pdf

The off-site credit risk team also developed a tool, the Integrated Monitoring System - SIM (*Sistema Integrado de Monitoramento*), to manage the warnings reported to on-site supervisors. The off-site supervisor used the tool to report its concerns to the on-site supervisor responsible for the institution where the suspicious evidence had been detected, and, in return, the on-site supervisor was required to register his/her feedback[146] (whether upheld or not). Initially restricted to off-site credit risk messages, SIM was gradually being expanded to comprehend the reporting processes from the other off-site areas, until, finally, being migrated to a corporate tool[147].

> "SIM has standardized the workflow between monitoring and supervision." (Rogerio Rabelo)

---

146. The on-sites supervisor's feedback was very important for the improvement of off-site tools' methodologies and calibration.

147. A 'corporate tool' is the one developed in appropriate language and managed by the IT area of BCB.

Off-site activities based on trade repositories' data:

The team responsible for managing information from the trade repositories focused, at first, on learning more about the securities and derivatives markets, the operations' behavior, and how fluctuations in traded values impacted the levels of liquidity and capital of financial institutions, due to their exposure to market risk. In this way, the first off-site processes developed aimed to identify patterns of normality and to flag the outliers. This was the only off-site team that has not developed periodic reports focused on expressing a conclusive opinion on a specific financial institution. Instead, the team produced lists of institutions with suspicious evidence to be investigated by on-site supervision.

Databases comprehended not only the registration of the institutions' custody positions, but also the individual register of each operation traded in the market, on a daily basis. For the derivatives, in particular, Brazilian regulation had established as mandatory the identification of the final holders and, in December, 8th of 2011, the Law 12,543 conditioned the legal validity of a derivative contract to its registry in a trading repository[148]. So, BCB had access to the complete information of all derivative contracts signed in the country.

> "The registration of financial assets and derivatives brings safety to investors. Having a third party assuring the registry of operations, as well as the supervision authority monitoring them, ends up being advantageous for the entire market." (Edson Teixeira)

In the beginning, trade repositories had processing limitations. They were able to record the operations, but it required a lot of machine time to process and report data to BCB. Fortunately, IT evolution has supported their continuous improvement in

---

148. Law 12,543 art. 1st § 4th states that the legal validity of a derivative's contract is conditioned to its registry in a trade repository or clearing house authorized by the BCB or CVM, among other requirements. (http://www.planalto.gov.br/ccivil_03/_ato2011-2014/2011/lei/l12543.htm)

performance, which gradually permitted, inclusively, the reduction of deadlines for sending information to the BCB.

> "Initially, Cetip's process to report information to BCB was not well organized and discussions regarding eventual problems usually took place at the operational IT level. At a given moment, BCB took the lead towards the enhancement of its data sources, even acting in the identification of some inconsistencies eventually not detected by Cetip. This initiative has contributed to significant improvements in Cetip's data quality and data management, as well." (Simone Acioli – CETIP)

At first, the off-site team developed metrics for monitoring the federal government securities' market. It established processes to identify operations traded out of the market's normal range[149] and to map 'day-trade chains', a sequence of purchases and sales of a same security carried out on a same day, where the traded security returns to the first seller at the end of the day. The objective was to identify excessive gains or losses among the participants. Afterwards, a similar process was developed to monitor interbank foreign exchange operations.

The team also developed processes to cross-check financial statements information[150] reported to BCB, by comparing them with data from independent sources, the trade repositories' registers. This routine, in addition to automatically processing all institutions at the same time, replaced a task normally performed by on-site supervisors during inspections, which opened space in their agenda for other activities.

Trade repositories' data was also used to monitor the FI's exposure to liquidity risk. Micro data was used at first to calculate the FI's liquid assets buffer. In a second step, the team developed a methodology to estimate the FI's liquidity needs under a stress

---

149. The team developed a methodology to identify the daily market price range, based on the operations traded in a same day, and to flag the outliers.
150. Several cross-checking routines were implemented, such as: the total balance of federal government securities' portfolio; balances of repo operations collateralized by government securities (assets and liabilities); balances of interbank deposits operations (assets and liabilities); and the total balance of time deposits' portfolio.

scenario of 21 working days[151]. The Liquidity Ratio - IL (*Índice de Liquidez*) was thus conceived as the ratio between those two values. A ratio lower than 100% meant that the liquidity buffer would not be sufficient to cover the FI's cash outflow in times of crisis.

IL was implemented in 2002. For its main data sources being on a daily basis with 1-day lag, the ratio had unprecedented timeliness. It was a very complex and advanced methodology for the time, as it comprehended the estimation of the worst idiosyncratic stress scenario for each institution, including losses in the value of liquid assets and derivatives outflows arising from market risk, and deposits runoff from wholesale and retail customers estimated separately. The early 2000s were hard times in Brazil and the financial market was highly volatile. Thus, besides being conceived with supervisory purposes, IL was also useful to the BCB Board for the assessment of impacts in monetary policy decisions.

> "We started to provide very important information to the Board. The off-site team could estimate the effect on the banks' liquidity level, resulting from changes in the exchange rate, in the interest rate, in the reserve requirements... this information was very helpful to Copom's[152] decision making process." (Tereza Grossi)

IL was implemented as a monitoring tool parameter, not a minimum requirement for banks. Thus, in addition to the natural difficulty in understanding its methodology, on-site supervisors did not have adequate regulatory support to demand action from institutions with IL below 100%, which impacted the effectiveness of

---

151. IL's stress scenario takes into account the deposits run-off, the perspectives on early redemptions, the market stress and the contractual outflows. Market stress is estimated as the amount necessary to cover losses arising from the impact of market fluctuations on the positions of liquid assets or those that may generate cash outflows in a crisis scenario. The losses encompass: i) margin calls; ii) settlements of derivatives contracts; iii) losses on marked-to-market values of the liquid assets. See https://www.bcb.gov.br/content/publications/financialstabilityreport/201810/FSR201810-fsrConcepMet.pdf for further details on the IL methodology.
152. The BCB Monetary Policy Committee - Copom (Comitê de Política Monetária) is responsible for setting the target for the policy interest rate – the Selic rate. (https://www.bcb.gov.br/en/monetarypolicy/committee)

off-site reporting concerns and the whole liquidity risk supervision process as well.

After the GFC[153], however, concerns about the need of an objective liquidity risk measurement gained space in the international forums' agendas and, in January 2013, the BCBS published the document 'Basel III: The Liquidity Coverage Ratio and liquidity risk monitoring tools'[154], which established the Liquidity Coverage Ratio (LCR) as a minimum liquidity requirement for internationally active banks.

While supervisors around the world finally counted with minimum standards for liquidity risk assessment, the liquidity risk off-site team celebrated how innovative and original IL was, as both were conceptually the same, with metrics quite aligned. When BCB implemented LCR requirements, on-site supervision finally got the missing regulatory support to take objective actions regarding the banks' liquidity risk management, as well as banks could easily understand why and what was being required of them.

Figure: Use of IL in Liquidity Monitoring during the Great Financial Crisis

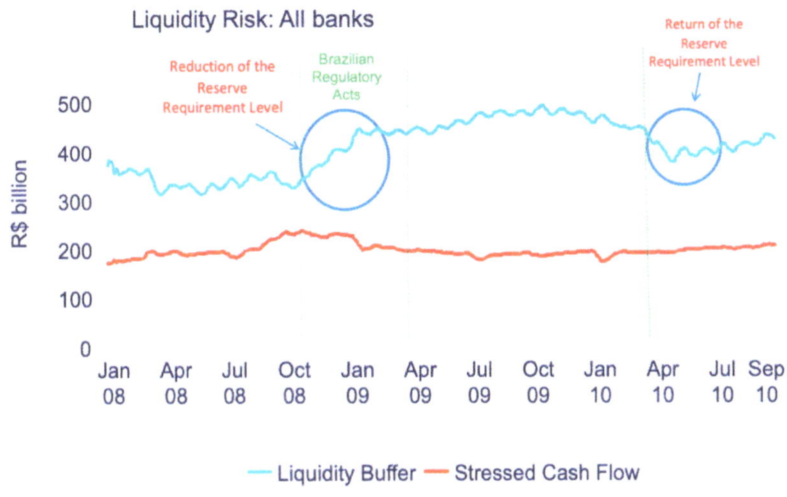

---

153. Brazilian banks with low IL level before the GFC were indeed those with severe liquidity problems during the crisis.
154. See https://www.bis.org/publ/bcbs238.htm.

Supporting decisions:

Oct/2008-Apr/2009: IL monitoring was able to timely report the effectiveness of the Central Bank's measures to mitigate the crisis effects and identify remaining fragilities

Mar-Jul/2010: IL monitoring was able to predict and timely report the impact of the return of the required reserves level in the liquidity buffer of the institutions

Identifying potential problems:

In April/2008, IL monitoring process identified 19 banks that would likely run into difficulties in a liquidity crisis. 14 FIs of that group actually faced liquidity problems during the GFC. FIs outside the identified group had no liquidity problems.

Liquidity Risk: Potential Fragility - 19 Monitored Banks

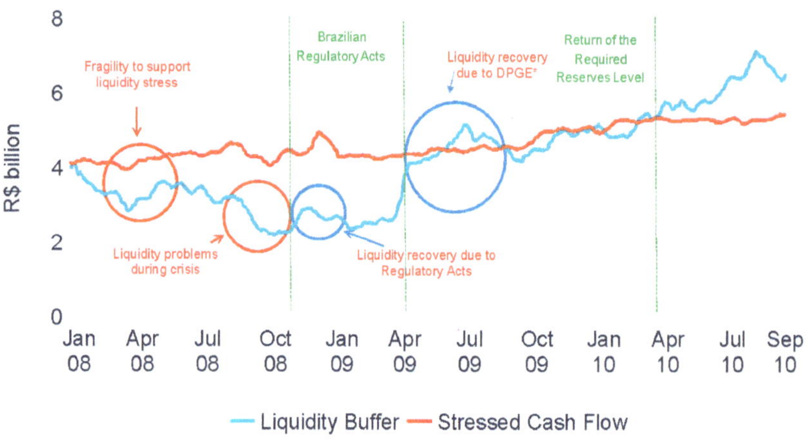

***DPGE[155] – Time Deposits with Special Guarantee from the FGC [Fundo Garantidor de Crédito], the Brazilian deposits insurance company.**

Source:Banco Central do Brasil

---

155. DPGE is a time deposit instrument covered by a special guarantee scheme, originally regulated by the BCB during the GFC (BCB Resolution No. 3.692 of 03/26/2009) to mitigate small- and medium-sized institutions' funding problems. In 2022, Applied Economics published the paper 'Financial innovation and moral hazard: the case of time deposits with special guarantee' by Gilberto Hanssen Androvandi, Carlos Enrique Carrasco-Gutierrez and Benjamin Miranda Tabak, which assesses the importance of the instrument as a crisis measure and its impact in the risk of moral hazard. (https://www.tandfonline.com/doi/full/10.1080/00036846.2021.2020712)

IL daily calculation routine was initially developed in Access and Excel macros. Processing problems were frequent and it was not unusual for the team to take a whole working day to produce the information, which shortly became outdated, as it would be replaced by new data processing on the next day. IL routine needed to migrate to a corporate tool, in order to be managed by an IT skilled team, with adequate processing tools and security controls.

The routine, however, was extremely complex: all financial assets existing in the database (which comprised, in fact, all financial assets traded in the Brazilian financial market) had to be priced and the worst scenario of each FI, due to fluctuations in market parameters, needed to be identified as well as its losses estimated, among many other cash flows estimations and calculations, in order to produce the IL ratio and an arsenal of information, such as the FI's exposure to market parameters, by index and maturity bucket. All information had to be at the computers' screen in the opening of each working day[156], to support liquidity and market risks' off-site supervision processes.

> "We used to get blood from stone to run the liquidity risk off-site routines. When we explained to the IT area what we wanted, they told us it was impossible to do. So, we told them we had already done it, in Access. All we needed was to migrate the tool to a more stable platform." (Gilneu Vivan)

Developing the System for the Monitoring of Liquidity and Market Risks – SMM (*Sistema de Monitoramento de Mercado*) was not a trivial task for the BCB's IT team, as it involved all operations traded in the financial market and required complex market risk calculations, as well. Programmers needed to understand the business rules in detail. The solution to speed work up came in the form of a mixed team, with off-site supervisors working side by side

---

156. Ideally, routines should start processing at the end of the day, right after the arrival of data from operations carried out on that same day, so that the information would be available to the off-site team in the morning of the following day.

with IT developers in structuring the databases[157] and even helping them to write the program codes of more complex routines.

Figure: SMM Workflow

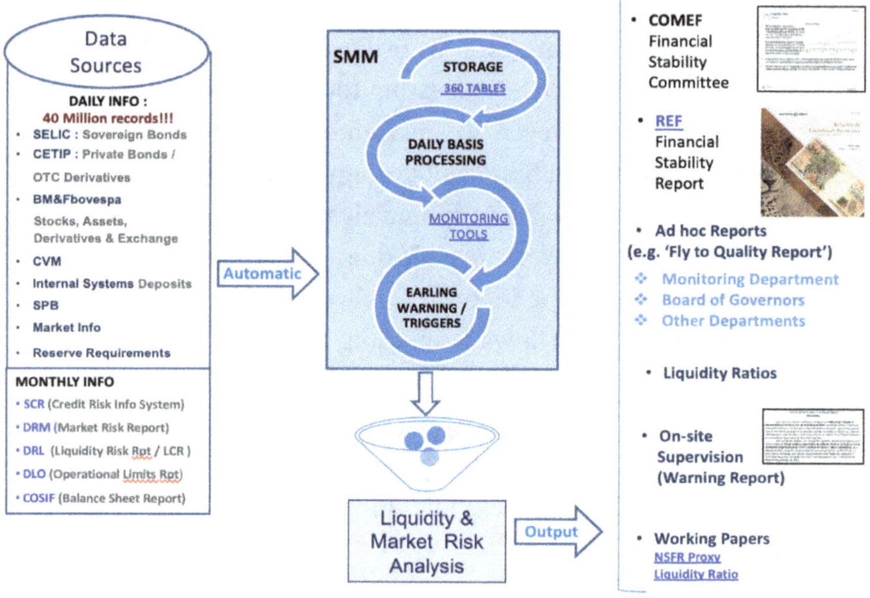

Source: Banco Central do Brasil

SMM implementation boosted the liquidity and market risks' monitoring productivity. The team, who barely had time to assess the outputs was finally able to focus on risk analysis, with data processing duties migrating to the corporate IT area.

> "In the first days of a crisis, we try to understand its dynamics, what is provoking the shock, in order to understand its behavior. Then, we replace the standard IL stress scenario by the specific scenario of that crisis. The sensitivity of the analyst is very important in this process." (Gilberto Androvandi)

---

157. SMM development also involved several negotiations with trade repositories, aiming the access to more information, as well as the improvement of data quality and reporting templates. Currently, SMM receives and processes over 100 different reports per day.

In October 2013, Law No. 12,865 delegated to the BCB the responsibility for regulating and supervising payment arrangements and payment institutions[158]. The regulation for these entities has evolved since then and contributed to the end of the natural monopoly of clearing houses and trade repositories in Brazil[159]. The arrival of new custodians and registrars, henceforth called Financial Market Infrastructure (FMI), raised competitiveness to this market and, consequently, reduced registration costs. On the other hand, it demanded an extra effort from BCB's supervision to collect and consolidate information from several sources.

---

158. A payment arrangement is the set of rules and procedures that govern the provision of a particular payment service to the public. The arrangements can refer, for example, to the procedures used to make purchases with credit, debit and prepaid cards, in national or foreign currency. Money transfer and remittance services are also payment arrangements. The non-financial legal entities that perform the payment services in the arrangement are called payment institutions and are responsible for the relationship with the end users of the service. Financial institutions can also operate with payments. (https://www.bcb.gov. br/estabilidadefinanceira/arranjospagamento)

159. Originally, there were 4 trade repositories, each one centralizing operations from a specific market: Selic, for the registry of operations with federal government securities; CBLC, for the stock market operations; BM&F, for the derivatives market; and Cetip for private securities operations and everything else not recorded by the other trade repositories.

Figure: Payment Arrangement Systems Authorized by the Central Bank

FMI	System	Market	Activity				
			PS	SSS	CCP	CSD	TR
[B]³	Câmara de Câmbio B3	foreign exchange operations	X		X		
	Central Depositária de Renda Variável B3	variable income financial instruments and derivatives		X		X	
	Sistema de Registro da BM&FBOVESPA	variable income financial instruments and derivatives					X
	Câmara B3	fixed income financial instruments and derivatives		X	X		X
	Sistema do Balcão B3	OTC derivatives		X		X	X
	Sistema de Registro de Ativos Financeiros - Unidade de Financiamentos	levies on guarantees of credit operations for automobile purchase					X
CIP	C3 Registradora	securitization		X			
	Sistema de Liquidação Diferida das	paymento order	X				
	Sistema de Transferência de Fundos	funds transfer	X				
Banco do Brasil	Centralizadora da Compensação de Cheques	clearing of cheques	X				
cielo	Sistema de Liquidação Financeira Multibandeiras	payment with credit/debit cards	X				
rede	Sistema de Liquidação Doméstica	payment with credit/debit cards	X				
serasa experian	Sistema de Registro da Serasa	record of payment defaults					X
CERC	Sistema CERC	receivables					X
crdc	Sistema de Registro CRDC	direitos creditórios					X
CSD BR	Sistema CSD BR	financial assets, llevies on guarantees of credit operations and insurance operations					X
CRT4	Sistema de Registro da CRT4	financial assets					X
TAG IMF	Sistema de Registro da TAG IMF	receivables					X

PS   Funds transfers

SSS   Settlement of transactions with securities

CCP   Central Counterparty

CSD   Central Securities Depository

TR   Electronic recording

Source:Banco Central do Brasil - https://www.bcb.gov.br/estabilidadefinanceira/sistemasautorizados_spb

Off-site activities based on payment system data:

In 1999, off-site teams were very excited about the new supervisory proposal and eager to know what data could reveal about the soundness of financial institutions. Thus, simultaneously with the exploration of trade repositories' databases, the liquidity risk off-site team mapped information from the entries in the banks' Reserves accounts, as a means of understanding the dynamics of money flow among the financial system participants and its impact on the banks' soundness.

> "Isney had mentioned to me that Depin[160] once carried out a transfer to Europe of a value much higher than those normally done. Before the transaction was settled, they received a call from the European settlement entity to confirm whether the amount was correct. At the time, he told me that he was impressed that there was a money transfer control in that entity at the operation-level. That comment inspired me. I decided to do something similar, that is, to identify patterns for the settlements in the banks' Reserves accounts." (Paula Oliveira)

In the first attempt to monitor Reserves account data, the daily settlements were plotted on a chart, taking debits as negative figures and credit as positive ones. The result was a group of curves with sharp ascending and descending moves, from which it was not easy to extract any useful information.

In the meantime, the team was struggling with a 40-working-days lag in the daily information reported by Selic, regarding the banks' TPF portfolio (government securities liquid assets). All other daily databases[161] were reported to BCB within a 1-day lag from the operations' settlement date. Thus, it was necessary to estimate the banks' TPF portfolio with 1-day lag as well, in order to have the banks' consolidated position to the most recent reference day.

Data from Reserves account was also collected on a daily basis within 1-day lag, including Selic operations' net settlement. Thus, adding Selic's daily settlements from day [-40] up to day [-1] would represent a *proxy* of the net result of a bank's operations with

---

160. The Department of Foreign Reserves (Depin) is responsible for managing Brazil's foreign reserves. Isney Manoel Rodrigues headed Depin in the 1990s.

161. The other data sources in the early 2000 were Cetip (interbank deposits operations and private securities market) and BM&F (derivatives exposures).

government securities (sellings and purchases) during this whole 40-days period. Adding this net amount to the balance of day [-40], informed in Selic database, would be an estimation of the banks' TPF portfolio value on day [-1].

Then, the revealing question was posed…

> "…and Cesar[162] asked me whether I could provide him the sum of Selic's net settlements from the last 40 days…" (Paula Oliveira)

The process to automate the production of Selic's 40-days net settlement was, in fact, replicated to every settlement system that impacted the banks' Reserves. Every day, entries were added to the sum of the previous day, and the results were displayed on a moving-window chart, starting at day [-180], and accumulating daily entries up to day [-1]. Each settlement system was represented by a curve in the chart.

> "I couldn't believe my eyes. All that tangle of curves in the form of an electrocardiogram[163] had been replaced by smoother lines, some taking an ascending shape, others descending, but with an harmonic, interrelated and symmetrical behavior! In fact, information had always been there, I just hadn't seen it yet from the best perspective!" (Paula Oliveira)

The chart, named 'Reserves Profile', revealed a very easy understanding of the financial market's cashflow. The events that required funds from the liquidity buffer, as well as the banks' strategies to restore the liquidity level were clearly visible in the curves' behavior.

Reserves Profile became the liquidity flow map, as it pointed out what should be investigated to understand the fluctuations in the banks' liquidity buffer, and whether or not it should be a concern

---

162. Cesar Viana was responsible for the monitoring of TPF data collected from Selic.
163. In the first attempt to monitor Reserves account' data, the daily settlements were plotted on a chart, taking debits as negative figures and credits as positive ones. The results were a group of curves with sharp ascending and descending moves.

to supervision. Since its implementation, it has been widely used as an off-site liquidity risk monitoring tool.

> "The Reserves Profile analysis provided us a clear understanding of the banks' cash flow. An upward trend in the Selic curve, for example, could mean liquidity loss along the time, while a sharp move of Selic's curve resulted in a sudden impact in the institutions' liquidity buffer. The events that provoked those changes in the bank's liquidity level (settlement of FX operation, funding instruments issuance, derivatives margin calls, cash withdrawals, etc.) could also be inferred by the curve(s) with a behavior symmetrically opposed to Selic's, as they represented the settlement of operations in a specific financial market, and operations in Selic were used to cover/store the cash flows provoked by them." (Paula Oliveira)

Figure: Reserves Account Profile

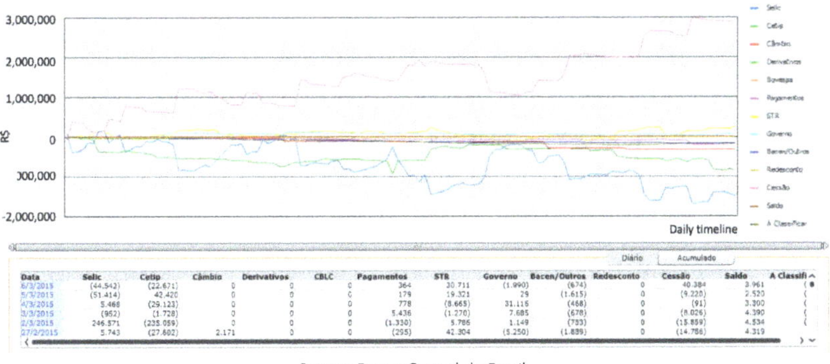

Data	Selic	Cetip	Câmbio	Derivativos	CBLC	Pagamentos	STR	Governo	Bacen/Outros	Redesconto	Cessão	Saldo	A Classifi
6/3/2015	(44.542)	(22.671)	0	0	0	364	30.711	(1.990)	(674)	0	40.384	3.961	(
5/3/2015	(51.414)	42.420	0	0	0	179	19.321	29	(1.615)	0	(9.220)	2.520	(
4/3/2015	5.468	(29.123)	0	0	0	778	(8.665)	31.116	(468)	0	(91)	3.300	(
3/3/2015	(952)	(1.728)	0	0	0	5.436	(1.270)	7.685	(678)	0	(8.026)	4.390	(
2/3/2015	246.571	(235.059)	0	0	0	(1.330)	5.786	1.149	(733)	0	(15.859)	4.534	(
27/2/2015	5.743	(27.602)	2.171	0	0	(295)	42.304	(5.250)	(1.839)	0	(14.766)	4.319	(

Source: Banco Central do Brasil

3.2 MONITORING & SUPERVISION MODEL – A NEW MICRO PRUDENTIAL APPROACH

After the Armistice[164], off-site supervisor's mission was no longer to assess the institution itself, but to assess the problem. The shift in focus has changed history. Whether the bank was going to fail was a supervisor's concern. Off-site teams were focused on

---

164. See Chapter 2 - 2.2 The implementation of the ongoing banking supervisory model in Brazil.

specific issues, like credit risk, liquidity risk or banks' compliance with operational limits, for example. Since the Armistice, the 'monitoring' perspective has been applied to all off-site working processes.

In this aspect, the greatest challenge was to adjust the process of monitoring the economic-financial situation, as it was the one that most carried the model of a comprehensive analysis of one bank. The tool developed for the economic-financial assessment of banking institutions and conglomerates was set up to run an automatic rating for each bank or conglomerate, but any off-site routine regarding analysis of outputs or adjustments on the automatic scores was discontinued. The automatic scores went straight to the supervisor, who was solely responsible for eventual adjustments.

The routine for the identification of significant variations in the financial statements evolved into two monitoring tools called 'Monitor' and 'Calculadora' [Calculator], which brought great autonomy and dynamism to the process of monitoring those variations. Calculadora, as its name implies, accesses information from several data sources[165] and calculates the indicators and parameters defined by the analysts[166]. In a second step, the Monitor compares the outputs with normality patterns, also established by the analysts, and flags the outliers. The Monitor works also as a routine management tool, as it records the analysis and eventual report to the on-site supervisor of each flagged event.

The flexibility and autonomy to develop working processes provided by Calculadora, together with the Monitor's capacity to manage them was the perfect combination to support any monitoring activity. However, each team worked independently and monitoring

---

165. Accounting documents, reports on operational limits (DLO - Demonstrativo de Limites Operacionais and DDR - Demonstrativo de Risco de Mercado), Market Risk Report (DRM), Liquidity Risk Report (DRL - demonstrativo de risco de liquidez), etc.

166. 'Calculadora' is a very flexible calculation tool where the user chooses the parameters and defines the formula to be processed, as well as its calculation frequency and scope of application. Similarly the raw data, all indicators and parameters produced by Calculadora are stored, and may be taken as data source for the creation of new formulas.

tools did not necessarily 'talk to each other'. Merging all monitoring processes into the Calculadora&Monitor framework, initially restricted to the assessment of variations in the financial statements, was a huge challenge and took time, but it was done and finally brought the long awaited integration to the micro monitoring area.

In 2005, on-site supervision activities were split into two different departments: one for the supervision of banking financial institutions and conglomerates, and the other for the supervision of credit unions and non-banking financial institutions. In terms of quantity and relevance, 97% of the SFN's total assets became the responsibility of bank supervisors, while non-bank supervisors took 93% of total supervised entities.

Figure: Scope of Supervision - December/2005

	Amount	Net Assets[1] (USD Million)
Banks and Banking Conglomerates	135	664.8
Credit Unions	1,416	10.0
Non-Banking Intitutions (except Consortia)	337	7.3
Total	**1,888**	**682.1**

(1) Net Assets = Total Assets - Financial Intermediation

Source:Banco Central do Brasil/IF.Data - https://www3.bcb.gov.br/ifdata/?lang=1

A supervision model that would require inspection routines one by one was absolutely unfeasible for non-bank supervisors. Thus, the development of monitoring processes focused on the non-banking sector seemed to be the best alternative to enable the supervision of this entire universe of institutions.

Monitoring tools and products had, however, been designed for the banking institutions. The non-banking universe comprehended a variety of peer-specific entities, with particularities that would probably imply complex adjustments in the tools' calibration. Monitoring teams did not count with the required expertise to do that. Furthermore, given the large volume of non-banking institutions, monitoring teams feared to lose focus on what was systemically relevant, should they incorporate the non-banking universe in their routines. Thus, an exclusive team was created to develop non-banking monitoring tools and processes, which encompassed credit, liquidity and market risks monitoring, and economic-financial analysis as well.

Tasks were distributed by type of institution among the team's groups, each one performing all monitoring activities regarding its scope of institutions. Groups produced reports with macro perspectives of each non-bank peer group, as well as individualized information and reports of identified concerns to the on-site supervisors.

Along the time, the evolution of metrics and technology helped non-banking working processes to gradually approach to the banks' monitoring models, until finally becoming ready to merge with the banks' monitoring processes in 2018[167].

> "In order to be able to encompass the entire non-banking universe, which is very large, reporting of concerns on credit risk issues to supervisors must be automatic." (Giovani Brito)
>
> "We expect a good adherence with the IL metrics for liquidity risk monitoring of some non-bank peers, such as SCFIs[168] and credit unions. For other types of institutions, we may need more adjustments and other sources of information." (Gilberto Androvandi)

In 2012, another split on supervisory activities resulted on the creation of a new department focused on Anti Money Laundry and Combat on Financing Terrorism (AML/CFT} issues, as well as the observation of the institutions' compliance with financial regulation[169]. In response, the monitoring area created a team to

---

167. By 2020, monitoring tools' calibration to incorporate non-banking institutions was still in process.

168. The Credit, Finance and Investment Companies (SCFIs) – also known as finance companies – are private non-banking financial institutions that provide funding for the acquisition of goods, services and working capital. Several SCFIs operate as financial arm of commercial or industrial corporations – such as department stores and vehicle assemblers – and concentrate their operations on the financing of their own products. (https://www.bcb.gov.br/en/financialstability/creditfinance)

169. Department of Conduct Supervision (Decon).

develop processes of cross-checking the various databases and flagging any suspicions of fraud or irregularities.

This type of investigation used to be carried out by on-site supervisors during inspection, using sample data collected directly from the bank's databases. Reporting concerns to supervisors within a fraud perspective were generally by-product of the financial markets and financial instruments' monitoring processes, where operations involving government bonds, investment funds, bank funding instruments, foreign exchange and derivatives were assessed in detail. The tools developed by this new monitoring team were specific for AML/CFT purposes and could process simultaneously all information from all supervised institutions.

> "We have an annual meeting with the supervision of conduct area where some aspects are discussed, such as what is being flagged by our FX market monitoring process, its effectiveness and eventual need of a metrics' review. They also take the opportunity to discuss with us their perception of the FX market's performance and risks."
>
> (Jose Luiz Loebens)

The team's first fraud investigation activity that produced concrete results derived from the application of a methodology known as 'Benford's Law', which evaluates the behavior of large numbers in a mass of data[170].

In 2010, the floor for individualized credit operation information in the SCR was R$5 thousand (USD 2.9 thousand), but a group of institutions had exceptionally reported to BCB detailed information with a R$ 100 (USD 53) floor, for a specific study. When the team applied Benford's methodology to this information, one medium-sized bank was flagged with a high concentration of operations having 4 as the initial number. A deeper investigation of these operations found out that they referred to amounts just below

---

170. Benford's law is an observation that in many real-life sets of numerical data, the leading digit is likely to be small. The number 1 normally appears as the leading significant digit about 30% of the time, while 9 appears as the leading significant digit less than 5% of the time.

the limit for submission to the SCR[171], so that they could not be identified in a regular monitoring process.

> "When I read 'The Drunkard's Walk'[172], I realized that Benford's Law was also used for supervision work. I got curious. We were about to work on a fraud investigation and I thought this law could be useful. Meanwhile, deputy governor Anthero sent us a 'paper' exactly on this subject. What a coincidence!" (Nizam Pfeilsticker)

Over the years, that team continued to follow step by step the cutting-edge technologies and was responsible for developing the first monitoring tools using artificial intelligence[173].

3.3 MONITORED ISSUES FRAMEWORK: A MAJOR STEP TOWARDS INTEGRATING THE SUPERVISORY MODEL

The boundaries between supervision and monitoring activities had been pacified since the Armistice, but communication gaps persisted and increased with models' sophistication. As the monitoring assessment of a particular issue improved, methodology became more and more complex. Variations in indicators and metric components were flagged to supervisors, without informing the potential problems they could bring to the institution, which were often not clear even to the reporting analyst him/herself.

> The monitoring perspective: "Supervisors couldn't understand the metrics' meaning, because they didn't think that way." (Gilneu Vivan)
>
> The supervisor's perspective: "Monitoring used to speak in a language very rooted to its models. The message was not clear to the supervisor." (Belline Santana)

---

171. The bank created false loan contracts of an amount a little below the floor for individual information to the SCR (R$ 5 thousand). These ghost operations led to the false accounting of the bank's assets in the amount of R$ 2.6 billion (USD 1.5 billion).
172. The Drunkard's Walk was written by Leonard Mlodinow in 2008.
173. See Chapter 7, item 7.2 - The use of machine learning techniques and its challenges.

.

The entire monitoring process urged for transparency, in a language that could translate the real supervisory concerns. For this purpose, a framework named 'Monitored Issues' – SM (*Situações Monitoradas*) was developed, in order to formalize every monitoring process, documenting the 'why', 'how', 'when' and 'for whom' of each monitoring routine.

Figure: Monitored Issues - Concept

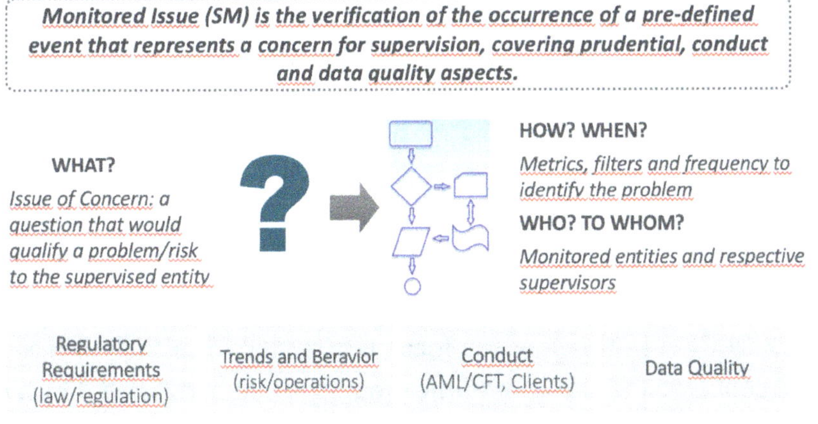

Source:Banco Central do Brasil

"The first Monitored Issues proposal was drafted for the development of monitoring processes for payment institutions. This was the event that conceived the idea of what should be an issue that had to be monitored." (Álvaro Freitas)

The Monitored Issues Framework had a simple concept, even obvious, but difficult to implement, as it required the reengineering of the whole micro prudential monitoring process. After all, monitoring teams had been born independent, each one developing its tools within its abilities and limitations. The teams' IT skills were not uniform and migrating to the Monitored Issues Framework would require each process to upload its results in a common database, within a standard template.

However, the most difficult step towards its implementation was previous to any IT challenge: getting the teams to identify the real supervisory concern they were assessing within each monitoring routine. Theoretically, why a particular monitoring process was being carried out should be a rhetorical question, but when teams were demanded to write it down, it turned out that it was not so obvious.

Each Monitored Issue had to be written objectively and in clear language, in the format of a question representing a supervisory concern: something other than the literal explanation of the metric used, such as 'Is the IL below 100%?', or the ultimate reason for micro prudential monitoring – 'Is there a risk of failure for the Institution?'.

The Monitored Issue should reflect the real concern of each procedure, so that both the monitoring analyst and the supervisor could understand exactly the same message: what was being monitored and why. Thus, 'Is the IL below 100%?' becomes 'Does the institution run the risk of not having sufficient liquid assets to honor its commitments in the next 30 days, in a stressed scenario?'[174]. In this way, the focus was shifted from the metrics to the concern, and the communication gaps that had lasted 15 years could finally be filled!

All teams faced some sort of challenge to capture the huge mindset shift provoked by the Monitored Issues Framework. The monitoring processes that flagged significant variations, for example, had been structured around single indicators. Each indicator had its own meaning, but not necessarily it alone was able to build up a supervisory concern. The characterization of a Monitored Issue could involve a group of indicators simultaneously.

> "We started to imagine what would be a concern and how to characterize it in the best possible way through our indicators. If the metrics proved to be efficient, it became a Monitored Issue. We gained a lot in efficiency. Events flagged for analysis jumped from 90% not relevant X 10%

---

174. The register of a Monitored Issue comprehends all information needed to formalize its routine: the question of concern, the metrics, the scope of application, the routine's frequency, etc.

reported to supervisor, to 20% not relevant X 80% reported. And there were no longer 600-700 flagged events/month, but 60-70." (Marcelo Bicalho)

There was yet another major communication gap that has been filled by the Monitored Situations Framework: the lack of the 'It's OK' information. Supervisors were able to access information about their institution in the monitoring tools at any time, but with the evolution of monitoring metrics, the verifications performed by the monitoring teams went far beyond the information available in the tools. Thus, consulting the data was not enough for the supervisor to infer what had been monitored on a given reference date and has not been taken as a concern. For safety reasons, some supervisors preferred to replicate routines that were already being carried out by monitoring teams.

Figure: Monitored Issues - Processing Output

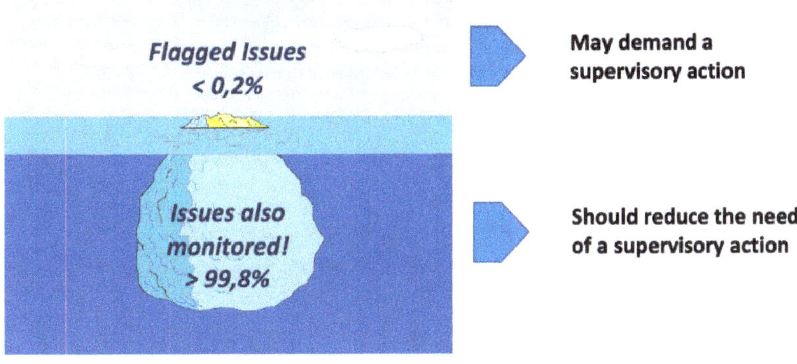

Source: Image from Josep Monter Martinez by Pixabay -https://pixabay.com/pt/users/josepmonter-1007570/?utm_source=link-attribution&utm_medium=referral&utm_campaign=image&utm_content=1321692

"Now, everyone can see the entire iceberg, not just its tip. And when something is reported, the report means the concern, no longer the metrics." (Gilneu Vivan)

In practice, most of the monitoring processes result in the conclusion that institutions are doing what was expected from them. Events that must be reported to the supervisor are exceptions. The information that an institution does not have a certain problem is very important to manage supervision actions more efficiently, as it allows to direct the workforce to where it is really needed.

Advances in technology and database integration were key to support the upgrade in the disclosure of monitoring results to supervisors. Each monitoring process was adjusted to register the results of all verifications, not just the flagged events anymore. A dashboard[175] was developed to display all results, providing the missing transparency of the entire monitoring process. From then on, supervisors could access everything that had been monitored, regardless if it has been reported or not to them as a concern.

Figure: Monitored Issues - Workflow

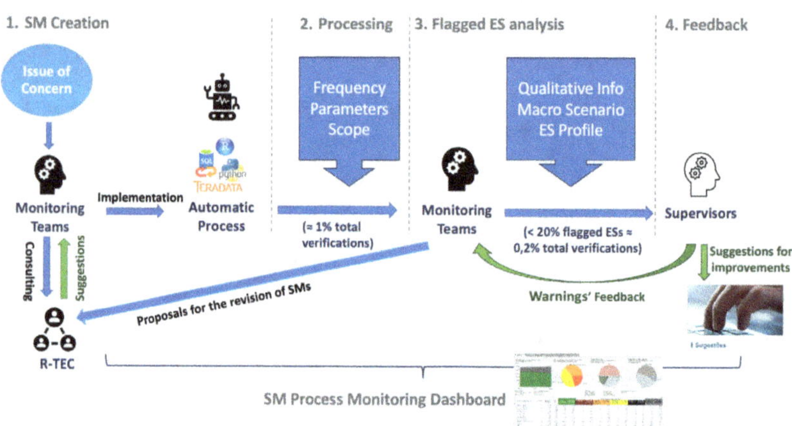

ES = Supervised Entity (*Entidade Supervisionada*)
Source: Banco Central do Brasil

After the implementation of the Monitored Issues Framework, the monitoring work processes were recognized as supervisory actions and won the status of 'remote inspections'. Thus, supervisors did not need to replicate them anymore, which brought efficiency to the supervisory model. From then on, supervisors could plan

---

175. The Monitored Issues Dashboard displays all monitored issues performed (and not performed) for a given institution at a reference date, as well as the assessment's result of the flagged events: "it is ok" (not flagged), "not reported because it has already been reported recently ", "reported to supervisor", "the flag is not a concern", etc.

their working schedule taking into account the results of the entire monitoring process carried out by the monitored issues.

> "When we created the Monitored Issues in the shape of questions, it was to give them the format of an inspection." (Paulo Sergio Neves)

CHAPTER 4

Information Management

"Information governance is something that gradually matures in several dimensions within the Institution."

(Gabriela Ruberg)

"Those who do not use the information cannot give quality to it."

(Sidney Marques)

"We only start to change history when we connect the user to the information.

(Gilneu Vivan)

In this chapter, the book's scope is extended beyond the boundaries of the supervision perimeter to highlight the importance of an adequate model of information management in an organization. In the case of the BCB, the supervisory area has played a key role in the creation of the current model, awarded internationally in 2018. The chapter also highlights the importance of data quality processes being designed as supervisory activities in Brazil and how the enactment of the Law on Access to Public Information (LAI) in Brazil has affected the prudential monitoring processes.

4.1 TRAJECTORY OF INFORMATION MANAGEMENT AT THE BCB

"There is a dissonance between the expectations of the financial institutions and the regulator regarding reporting information. Institutions often do not see the benefits of data for financial stability management. A communication effort is recommended, highlighting its importance. At the same time, it is necessary to monitor data requirements, in order to ensure efficiency. In this sense, it is important to have a permanent agenda for discussion between the regulator and those who provide information, in order to reduce redundancies and operational costs, without compromising the soundness of the financial system." (Everton Goncalves – ABBC)

Information management has always been a relevant issue within the BCB, which motivated the continuous search for improvement. In the model in force until the 1980s, departments had ample autonomy to regulate issues related to their working processes and to require the necessary information to support their activities. Independently, they defined what to collect, how and when. Databases had 'owners'. Rationalization and information sharing were still utopian concepts, far away from practice. As a consequence, it was not uncommon for financial institutions to send the same information to different departments, or worse, with small differences, which made the process of reporting information to the BCB confusing and dissonant.

In an attempt to minimize the cost of compliance with information requirement rules, in 1987, BCB centralized these activities in a single department created exclusively for this purpose, and subordinated to the Deputy Governor for Regulation.

The new department established standards and routines for the creation of reporting templates as well as to the data delivery process[176]. It also actively participated in the design of new templates, such as the standard financial statements report, the Cosif, that in 1987 replaced the different existing templates of each type of financial institutions[177].

> "We scanned all the several financial statements' templates to list the accounts that would remain in Cosif. We wanted to eliminate the unused ones. There was a liability account named 'Marked Checks'. Zero balance for all institutions. Nobody knew what this account was for. My father-in-law, who had worked in a bank since 1935, was the one who explained its purpose to me: in the past, when a customer came to the bank to withdraw money, but the bank had no sufficient cash, they agreed with the customer a day to come back and get the money. Then, my father-in-law had to take a train up to the city where the bank had a larger branch, to get money. The accounting rules required that the amount to be withdrawn were transferred from the bank's 'Deposits' account to 'Marked Checks' account, until the money was delivered to the customer. In the elaboration of Cosif, we have eliminated this account." (Alvir Hoffmann)

Cosif pioneered the implementation of some procedures for receiving data that became BCB standards, such as electronic

---

176. The process basically checked the upcoming reports in the list of expected remitters and applied penalties (fines) for delays in delivery.

177. Cosif permitted the standardization of accounting registries among the different types of financial institutions, which helped the implementation of Multiple Banks in Brazil. Before Cosif, even the areas responsible for the supervision of banking and non-banking institutions were subordinated to different Deputy Governors.

remittance, instead of the physical delivery on a floppy disk, entrance validation rules and pecuniary fines for late delivery.

> "In the implementation of Cosif, we created 27 very simple automatic validations, such as 'Total Assets = Total Liabilities' or 'The amount informed in the clearing account X must be equal to the amount of Assets account Y'. Any report could pass the validation in the first remittance. It took us more than 10 months to gather information from all institutions for a single reference date! With the application of fines, delivery was gradually being improved." (Alvir Hoffmann)

Demands for new information increased with the advance of technology. The rhythm of new reports increasingly exceeded the elimination of obsolete ones. Thus, although standardized and automated, operational routines for data collection demanded more and more personnel. Having the agenda taken over by these procedures, teams were gradually distancing themselves from decision-making processes and losing the information user's perspective. Consequently, the lack of 'intimacy' with data had its effects in activities for the improvement of data quality. Since the teams no longer knew what data was for, they had no idea of what kind of error could be avoided or should be corrected.

> "Only the person who uses the information can bring quality to it. Anyone else is not able to understand whether the number is good or bad, if it's weird, if it makes sense going up so fast or not. And to question the data provider, you need to understand what the person is talking about, otherwise, you take any answer as gospel." (André Maurício)

At the turn of the century, the biggest critic of data low quality was the supervision area, a fact that even contributed to the supervisor's lack of interest in the development of off-site analysis tools and disbelief regarding eventual outputs, such as the financial indicators produced by Indicon[178].

With the segregation of supervision activities into on-site and off-site in 2000, investments in data quality became essential to the success of the new supervisory model. Therefore, the decision of moving the information management department from Regulation to Supervision area was very strategic, as it gave autonomy to supervision to take the lead towards data quality improvement. However, supervision took responsibility for receiving all data remitted to BCB, regardless of its usefulness for supervisory purposes.

Under new management, data entry processes migrated to the supervision area, although still segregated from supervisory processes. The teams modernized data reception procedures, but at the end of the day, they continued restricted to this type of activity. Initiatives towards the improvement of the consistency and completeness of information were not in their scope, and the consequences of this gap continued to be felt by the off-site supervision area. Despite being closer to the user, the lack of intimacy with information of those responsible for data management remained unchanged.

> "The information management department did not succeed for a very simple reason, because people did not take care of information, they simply received it." (Ailton Aquino)

It took five years to a structural reform provoke real changes in mindset and allow for advances in the information management model: the merger of the off-site supervision and the information management departments.

At first, offsite and data management activities were put 'under the same roof', but did not necessarily interact. On the contrary, exclusive teams for data management were formed. The two areas were even physically separated by a glass wall, which in a short

---

178. See Chapter 1 - 1.3 Structure and functioning of supervision.

time was named the 'Berlin Wall'. It was a common belief that off-site supervision activities were confidential and, thus, they should not share the same physical space as the teams that provided data to them. In those times, only a few people could see information management as part of the supervisory process.

> "I asked myself: how can we convince people that without information management, it would be impossible to do everything that monitoring does?" (Carine Bastos)

Historically, information management models used to swing along the time between a centralized model, where the management of all information is carried out by a single component in the organization, and a decentralized model, where each area is responsible for its own information. BCB was no exception. Off-site supervision started to feel some sort of 'wish for decentralization', as soon as they had to share time and personnel with the capture of information out of scope of supervision.

In fact, there are advantages and disadvantages of both models. In the BCB, the centralization implemented in the mid-1980s had been a good response to the problems caused by the existing decentralized model. However, the increasing involvement of information management personnel with operational procedures and the consecutive distancing from information users have compromised data quality.

Even the attempt of having both activities in the same department seemed unfruitful. Data management needed to be really incorporated by the off-site process.

In an attempt to do so, each data user was designed as responsible for the reception and quality of his/her own data source. At first, off-site teams were concerned that incorporating this new activity would blurr the focus on monitoring issues. Over time, however, they could experience the synergy among processes and, finally, found out that ensuring the quality of information was really a supervisory duty.

But, what to do with information not destined to supervision? The teams responsible for managing it worked totally apart from the off-site department's activities. Should the same strategy be applied, they had to return to the BCB areas they belonged. In other words, a step backwards to the pre-1980s decentralized information management model…

> "As the off-site deputy head responsible for the information management teams, I coordinated all transfers of information we didn't use, and the correspondent data management team, to the respective non-supervision users. That is, my job was to extinguish my own job!" (Reynaldo Furlani)

In fact, the perception of problems in the BCB's information management model transcended the supervision borders as soon as the off-site's 'to Cesar what belongs to Cesar' approach reached the non-supervision areas.

The need for a model review at the BCB's strategic level was urgent. Otherwise, it would be a matter of time before the return to the ancient problems inherent in a decentralized model. Yes, information had to be close to the user, no one disagreed about that, but it was also common sense that some sort of governance needed to exist.

Along the process of returning data to the user, there were databases and systems with multiple users. To some of them, off-site supervision identified more than one interested in assuming the database, and to others, nobody volunteered. Unicad, the BCB's Registry System of Financial Institutions, was the most critical example of the latter. The whole BCB accessed Unicad, thus, every department considered itself in the same user-level as the others, and no one wanted to take the responsibility for it. Being an 'orphan' system, demands for improvements in Unicad were often taken as low priority and postponed, up to the day the system continuity depended on a technological updating that would involve its rebuilding. As no one volunteered to conduct a project at this proportion, the IT area took the lead on the problem. This event was the kick-off for the design of a new information governance structure for the BCB.

> "Structuring information governance at the Central Bank was a long but successful process." (Anthero Meirelles)
>
> "Unicad was the trigger for information governance at the BCB." (Haroldo Cruz)
>
> "We've interviewed all heads of department to map out the big issues and we've detected several. For example, there were 69 financial institutions' registry databases, not necessarily integrated!" (Gabriela Ruberg)

The BCB's 'Information Governance Policy'[179] was published on February 19th, 2013. It has created one strategic and deliberative forum, the Information Governance Committee[180] - CGI (*Comitê de Governança da Informação*), responsible for deciding on matters related to the report of information to the BCB or any conflict forwarded by data users, as well as dealing with omission events, and one operational office, the Information Governance Office - EGI (*Escritório de Governança da Informação*), responsible for CGI's secretariat[181].

---

179.   See the full document at https://www.diariodasleis.com.br/legislacao/federal/222425-polutica-de-governanua-da-informauuo-do-banco-central-do-brasil-fica-divulgada-a-polutica-de-governanua-da-informauuo-do-banco-central-do-brasil-na-forma-do--anexo-a-esta-portari.html.

180. CGI is composed of heads of department or heads of executive offices appointed by each BCB deputy governor and is coordinated by the BCB's Executive Secretary.

181. EGI is composed of employees from the IT department. Among other attributions, it provides technical support to data curators and manages the procedures for data capture and integration, the BCB's Information Catalog, the BCB's master-data and the data quality platform.

Figure: BCB's Information Governance Framework

Source:Banco Central do Brasil - https://www.bcb.gov.br/detalhenoticia/291/noticia

The key point of the model, which enabled the real change in the entire information management framework, was the extinction of 'data property' behavior. 'Data owners' used to have absolute control over 'their' information. That was the core of major problems, such as financial institutions reporting the same or similar information to different areas of the BCB; reports still being required, even long after information became obsolete; or 'data owners' changing templates and databases, without consulting other users.

According to the new perspective, information no longer belonged to the BCB, or to department X, it belonged to the reporting financial institution, which reported it to BCB, in compliance with regulation. Thus, it was solely a 'regulated information' from a 'reporting institution'. A bit obvious, but at the same time so revolutionary, that the 'Central Banking FinTech RegTech Global Awards 2018'[182] was awarded to BCB's Information Governance Framework, as the 'Best Data Management Initiative'.

---

182. https://www.centralbanking.com/technology/3711046/best-data-management-ini-tiative-central-bank-of-brazil.

> "The PGI is impressive not only because it has helped streamline the central bank's data management processes, but also because it helped mitigate a number of operational risks through the reduction of information exchanged between the central bank and public agencies mandated to submit certain data to the regulator, a major cost for both parties." (Central Banking Awards – 2018)

Regulated Information should be accessible to everyone who needs it to exercise its institutional competence, instead of being restricted to those who took the initiative to require it. 'Data owners' were replaced by 'data curators'[183], with the responsibility of keeping the information alive, timely, correct, accessible to any user, with an adequate level of security, disclosure and compliance costs.

> "Databases used to have names and surnames! Nowadays, there are around 500 formally designated curators. It took us a lot of work to make them realize the importance of their new role." (Gabriela Ruberg)

Dismissed from the responsibility of managing BCB's entire database, off-site supervision could focus on the organization of those ones under its curatorship. After all, being the curator of all information of interest to supervision would by far be a small or trivial task.

> "We started to think of information as a process. When someone needed to require new data, he/she contacted us to formalize the demand and his/her eventual intention to be designated as curator.

---

183. Data curators must have a direct interest in using the data source to carry out his/her activities, as well as sufficient skills and commitment to ensure data quality. They are responsible for: ensuring and controlling data quality, such as the definition of prerequisites, business rules and metrics for data quality assessment; assisting users regarding data analysis and the improvement of its quality; identifying and solving any issue regarding data; setting reference values for data attributes; keeping updated all documentation (metadata) disclosed at the BCB's Information Catalog; defining rules for data access; and assuring to all users that data suits their needs. In the case of shared curation among two or more users, a master curator is designated as the curators' representative in other instances.

This was the trigger to our routines: contacting other people involved in its approval and regulation, such as the reporting standards' team, the IT area and the CGI; verifying whether and where the information would be published; classifying its level of confidentiality; etc." (Clara Rizel)

4.2 FINES, A BAD STRATEGY TO ENSURE DATA QUALITY

Data reception routines had been established at the time reports were physically delivered[184] at the BCB. Thus, there was a team in each of the 10 Regional branches responsible for receiving all documents reported by the financial institutions which head office was located inside the branch's perimeter[185]. The team carried out the complete reception process for all documents: checking the list of reporting institutions, monitoring the report's delivery, applying penalties for delays and answering eventual questions.

> "We were replicating data reporting processes just to have delivery units close to reporting institutions, which made no sense, as delivery was virtual." (Clara Rizel)

Among several inefficiencies, the data reception process had a bottleneck: the approach to mitigate delays and to reinforce data quality was not effective. A penalty of R$ 150[186] per day of delay[187] had been instituted in the late 1980s to push compliance with Cosif reporting, and over time it became standard to all reports required by BCB. Due to its negligible value, the amount charged did not even cover the cost of BCB's personnel involved in the task, and

---

184. Before the implementation of SISBACEN in 1986, each financial institution had a pigeonhole at the respective Regional branch's building to exchange information with the BCB, also used for reports' delivery purposes. Initially, reports were delivered on paper and later, on floppy disks.

185. See map of Regional branches' perimeters in Chapter 1 - 1.3 Structure and functioning of supervision.

186. About USD 57, in January/2005.

187. Information reported with errors needed to be replaced. In terms of penalty application, a report's replacement was taken as a delay. Days of delay were counted from the final date for remittance up to the report's replacing day.

some institutions preferred to pay the fine rather than to send the documents on time or to replace incorrect information. Thus, while the volume of fines grew exponentially, its intended purpose, i.e., data available in time and with quality, was less and less being achieved.

When monitoring incorporated the information management area in 2005, there was a huge stock of due and not collected fines, many of them already overdue, which could provoke, indeed, legal risk to the BCB.

> "When we measured the stock of outstanding fines, we realized that there were close to 50,000 fines to be charged, I looked at it and said to myself: 'this is impossible! We're going to put a world of people charging fines and it won't solve the problem!'" (Edson Teixeira)

Routines for the application of penalties were not uniform among the BCB branches and very little was done without manual intervention, which made the procedure uneven, slow and inefficient. It was necessary to harmonize and speed up the approach. To this end, a system for automated collection of fines, the SGM (*Sistema Geral de Multas*), was developed.

At first, SGM helped to mitigate the legal risk involved in fines prescription, however, the system did not get to the root of the problem: institutions remained willing to pay the penalty instead of reporting correct information on time.

In the search for another strategy, once more, the obvious proved to be revolutionary: If the provision of information to the BCB was regulated, the submission of poor quality or delayed data was, in practice, a violation of the rules. It was therefore sufficient to include reporting information in the scope of supervision, that is, subject to the same penalties applied to irregularities identified in supervisory work.

Under the new approach, named 'Audit of Compliance', the existing process of charging fines could be extinguished and institutions with recurring reporting problems would finally be pushed to invest in improving their data provision processes.

Issues that used to be discussed with the bank's employee responsible for the report's elaboration, were now in the agenda of the bank's director responsible for data reporting. In presential meetings at the BCB, the director was formally informed about the bank's failure in reporting timely and correct data, and required to sign a Memorandum of Understanding (MoU), which formalized his/her commitment on the implementation of concrete actions for its regularization. Should the bank not comply with the agreement, supervisory administrative proceedings could result in either a warning, a penalty, or even the disqualification, both of the institution and the director him/herself.

> "We have completely changed our approach to deal with reporting gaps. We called the director to a meeting at the BCB and said: the information is relevant, there is a regulatory obligation to report this data timely and correctly, your bank is not compliant, so you need to change your process." (Edson Teixeira)

> "I didn't want to apply penalties, all I wanted was correct and timely data. The Audit of Compliance was a better approach, as it penalized the banks' top management. They needed to be interested in sending us the information and to understand that it was good for them too." (Marcelo Fernandes)

Currently, BCB's framework that ensures excellence in data reporting consists of three pillars: the CGI, which requires adequate planning in the design of new reports; the curator, who is primarily responsible for interacting with the information provider to ensure that it is being delivered on time and with quality; and the Audit of Compliance, which raises discussions to the top management, whenever curators' attempt to solve the problem is not successful.

> "Today, 99.9% of institutions comply with information reporting requirements. The problem practically no longer exists." (Andreia Lais Vargas)

4.3 APPROACHING DATA TO THE USERS

When data management and off-site supervision merged, the replication of data reception routines contrasted with the monitoring processes' thematic distribution[188] among BCB's Regional branches. Therefore, it was necessary to align data reception with the monitoring model, that is, each regional would centralize the whole reception of one or a few reports, preferably used by the 'neighbor' monitoring team . This rearrangement gave greater independence to the regional teams, allowing them to invest in harmonizing the process for receiving the reports and in actions to improve data quality.

BCB's approach towards regulated entities has also evolved, as it opened the floor for discussions during the elaboration of a new regulation or data requirement. The practice of designing templates with the participation of reporting institutions also contributed to add value to their internal process. Quality checks carried out at the BCB are important, but when the information to be reported is also useful to the institution, it is much easier to achieve a higher level of quality. SCR is a good example of this phenomenon, as it became the most complete and reliable database of credit operations in the country because it is also used by reporting institutions in their credit risk management processes.

> "Discussing with the market a reporting template that makes sense for them contributes to the evolution of all involved. For example, in order to know what is being directed towards the green economy, we need to find out together a way to identify these operations. Taking into account that 'the best is the enemy of the good', we started by requiring data only from the large institutions, so that everyone could develop adequate data collection and data quality processes. Afterwards, we will gradually add more institutions, until we achieve the whole reporting universe." (Marcelo Fernandes)

---

188. The monitoring teams were specialized in topics such as credit risk or foreign exchange market, for example, and used certain databases to carry out their processes.

> "Before the DRM[189], there was no information on market risk at the Central Bank. We had several meetings with the banks to design its template. It was a very enriching experience. We learned to create the information together." (Getúlio Fialho)

4.4 MULTIDIMENTIONAL TEAMS

The thematic alignment of curation and monitoring processes[190] permitted the rearrangement of Regional teams, in order to bring together related activities. Monitoring teams became a mix of three types of specialists: monitoring analysts, tool developers, and data curators. The new composition boosted the teams' autonomy to plan, conduct and improve their working processes.

In fact, mixed teams caused the boom of micro and macro monitoring activities in BCB. Ongoing technological advances pushed database integration, which improved more and more in timeliness and accuracy the monitoring capacity to meet the demands both from supervision and the Board.

As information reports have been created at different times and by different areas, each one had its own reception process, including different rules for data substitution[191]. The IT-Experts team[192] standardized the processes and developed a tool, the Gedoc System, to control the reception of reports. Gedoc was an important milestone, as it standardized the procedures for receiving the documents created to meet supervision needs.

---

189. Report on Market Risk Management [*Demonstrativo de Risco de Mercado*].
190. With the implementation of the new Information Governance model, curators replaced the former data managers, and off-site supervisors became monitoring analysts, with the implementation of the Monitoring&Supervision model.
191. Some reports could be directly replaced in the database, others had first to be excluded, to permit the reloading of the new report.
192. The creation of the IT-Experts team is described in Chapter 3, 3.1 – The off-site supervision implementation.

> "The success of monitoring processes is based on the ability to organize information. Nothing would stand if we hadn't structured our databases." (Elvira Schulz)

4.5 LAW ON ACCESS TO PUBLIC INFORMATION - LAI (*LEI DE ACESSO À INFORMAÇÃO*) AND THE MANAGEMENT OF DEMANDS FOR INFORMATION

> "The free flow of information and ideas is at the very heart of the notion of democracy and is crucial for effective respect for human rights. The principle that public bodies hold information not for themselves, but on behalf of the people, is fundamental to guarantee this free flow. These bodies have an immense wealth of information that, if kept secret, the right to freedom of expression is seriously compromised. [193]" (Abdul Waheed Khan – UNESCO Assistant Director-General, Communication and Information Sector)

As monitoring databases were increasing in scope and granularity, the responsibilities related to the proper use of information were gaining space in the curators' agenda. Thus, concerns regarding confidentiality, transparency and access permission according to the user's profile were concentrated in a single team[194].

In 2011, LAI regulated the disclosure of public information in Brazil, based on the principle that everyone has the right to access public information. As a result, demands for public information grew exponentially in the whole country, which brought excessive

---

193. Preface to the book 'Freedom of information: a study of comparative law', by Toby Mendel, published by Unesco in 2009. See the full document at https://unesdoc.unesco.org/ark:/48223/pf0000158450_eng.

194. Frequent management problems to control the access to databases, such as permissions still valid even after the employee has left the team or access denied to someone occupying a temporary position, were solved by establishing the 'database access kit' of each monitoring activity. Every day, each user would have permission to access only the information necessary to carry out the activities related to his/her current position and function. In order to automatically and timely control permissions, a system was developed to daily capture the current functional status of each monitoring employee in the BCB's database and provide him/her the correspondent access kit.

costs to public entities, inclusive the BCB, and, of course, the monitoring area was heavily impacted.

> "The State must guarantee the right of access to information, which shall be provided through objective and agile procedures, in a transparent, clear and easy-to-understand language." (Article 5 of the LAI)

> "In the beginning, it was very difficult to convince our teams that LAI was a good thing, as it brought transparency to the Public Service. The media emphasized that we could not deny any information request, but data was normally required as 'in the format of the attached file'. Thus, we had to stop our activities just to meet the specific demand of a single citizen!" (Clara Rizel)

According to the LAI, all confidential information had to be classified in terms of its secrecy level, which established a correspondent maximum period of restriction to its access[195]. Citizens had three instances of appeal against a possible denial on information request: 1st- the head of the curator department; 2nd- the governor of the public entity; and 3rd- the Comptroller General of the Union - CGU[196] (Controladoria-Geral da União). Despite the fact that the LAI established criteria to support a denial of access to information, in practice, CGU used to revert the denials from previous instances.

> "The three instances of appeal prescribed by LAI made things very hard for us. We had to be aligned with all instances to be able to sustain a denial of information." (Clara Rizel)

Shortly after LAI implementation, the volume of requests for information was overwhelming monitoring activities. All teams

---

195. Article 24 established the confidentiality levels and respective restriction periods as follows: I - top secret: 25 (twenty-five) years; II - secret: 15 (fifteen) years; and III - reserved: 5 (five) years.
196. CGU is a branch of the Brazilian federal government tasked with assisting the president regarding the treasury and public assets' protection, as well as the government's transparency policies.

were crammed with individual requests that required accurate analysis, even for non-granular information, as the type of data aggregation could not violate any confidentiality hypothesis. The better strategy would be to avoid the arrival of information requests at the BCB. In other words, it was necessary to make information available to the public before there was a request for it.

The movement towards more transparency experienced in Brazil was, in fact, a worldwide trend[197]. The great financial crisis had revealed that gaps in financial information prevented the timely detection of risks to which economic sectors and market participants were exposed. International entities created specific forums to encourage discussions and share best practices on information disclosure, such as the International Financial Information Forum, created in October 2014 by the Center for Latin American Monetary Studies - CEMLA[198].

> "It was evident the need for increased available and detailed information on financial systems to understand and analyze in an opportune and proper way its interactions with the macroeconomic stability and the mechanism of monetary policy transmission." (CEMLA/Financial International Forum. https://www.cemla.org/fif/english.html)

Central banks started to foster market discipline with broader transparency requirements, and, at the same time, to invest in improving their own skills for collecting, producing and using economic and financial information. Basel expanded the scope

---

197. Transparency or open data laws vary from country to country. Usually, requests are free of charge and the respondent entity has a deadline for response. The Global Investigative Journalism Network website provides links to information requests in over 60 countries. (https://gijn.org/gijns-global-guide-to-freedom-of-information-resources/)

198. The Financial Information Forum aims at strengthening the financial information models of Latin American and the Caribbean central banks, and thus contribute to: 1) improve the analytical capacity for monetary policy and suitable macroprudential regulation and supervision; 2) harmonize the national financial statistics in light of the major financial integration and interconnectedness across the Region; and primarily 3) foster technical collaboration among the Forum members for the debate of relevant issues, international standards and recommendations, seeking its adoption into the Region's financial information models and systems on a thoughtful way. Source (https://www.cemla.org/fif/english.html).

of Pillar 3[199], defining standards for the disclosure of information, inclusive of those taken as sensitive and strategic, such as liquidity risk quantitative data. Motivated by the global trend, BCB put further efforts on the disclosure of public information existing in its databases, combining the objectives of promoting market discipline and reducing the cost of responding to requests for information.

In Brazil, the supervision area had long taken its first steps towards active transparency[200]. The first table of bank fees was published in 1998, in order to allow customers to compare banking service costs among banks, and the accounting information for the 50 largest banking conglomerates, known as 'Top50', became publicly available shortly after the turn of the century.

The disclosure of information reported to supervisors continued evolving along the time and providing relevant information to the public, such as the IF.Data[201], the evolution of Top50, and the SCR.Data[202], which comprehends more than 700 thousand series of information on credit operations. In terms of priority, however, disclosure was still seen as a byproduct of monitoring activities.

> "The disclosure of information needs to be well planned, to mitigate questionings and even the probability of new information requests. Whoever discloses an information becomes responsible

---

199. The Pillar 3 disclosure framework seeks to promote market discipline through regulatory disclosure requirements. The enhancements in the standard contain three main elements: (i) consolidation of all existing Basel Committee disclosure requirements into the Pillar 3 framework; (ii) introduction of a "dashboard" of banks' key prudential metrics and a new disclosure requirement for banks which record prudent valuation adjustments; and (iii) updates to reflect ongoing reforms to the regulatory framework, such as the total loss-absorbing capacity (TLAC) regime for globally systemically important banks and the revised market risk framework published by the Committee in January 2016. Source (https://www.bis.org/press/p170329.htm).

200. BCB's IT area is responsible for leading the dissemination of information from public entities in Brazil, with the development of advanced tools that follow the latest trends in technological evolution.

201. IF.Data data can be accessed through the link: https://www3.BC.gov.br/ifdata/.

202. SCR.Data provides information on credit operations reported to SCR and can be accessed through the link: https://www.bcb.gov.br/estabilidadefinanceira/scrdata/.

for its data consistency and shall be at the public disposal to answer eventual questions." (Clara Rizel)

Motivated by the global trend for 'transparency' and pushed by the huge amount of information requests, the IT-Experts team decided to map all monitoring information that could be made public, organize them into data-kits and establish a publication schedule[203] for them. Thus, 36 data-kits, such as reports on credit operations, total claims from public and subnational entities, among others, are gradually being disclosed at the BCB website.

> "We've disclosed the 'Bank Fees' information for bank customers, but the banks themselves also accessed the information to check their competitors." (Mauricio Soares)
>
> "IF.Data is broadly used, either for academic purposes or for bank analysis itself, both by investors and depositors. It is really an effective product." (Marcelo Bicalho)
>
> "I use IF.Data to get an idea of the risks that FIs are running, not only in relation to capital and liquidity indicators, but also to know the borrower profile." (Everton Gonçalves – ABBC)

---

203. The disclosure schedule was prepared in partnership with the IT area, responsible for its operationalization, and with BCB's Ombudsman, responsible for conducting actions related to LAI.

Figure: IF. Data Scope

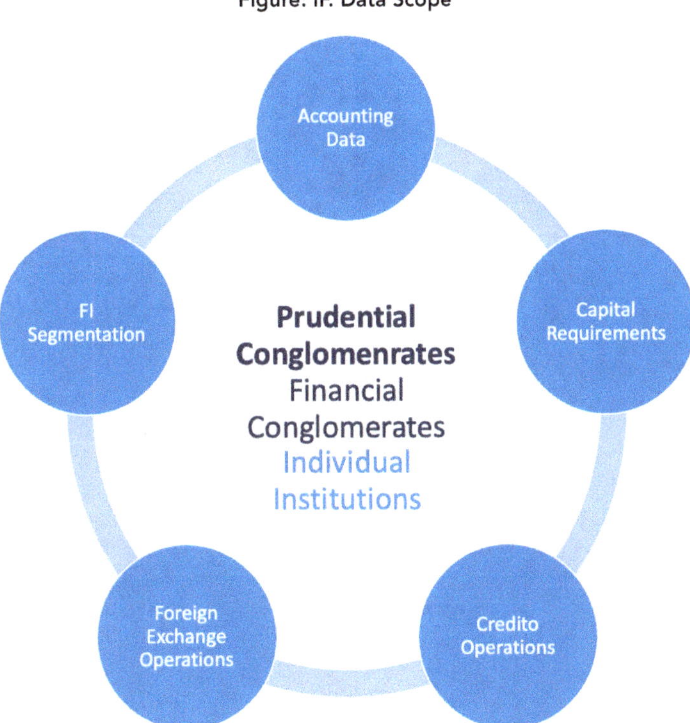

Source: Banco Central do Brasil/IF.Data. https://www3.bcb.gov.br/ifdata/?lang=1

On May 11, 2016, the Brazilian government instituted the Open Data Policy of the Federal Executive Branch[204], which comprised a series of normative, planning and guidance documents for the disclosure of open federal executive data, based on LAI. Guided by this policy, BCB developed an Open Data Portal, which consolidates the links of all information disclosed by financial institutions in their websites[205].

---

204. The Open Data Policy of the Federal Executive Branch aims to promote the disclosure of data from agencies and entities of the federal government in the form of open data, as well as enhance public transparency. More information at the link: https://wiki.dados. gov.br/Politica-de-Dados-Abertos.ashx.

205. The BCB's Open Data Portal (https://dadosabertos.bcb.gov.br/) discloses more than 3,000 datasets in Portuguese and about 2,860 datasets in English, mostly regarding data on 'Financial inclusion' and 'Economy and finance'. Data is available in its original format and financial institutions are responsible for publishing their own information catalogs. BCB consolidates all catalogs and discloses their links.

Figure: BCB Open Data

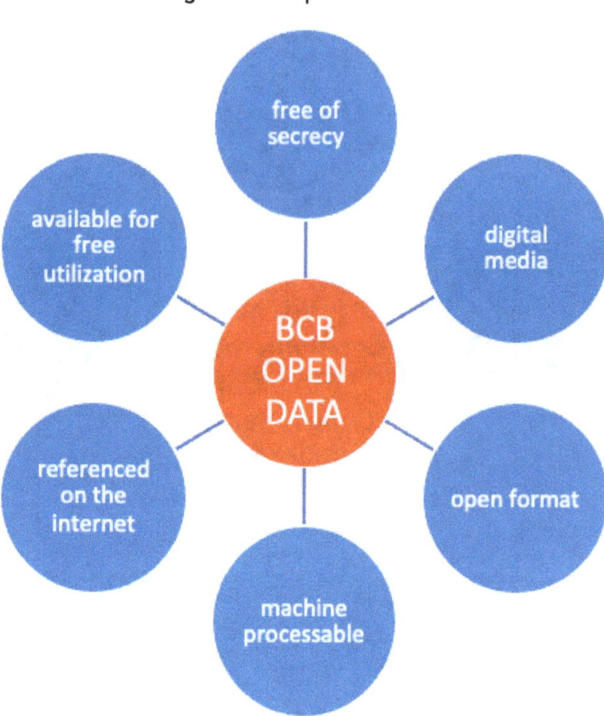

Source: Banco Central do Brazil. https://www.bcb.gov.br/acessoinformacao/dadosabertos

4.6 THE INCORPORATION OF DATA QUALITY IN THE MONITORED ISSUES FRAMEWORK

For many years, the development of data quality routines were out of the list of priorities. Monitoring teams were focused on producing analyses, warnings, reports. Allocating people to check data quality meant missing the workforce. Over time, very little was done towards the enhancement of data quality routines, especially when compared with the huge development of monitoring tools and processes. The real mindset shift was triggered by the implementation of the BCB's Information Governance Policy in 2013, which helped to put together data users and data curators.

"The new information governance model was a springboard for data quality processes, because it states that the Central Bank has to worry about it, and has to put efforts on it. I used to hear: 'once things are stable, I'll worry about quality, because it's very important!', but this moment never came… Today, all reports we receive are subject to a very comprehensive data quality process." (Helton Maciel)

Although in the agenda, the fact is that improvements on data quality processes evolved slowly. The commitment of the reporting institutions' top management and eventual signatures of MoUs[206] have been very important instruments at the beginning of the data cleaning process, but they were time-consuming and very punctual to withstand the frequency and volume of data received. It was necessary to establish a more dynamic and prophylactic process.

"As much as we worked to correct data and the errors represented a small portion of the database, finding an error raised doubts about the accuracy of the whole information. These problems encouraged the false idea that it was necessary to do on-site inspections to confirm the information received." (Gilneu Vivan)

Quality issues were being addressed by topic. Task forces were formed to solve a different problem at a time. This strategy, however, resulted in an infinite process, as errors supposedly exterminated, happened again. This approach was proving itself increasingly fruitless. The only way to avoid recurring errors would be the implementation of ongoing data-check processes.

"Many things can provoke recurrent errors in the database: new reporting institutions, changes in service provider or personnel responsible for the report elaboration… Besides, people may also make the same mistakes over time." (Marcelo Fernandes)

The shift in approach occurred when the Monitored Issues Framework[207] was extended to data quality routines, creating the Monitored Quality Issues - SMQ (*Situações Monitoradas de*

---

206. MoU is the acronym for Memorandum of Understanding.
207. See Chapter 3 - 3.3 Monitored Issues Framework: a major step towards integrating the supervisory model.

Qualidade). From this moment on, the quality process could be effectively integrated into the monitoring activities, as the same procedures started to be used to address prudential and quality-related issues.

There was, however, a peculiarity that required the SMQs procedures to be structured a little differently. While in a regular Monitored Issue the monitoring analyst directly reports to the supervisor its concerns regarding the issue identified in the monitoring process, those identified by a SMQ process, prior to being reported to the supervisor, are checked with the respective institution whether the reported information is correct.

The implementation of the SMQ Framework favored relevant advances in data quality processes. Validation checks that were previously limited to cross check information of a same document at its delivery, could expand to more complex algorithms, performed after the report had been uploaded, such as: assessing the evolution of one specific information along the time; cross checking information among different documents and data sources; or even comparing theoretical versus actual behavior of a specific data.

Gedoc System, which was developed to control reports delivery, evolved into a more robust system, the System for the Control of Documents' Delivery - CRD[208] (*Sistema de Controle de Remessa de Documentos*), which besides controlling delivery is also able to access any BCB's database needed to carry out the various data quality algorithms, regardless of their complexity level. CRD is also used to process and manage SMQs' routines.

Upon the delivery of a new report, CRD processes all SMQs related to it. In case of suspected inaccuracies, the system automatically forwards them to the reporting financial institution, asking for a justification or its immediate correction. Should the

---

208. Reporting institutions may access CRD to monitor their report's delivery. They have access to the list of required reports, deadlines for delivery, as well as it records the effective date of delivery and replacements of each report uploaded at the BCB. CRD also works as a communication channel with the BCB, for delivery protocol messages, like error messages and the report's current processing status.
(https://www.BC.gov.br/estabilidadefinanceira/controledocumentosif)

institution justify it, the data quality analyst decides whether it is or not a concern that needs to be reported to the supervisor.

Figure: Monitored Quality Issues - Workflow

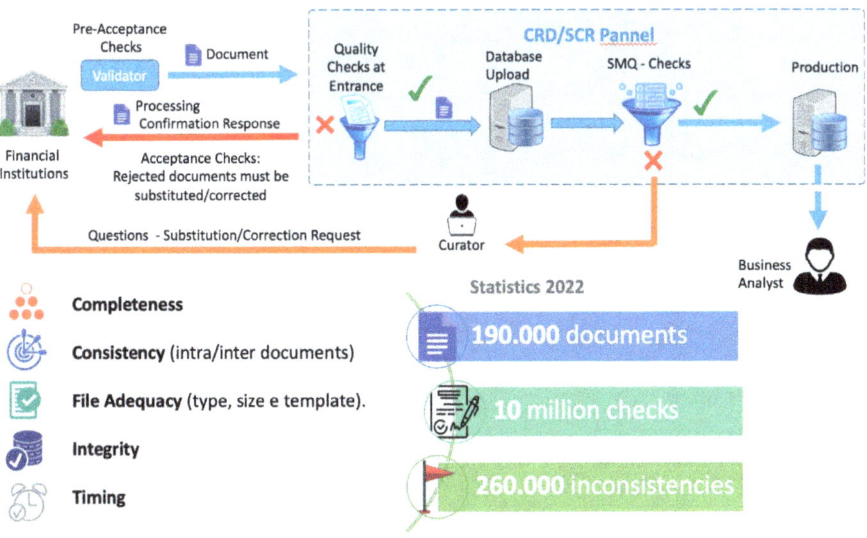

Source:Banco Central do Brasil

"Any user is allowed to create a new SMQ in the CRD system, and it goes live immediately." (Helton Maciel)

"SMQ framework favors the increase of validation checks over time. And we give transparency to this process, by disclosing in advance the checks that we will carry out." (Marcelo Fernandes)

CHAPTER 5

Supervision

"In the accounting inspection model, we looked backwards. When we shifted our focus to risk, we started to look forwards, but still focusing on risks, without exploring the business environment. Now, we are moving towards a more prospective view."

(Paulo Sérgio Neves)

This chapter describes the trajectory of the 'Supervision' activities of the M&S model (the former on-site supervision) and the development of the supervision process on a continuous basis. It also presents the allocation of supervision activities into three different departments, as a strategy to optimize its workforce not only proportionally to the systemic importance of the supervised entities (banking vs. non-banking institutions), but to adequately address issues related to compliance, consumer, fraud, money laundering and combating the financing of terrorism, as well. The innovations implemented for the supervision of non-bank financial institutions and credit unions in large-scale are also a prominent topic in this chapter.

5.1 THE IMPLEMENTATION OF A SUPERVISORY MODEL ON A CONTINUOUS BASIS

The IGC supervisory model[209] had been very important within the historical context, as supervisors needed to deeply understand how a bank operated. However, it was not a sustainable model. IGC planning and execution required a high cost and a lot of time to carry out a point-in-time assessment of a single financial conglomerate, while keeping the rest of the financial system on the waiting list.

Figure: On-site Supervision Activities Carried Out in the First Semester of 2001

Inspection Modality	Quantity (Qt)	Working Days X Employee (DUH)[1]	DUH / Qt
IGC - Consolidated Global Inspection	4	5969	1492.3
IGC Preparation	5	3361	672.2
IGC Follow-up	10	97	9.7
General Inspection	4	3900	37.5
Modular Inspection	55	839	15.3
Special Verification[2]	201	9115	45.3
Verification under request	60	19	0.3
Citizen's Complain	50	56	1.1

1/ DUH (man X day) is equivalent to the traditional measure man x hour (HH), corresponding 1 DUH to 8 HH

---

209. See Chapter 1, 1.4 Consolidated Global Inspection - the X-ray of the financial institution, for more details on the IGC model.

2/ Special verifications are carried out whenever further investigation is necessary, due issues regarding the economic and financial situation of the supervised entity or warnings reported from the monitoring area.

Source:Banco Central do Brasil

The Netherlands had developed a supervisory model that basically consisted of segregating financial institutions activities into business lines, and comparing the risks inherent to each business line with the controls used to manage these risks. Each assessment was converted into a score, and the institution's final rating would be an average of all business line's scores. The 'Rating Model' had presented good results among the supervisory entities that had implemented it, which has contributed to BCB's decision to also adopt the model.

> "I was one of the first supervisors to apply the Rating Model in Brazil. The manual was still very tied to the European financial market, as it did not comprehended the operations that I wanted to analyze and the bank's portfolio did not have the operations that the manual recommended us to inspect. But, in general, it was good, because we had to discuss liquidity, market and credit risks with the bank. It was also the first time we dealt with reputational risk." (Paulo Sérgio Neves)

Supervision had migrated from the accounting inspection model to the IGC model in the late 1990s and, in less than 5 years, the model was being replaced again. Those frequent shifts provoked confusion and discomfort amongst supervisors. They felt compelled to advocate for one of the models, convinced that 'his/her' model was the right one!

In fact, the IGC model gave supervisors the feeling that they were playing the leading role of the supervisory process, as it should be. An IGC was an invasive action, where the supervisor him/herself extracted information from the institution's database to form an opinion about it. The Rating model, in its turn, abandoned the need to 'get the hands dirty', as the supervisor's assessment would be based on interviews with the institution, focused much more on controls and governance than on assets' quality. In fact, according to the new approach, asset quality would be a consequence of how the institution was being managed, especially the risk management. Thus, supervisors did not take the Rating model as a supervisory methodology per se, but as a preliminary diagnostic tool, to guide the planning of the 'real' supervisory work. After all, no one was comfortable with rating an institution without carrying out a detailed on-site inspection.

> "It was a mindset shift. For a while, supervisors thought that on-site inspections were prohibited." (Osvaldo Watanabe)

Although the technical teams took the Rating model as preliminary work, the senior management of supervision knew that its scope was more comprehensive and adequate. Nevertheless, it was necessary to adjust the model to the Brazilian financial market characteristics. Thus, supervisors were allowed to rate institutions in experimental mode, while adjusting the model and, as long experience and confidence in the new methodology were advancing, IGC works were gradually losing purpose until finally falling into disuse[210]. As a result, the Rating model evolved towards a sound ongoing supervision framework that, in 2003, was consolidated as the System for the Assessment of Risks and Controls - SRC[211] (*Sistema de Avaliação de Riscos e Controles*).

> "The SRC is much broader than a supervisory process, it is an organized infrastructure to bring and consolidate all the knowledge supervision has about the institution." (Belline Santana)

---

210. The last IGCs were held in 2003.
211. SRC consists of a set of criteria and structured procedures, in order to consolidate and keep up-to-date the risk profile of banking institutions, as well as it permits to timely identify risky situations.

Figure: SRC Cycle

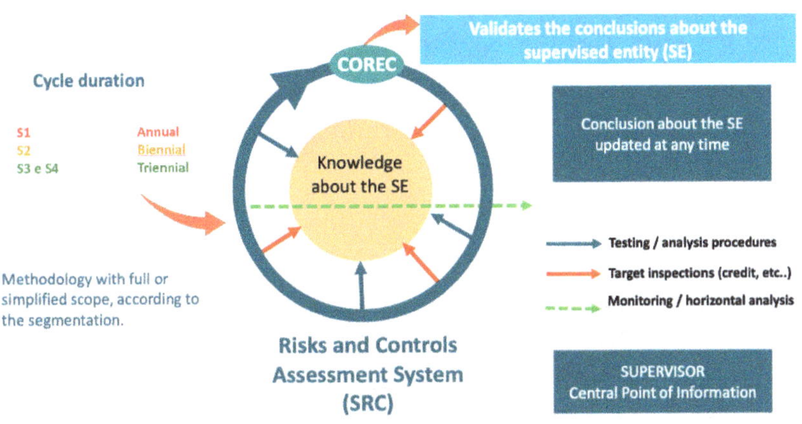

Source:Banco Central do Brasil

SRC continuously updates the institution's rating with each new assessment input by the supervisor in the System. At the end of one cycle that can vary from 1 to 3 years, depending on the size of the institution, the rating must be ratified by an internal supervisory committee, called the Risk and Control Assessment Committee - Corec[212] (*Comitê de Avaliação de Riscos e Controles*).

Up to 2021, the SRC methodology comprised two groups of analyses: the Economic-Financial Assessment - ANEF (*Avaliação Econômico-Financeira*), where the monitoring area contributed with a 'quantitative' score, calculated automatically by its scoring system, which the supervisor could adjust if deemed necessary; and the Assessment of Risks and Controls - ARC (*Avaliação de Riscos e Controles*), which comprehended the supervisor's analysis of the various risks associated with the institution's activities and the respective controls to manage them. The exception was the evaluation of controls and actions to combat money laundering

---

212. The composition of the COREC also varies according to the size of the assessed institution: in medium-sized banks, it is composed of 5 people, comprising the deputy head of Banking Supervision Department, the bank's supervision manager and 3 heads of division; in large banks, the department's head is also part of the committee and, in small banks, it is made up of 3 participants, being the bank's supervision manager, his/her deputy, and another member of the bank's supervision team.

and terrorism financing (AML/CFT), which was carried out by the BCB department responsible for those issues.

Recently, ANEF evolved to a more prospective view and encompassed the analysis of the institution's business model, assessing not only its strategy and results, but also the sustainability of financial results over time.

Figure: SRC Model

Source:Banco central do Brasil/Difis

5.2 SPECIALIZED TEAMS

Figure: Specialized Teams' Scope[213]

CREDIT RISK

MARKET RISK

LIQUIDITY RISK

CAPITAL

CORPORATE GOVERNANCE

ACCOUNTING

BUSINESS MODEL ANALYSIS

SOCIO-ENVIRONMENT RISK

LEGAL ISSUES

CYBER RISK

FMI'S NON-FINANCIAL RISKS

DATA INTEGRITY

Source:Banco Central do Brasil

---

213. The specialized teams are divided into two areas, one focused on operational risks, mainly cybernetic and financial market infrastructure, and the other focused on other risks and topics: credit, market, liquidity and legal risks, capital, governance, socio-environmental and climate risks, accounting and auditing, economic and financial analysis, among others. The specialists in FMIs are also the on-site supervisors of these entities.

Specialized teams were created by the IGC model, with the objective of assisting supervisors on the assessment of relevant topics, such as credit, foreign exchange operations, ALM and IT[214]. Supervisors' uneven skills and focus could imply into different approaches and conclusions among supervised institutions, for the same inspected issue. Thus, as the works were becoming more complex and demanded higher levels of expertise, new specialized teams were being created to meet those new demands[215] and to guarantee the supervisory model's level playing field.

> "The IT-specialists team was initially destined to provide operational support to inspectors, when they were not yet technologically skilled. The team helped them, for example, to manipulate data or to use Excel and other Office Package tools. Gradually, supervisory teams improved their IT-user skills and the IT-specialists could focus on the assessment of IT governance issues." (Harold Espinola)

> "I was a 'founding partner' of the off-site specialist team, which later evolved to assess corporate management efficiency and then internal controls. The team has really evolved over time. When I left, they were focused on issues like governance, operational risk and analysis of the bank's financial results." (Belline Santana)

The specialists carried out inspections related to their topics and prepared reports pointing out the identified problems and determining the necessary actions to solve them. The supervisor

---

214. Initially, the activities of the specialized teams were limited to compliance check, such as whether the custody of bonds and securities really existed, whether the exchange operations were duly registered, whether the credit files had complete documentation, or whether the guarantees really existed. The arrival of the ACL tool permitted them to upgrade both in autonomy, as they became able to extract information directly from the institutions' databases, and in performance, as they could develop risk analysis procedures, based on the collected data.

215. The specialized teams are composed of two areas, one responsible for operational risks, most focused on cyber risk, and financial market infrastructures (FMI), and the other responsible for the remaining risks and topics: credit, market, liquidity and legal risks, capital, corporate governance, socio-environmental and climate risks, accounting and auditing, economic-financial analysis, among others. The FMI specialist division is also responsible for carrying out the supervision of these entities.

responsible for the institution consolidated all reports into two documents: the IGC internal report and the inspection letter, which comprehended the determinations to correct all identified problems. At the conclusion of the IGC works, the supervisor delivered the inspection letter to the institution, and afterwards, supervised its compliance with the determinations.

Each specialist team was focused on specific issues and the supervisor had the holistic understanding of the various problems together. Thus, he/she could perceive the relevance of each one for the soundness of the financial institution as a whole. Although supervisors needed the experts' technical support to properly cover the entire spectrum of issues addressed in an IGC, in some way, this arrangement put them as hostages of the expert's opinion.

In general, experts' recommendations were considered too severe in the supervisor's perspective, however, their technical supremacy made any opposing view unarguable. In practice, whether or not the supervisor agreed, he/she had to sign the inspection letter with the experts' determinations and make the institution comply with them.

This nature of conflict was recurrent and worsened over time, which raised questions on the existence of specialized teams and a few proposals for their extinction. When the Rating model was finally consolidated in 2008, a great dilemma was raised: how to adjust the work of specialized teams to the new model? After all, they had lost the purpose for which they had been created and the pressure to extinguish them was growing strong. They needed to reinvent themselves, should they want to survive.

> "Supervisors wanted the specialized teams to be dismantled and experts relocated to the banks' supervisory teams, but when the Rating model replaced the IGC model, they remained." (Harold Espinola)

The solution to avoid extinction came with encompassing other activities, such as reviewing the Rating procedures guide or providing consultancy for on-site inspections. Evidently, experts continued to be demanded for the most problematic issues and entered into action with all their traditional tools whenever there was a suspicion of something more serious. However, most inspection activities had been replaced by interviews, which made those opportunities increasingly rare.

Historically, on-site supervision processes had been structured to focus on one supervised institution at a time. Comparative analysis of the institution over time or in relation to its peers were out of the supervisor's agenda, and it was precisely this lack of comparability that caused the need to migrate to a more comprehensive model that encompassed the assessment of all institutions simultaneously.

Thus, in 2013, supervision adopted a matrix approach: the bank supervision teams would keep the classic 'vertical supervision' approach, i. e., assessing institutions as a whole, one-by-one; and the 'horizontal supervision' approach would be performed by the specialized teams, each one assessing issues under its expertise, across all institutions.

The rearrangement of activities rescued the relevance of the specialized teams and brought any discussion for their extinction to an end. Specialized teams increased in number, strengthened their workforce and gained autonomy to develop methodologies for horizontal assessment.

> "The idea was to have teams with different but complementary views, questioning issues not yet addressed by one or the other." (Lucio Capelletto)
>
> "It was nice when people from a bank's supervision team participated in our work [specialized in market and liquidity risks], because we were able to anticipate eventual conflicts and reach an agreement still on the course of the work. It was also an opportunity for us to share some specific knowledge with them." (Nelio Magina)

Having two opinions about the same institution seemed to be a good strategy to mitigate the risk of a relevant problem going unnoticed, but, in practice, it turned out to be a recurring and inevitable source of conflicts. In fact, the matrix approach had been developed exactly to raise this kind of debate, but once more, the supervisor became a hostage to the expert's opinion.

> "The specialist has in-depth knowledge, as he/she is very dedicated to a particular topic. Therefore, in some situations, he/she may have some difficulty to follow the supervisor's generalist position. Sometimes, something relevant and legitimate that the expert is claiming, may not be so significant when considering the financial institution as a whole. In certain situations, attacking the problem as required by the specialist can be a bad strategy, as there may be more serious problems to address first." (Marco Verrone)

Once again supervision was struggling with the same problems that caused the rupture of the on-site & off-site supervision model years ago: the responsibility of an opinion about the supervised entity relied exclusively on the supervisor and there was a third party pointing out what to do.

In fact, according to the Monitoring & Supervision model's original plan, specialized teams had to move to the strategic department, so that they could provide expert support and centralize technical discussions among all departments of the supervision area. However, they have always been exclusively focused on banking institutions, partly due to their origins and partly due to the banks' systemic relevance in terms of financial stability. Besides, these experts had become the supervision department's technical skills, not only internally, but before other departments within and outside the supervision area. They were the supervisor's voice in discussions for the implementation of international standards[216] and other banking regulations, they represented the department in

---

216. Also called "Basel Accords", the international standards are recommendations on banking regulations issued by the Basel Committee on Banking Supervision (BCBS).

interdepartmental projects etc. For those reasons, the migration of specialized teams to the strategic department was delayed for many years.

> "Nowadays, the specialist summarizes his/her notes as a suggestion, to be submitted to the supervisor's discretion. Under this new approach, conflicts have lessened." (Nelio Magina)

5.3 SUPERVISION OF NON-BANKING FINANCIAL INSTITUTIONS

The evolution of the supervision model did not happen in peaceful times. On the contrary, several crises and problems that impacted the SFN[217] occurred during its metamorphosis. However, BCB's supervision managed to keep alive the flame of trying to solve the internal problems, even though it was constantly being trampled by countless demands arising from a turbulent environment.

With efforts continuously focused on institutions with systemic impact (banks and banking conglomerates), the lack of relevance of supervisory activities aimed at credit unions and non-banking institutions became more and more evident over time. Many of them repeatedly did not meet the minimum regulatory requirements, and little supervisory attention was given to their problems. Thus, credit unions began to pressure Congress[218], claiming for an exclusive supervisory and regulatory agency.

This was the trigger that moved BCB to split on-site supervision activities into two departments: one focused on banking conglomerates and financial institutions (Desup), and the other, on credit unions and non-banking conglomerates and financial institutions (Desuc) [219].

---

217. Asian Tigers (1997-1998), Russian crisis (1999), Dot-com bubble (2000), Argentina crisis (2001-2002), President Lula's inauguration (2002) etc.

218. Parliamentary representation of credit unions has always been very strong in Brazil.

219. The new component assumed the supervision of a wide range of financial institutions: Development Agencies; Savings and Loans Associations - APE (*Associações de Poupança e Empréstimo*); Credit Unions; Exchange Brokers; Securities Brokers; Mortgage Companies - CH (*Companhias Hipotecárias*); Leasing Companies - SAM (*Sociedades*

"The concentration of non-banking supervision in an exclusive component allowed for the dedication to institutions that, due to their heterogeneity, were hard to supervise together with the banking segment." (Donizeti Maia)

"The on-site supervision split was the root of the 'segmentation and proportionality' approach[220] that we came to implement years later." (Paulo Sergio Neves)

Figure: Segmentation of Financial Institutions and proportional application of prudential regulation

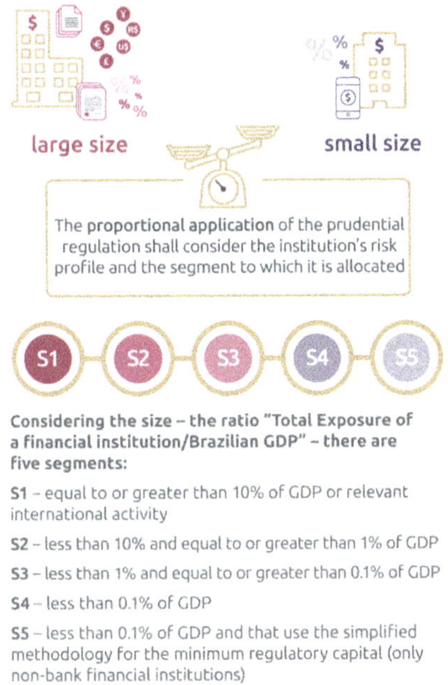

---

de Arrendamento Mercantil); Credit, Financing and Investment Companies - SCFI (*Sociedades de Crédito, Financiamento e Investimento*); Credit to MIcro and Small Business Companies - SCMEPP (*Sociedades de Crédito ao Microempreendedor e à Empresa de Pequeno Porte*); Real Estate Credit Companies - SCI (*Sociedades de Crédito Imobiliário*); Consortium Managers. Over time, the new forms of financial intermediation that emerged from the evolution of financial regulation and means of payment were also included in its supervised universe: Payment Schemes; Payment Institutions; Direct Credit Company - SCD (*Sociedade de Crédito Direto*); and Peer-to-Peer Loan Company - SEP (*Sociedades de Empréstimo a Pessoas*).

220. Resolution No. 4,553/2017 establishes the segmentation of financial institutions and other institutions authorized to operate by the Banco Central do Brasil for the purpose of proportional application of prudential regulation, according to their size and international activity level.

Desup's scope: S1 to S4 banking and banking conglomerate institutions

Desuc's scope of action: S2 to S5 credit unions and non-banking financial institutions and conglomerates

Source: Banco Central do Brasil - https://www.bcb.gov.br/en/financialstability/regulation

Non-banking on-site supervision was born in 2005, on the apex of the conflict between on-site and off-site activities. With a large contingent of institutions to supervise, non-banking supervisors needed to rely on remote and automated procedures to be able to carry out the work. Thus, its first strategy was to seek for an off-site partnership, and, in the blink of an eye, off-site supervision had gone from being rejected to being desired!

> "Bank supervisors used to say: 'only report to me what is relevant and I'll ask you when I need it'. Non-bank supervisors wanted us to do all the work: 'tell me what happened and whether it was a problem or not!'" (Álvaro Freitas)

Although flattered, some factors prevented off-site supervision from being able to immediately and satisfactorily encompass the non-banking universe. First of all, off-site routines were also focused on banking institutions. Tools and analyzes had been built to assess banks and they were improving skills towards macro prudential monitoring, for the assessment of financial stability. Secondly, the non-banking universe comprehended a variety of types of institutions with very specific particularities that had not been calibrated in the off-site metrics. Furthermore, the granularity of non-banking information was much less detailed and the initiatives to bring them to the same level of banks' micro data were limited by compliance costs.

> "When I was appointed as credit unions' supervisor, I realized that there was no off-site support for us. We felt completely ignored because we had no systemic relevance." (Fabio Lacerda)

An exclusive off-site team to monitor the whole universe of non-banking institutions was the only viable option. Then, the team was formed and its first challenge was to adapt the bank's economic-financial analysis model to the new 'customer'. However, the team's inexperience, added to the countless particularities of the non-banking sector, and combined with the non-banking supervisors' uncertainties regarding the supervision model to be implemented, were strong obstacles for them to be able to quickly implement an effective supervisory process.

> "The biggest problem was the large number of different institutions. A consortium is completely different from a development agency, which is different from a foreign exchange broker, and so on. Methodologies were very different from what we were used to applying for bank's off-site supervision." (Álvaro Freitas)

The implementation of non-banking off-site routines evolved with slow steps until the signing of the Armistice in 2006, when on-site & off-site supervision gave way to the Monitoring & Supervision model. Under the new approach, the off-site supervision routines were discontinued and the monitoring area focused on reporting to supervisor eventual concerns resulting from the micro prudential monitoring processes, as well as on developing skills to perform macro prudential analyses. The extinction of an off-site supervision component was the final straw for non-banking supervision move towards the development of its own supervision tools and models.

Similar to the ancient banking supervision framework, non-banking supervision was primarily organized in the form of traditional inspections, with teams distributed geographically. Each regional team was responsible for several types of institutions, although the number of inspectors was not sufficient to supervise all of them. Once again following the banking supervision steps, the first challenge would be the harmonization of the supervisory processes. Thus, standardized inspection and assessment scripts were created[221], where each topic (credit risk, ALM, economic-

---

221. The first script created was called '*Método de Avaliação de Cooperativas*' - MA-COOP, a credit union assessment method. Then they created MACOR for the brokers' assessment, and so on..

financial situation, other assets and liabilities etc.) was step-by-step fully described, taking into account, of course, the particularities of each type of institution.

> "We incorporated into the scripts the obligation to score the institution, so that a conclusion on the assessed topic became mandatory. From then on, reports couldn't no longer be merely descriptive. The inspector had to give his/her opinion on each inspected topic." (Sandra Castro)

In view of the lack of sufficient personnel to cover the wide non-banking universe, institutions were classified according to their risk and impact levels and an inspection cycle was established to each Risk&Impact category[222]. Regional teams have also abandoned the geographic distribution and were rearranged by institution type, similar to the changes occurring in the monitoring area.

Despite all the efforts to implement the non-banking supervision framework, the continuous growth of the supervisory universe was always overcoming supervisors' working capacity. Especially when fintechs and payment schemes[223] started to be regulated and supervised by the BCB, as all entities arising from these new forms of financial intermediation were automatically attached to the already inflated non-banking universe[224].

---

222. The 'Continuous Cycle' comprises institutions with the highest risk and greatest impact. High risk institutions are inspected every 3 years and medium risk institutions, every 5 years. Low-risk institutions do not have a predefined inspection cycle and are allocated in the 'No Cycle' category. Eventual on-site activity in them would be triggered by the identification of a concern in an off-site supervision (performed by the non-banking supervision department itself) or monitoring (performed by the monitoring area) routine.

223. A payment scheme is a set of rules and procedures that regulates the provision of certain payment services to the public, which is accepted by more than one recipient/payee, by means of direct access by end users, payers and recipients/payees. Law No. 12,865/2013 regulates the payment schemes and payment institutions as part of the Brazilian Payment System (SPB). Source: https://www.bcb.gov.br/en/financialstability/paymentschemes.

224. Non-banking supervisors have encompassed the supervision of Payment Schemes, Payment Institutions - IP (*Instituições de Pagamento*), Peer-to-Peer Loan Company - SEP (*Sociedade de Empréstimo entre Pessoas*) and Direct Credit Company - SCD (*Sociedade de Crédito Direto*).

Figure: Payment Schemes

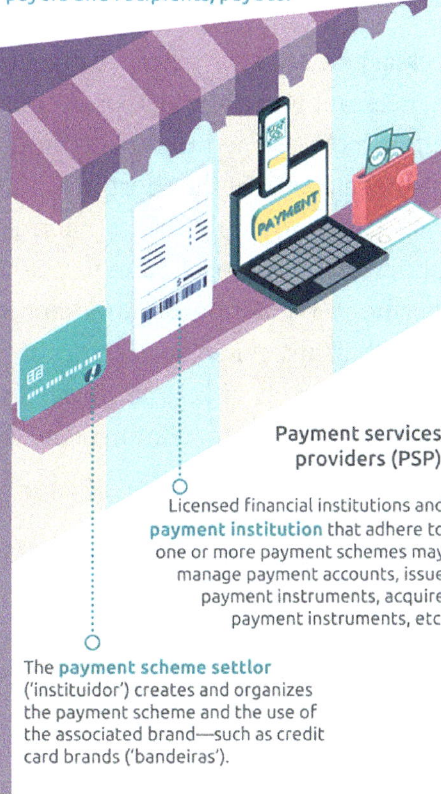

Source:Banco Central do Brasil - https://www.bcb.gov.br/en/financialstability/paymentschemes

> "The new conglomerates are arising from payment schemes. They start by providing payment services, and gradually add other financial products, until they become a financial conglomerate, that may or may not have a bank in its composition, but just as a business line. Today, non-banking supervisors are discussing issues such as the entry of WhatsApp as a Payment Institution." (Harold Espinola)

It was necessary to seek for external partnerships, in order to overcome the incessant growth in demand, since the alternative of increasing staff number seemed unfeasible in the long run, and completely out of the question in the short run.

The external auditor would be a natural partner for a public&private supervisory approach, due to his/her function and capillarity. Furthermore, regulation required auditors to formally communicate to the BCB any evidence of errors or fraud, that could put the audited institution at risk[225]. Historically, however, they were seen just as a mechanism to reinforce the credibility of the institution's financial statements disclosed to the public.

The credit unions were chosen as the target to the implementation of the new approach. Besides being the most organized institutions of the non-banking supervised universe[226],

---

225. CMN Resolution 607 of April 2, 1980 extends the requirement of an external auditor to all financial institutions authorized to operate by the BCB. Auditor's opinion regarding the institution's financial statements attests its accuracy, although it does not exclude or limit BCB's supervisory action.
"… The CMN promoted, through Resolution No. 3081, of May 29, 2003, a major transformation in the regulation of external audit services for financial institutions and other entities authorized to operate by the BCB, instituting a regulation that consolidated the requirements that were already in force and included, among others, the following innovations: … determination that the external auditor and the Audit Committee must, individually or jointly, formally communicate to the BCB the existence or evidence of error or fraud represented by: non-compliance with legal and regulatory standards that jeopardize the continuity of the audited entity; fraud of any value perpetrated by the institution's management; material fraud perpetrated by the entity's employees or third parties; errors that result in material inaccuracies in the entity's financial statements." (Evolution of Regulation of External Auditing in Brazil: Critical Analysis, from the Theory of Regulation, Jorge Katsumi Niyama et al.).
226. In Brazil, credit unions can be Singular, when they act individually, be organized in the form of Credit Union Centers or Federations, composed of at least 3 singular credit unions, or even grouped in the form of Confederations of Credit Union Centers, composed of at least three credit union centers or federations.

they had been the ones that raised the flag for a more active regulatory and supervisory framework.

Figure: Credit Union Infrastructure in Brazil

Credit Union National System

Source:Expert XP – 'Cooperativas de Crédito: o que são e como funcionam?' - https://conteudos.xpi.com.br/renda-fixa/relatorios/cooperativas-de-credito-o-que-sao-e-como-funcionam/

However, the establishment of links between the work of the external auditor and BCB supervision ran against the auditor's independence. Auditors were not subordinate to the audited credit union nor to the BCB and, consequently, the supervisor could not and should not have any control over his/her work.

This gap was closed in 2015, when Resolution 4,454 created the 'Credit Union's Auditor'. Despite being independent from the point of view of the audited institution, the credit union's auditor was licensed by the BCB, which means that BCB had the power of disqualifying or not renewing an auditor's license, in case of bad performance. From then on, supervisors got greater control over the quality of the auditor's work. They could, for example, require the credit union either to demand the auditor to redo some work or to hire another auditor to do it with the scope defined by the supervisor[227].

> "There are many organized infrastructures that give support to the non-banking activities and we have been working hard to make them work properly. While we do not have the 'financial auditors' for other institution types, we are working with internal auditors to fulfill this role. We demand them for results and check whether the work was adequate and sufficient." (Sandra Castro)

The 'partnership' approach applied to the credit unions brought important reflections to the supervisory working process, as supervisors began to realize that many identified issues would only be regularized with the involvement of the respectives credit union centers and confederations.

> "Inspecting one credit union, then another, then another was like 'beating a dead horse', as supervisors always ran into the same problems." (Sandra Castro)

Supervisors began to carry out consolidated inspections, that is, they investigated the same issue in all affiliated credit unions, simultaneously[228]. Thus, they could identify problems more easily, and also their roots[229]. Besides, the solution often required changes in systems or methodologies used for risk management, which used to be under the unions' center or confederation's responsibility. In

---

227. Supervision has also established partnerships with credit unions' centers and confederations, in order to properly exercise an auxiliary supervision function of the individual credit unions under their umbrella. Those entities are responsible not only for monitoring their affiliates, but also for monitoring the notes made by the credit union auditors, for requiring them the elaboration of a recovery plan, for monitoring its execution and, if necessary, communicating to the BCB relevant facts.

228. The automation of the supervision process (described in Chapter 7) allowed inspections to be carried out remotely, where all interaction between supervisor and supervised entity is virtual. This new work process broke with personnel, time and budget limitations, and provided the appropriate technological environment for consolidated inspections, as well.

229. Problems regarding risk management issues, for example, would normally affect all affiliates and be related to the risk management system adopted by the unions' center or confederation.

other words, the consolidated work better identified the problems and also directed supervisors to demand corrective actions to the real responsible for its implementation. The increase in productivity offered by the consolidated approach led to its application to other types of institutions, like the financial companies, also bringing good results.

5.4 SUPERVISION OF MISCONDUCT

Since the end of the 20th century, issues related to money laundering have been gaining strength. In 1999, the supervision area created an exclusive component to fight against currency and financial illicit activities. However, how far one should go in the mission to combat and track illicit acts was subject of great internal debates. Theoretically, the Federal Police is the responsible for tracking illicit activities and the BCB should only verify whether banks had adequate controls to identify suspected illicit transactions. In practice, however, supervisors were used to do investigative work. Thus, it was natural for them to apply a similar approach to carry out the supervision of financial illicits.

Seven years later, the same supervision component incorporated the responsibility of managing BCB's call center for information requests and financial consumers' complaints. The activity was far from heading the supervisor's priority list, thus, routines were established in order to merely manage the middle ground between the demanding citizen and the responding supervisor. Meanwhile, the subprime crisis broke out in the United States, and at the heart of it was a major consumer relationship issue: the offer of inappropriate products to a huge range of customers. That event revealed the supervisor's lack of attention to problems that could arise from consumer issues. Until then, it was believed that consumer protection could be achieved by ensuring the soundness of financial institutions.

In response to the crisis, regulators and supervisors reinforced minimum standards' requirements, internal controls and transparency of financial institutions, as well as improved the monitoring of financial stability from a macro prudential perspective. However, these actions would not be sufficient should the attention focused on consumer issues were not equated in relevance and importance with prudential issues. The 'Twin Peaks'[230] supervision model proposed by Michael Taylor in 1995 regained strength and some jurisdictions moved towards it.

> "One cannot mix resources to prudential supervision, which deals with economic-financial issues, with those destined to support supervision of conduct, focused on the financial customer. Prudential supervision always ends up consuming all resources." (Andreia Lais Vargas)

In Brazil, despite the existence of a supervision component focused on financial crimes and consumer issues since the turn of the century, its scope and working processes required adjustments[231]. With regard to AML/CFT, for example, they were responsible for assessing the institution's controls, within the ongoing SRC supervision model. However, the proper management of this topic within the supervision cycle ran into conflicts of agenda and scope with the bank supervisor. AML/CFT supervisors advocated for more extensive and in-depth inspections, which generally was not possible to fit into the bank's assessment program schedule. Thus, on many occasions, the bank supervisor preferred to assess the topic him/herself, in order to avoid delays.

In 2012, the FSAP pointed out this mismatch as a point of improvement of the Brazilian supervision model, which raised

---

230. The 'Twin Peaks' model consists of the existence of two autonomous and independent supervisory entities, where both have transversal powers over all sectors of the financial system. The 'peaks' correspond to two objectives, financial stability and consumer protection. The core of this model lies in the division of prudential supervision and behavioral supervision into two different regulators, with specific competence to exercise competences related to each type.

231. Some working processes went beyond the classic supervision scope, by establishing police-like investigation procedures against financial crimes. On the other hand, others fell short of expectations, by not taking a more proactive approach in the conduct of consumer-related issues.

internal debates in the search for a solution. Meanwhile, the 'Twin Peaks' model had already been adopted in Australia, the Netherlands, Portugal and Canada, and was on the way to being implemented in the United Kingdom. Thus, Brazil decided to follow the trend and restructured its approach related to AML/CFT and consumer protection issues. The 'Supervision of Conduct' component was therefore put apart from the prudential supervision and monitoring components, with the following responsibilities: preventing the use of the financial system in activities that could bring reputational risks to the supervised institutions; improving the institutions' compliance with financial regulation; and encouraging actions aimed at reducing complaints from society.

> "Without adequate regulation and supervision, any minimally relevant money laundering event could lead to very high losses to the involved institutions." (Sidnei Marques)

Few people, a large scope of activities and a huge universe of institutions to cover were not new challenges to the supervision area, and, for the development of supervision of conduct routines, the scenario was not different.

Thus, the implementation of an Ongoing Conduct Monitoring - ACC (*Acompanhamento Contínuo de Conduta*) process, with one supervisor full-time dedicated to each institution, was restricted to the 15 largest institutions, which, in fact, represented more than 90% of customer-related issues. Besides, twice a year, the head of the department of conduct supervision has individual meetings with senior management and the audit committee of each of the 5 largest banks, to personally give them feedback on actions already implemented and to discuss what still needs to be done. For smaller institutions, the supervisory approach is reactive, that is, supervisors take action triggered by denouncements, complaints or news published in the press.

"The semestral meeting with banks is a very successful procedure, because it involves the bank's top management and they become committed to the improvements." (Andreia Lais Vargas)

Another relevant step towards consumer protection was the disclosure of BCB's Rankings for Customer Complaints and Ombudsman's Quality.

In order to give transparency to citizens about the complaints and denouncements received, BCB started to publish rankings on its website, listing: the most complained institutions; the most frequent complaints; and the efficiency of ombudsman services in solving problems[232].

Figure: Demands Received by the Ombudsmanship (2015-2017)

Type of demand	2017	Δ%	2016	Δ%	2015
1. Suggestions	269	10,2%	244	-7,2%	263
2. Compliments	107	-37,1%	170	-2,3%	174
3. Whistleblowing	17	142,9%	7	16,7%	6
4. Complaints	796	-7,3%	859	38,8%	619
Total of demands to the Ombudsmanship	1.189	-7,1%	1.280	1,7%	1.259
5. Incorrect channel (a)	926	-8,7%	1.014	-18,8%	1.249
6. Request for information (b)	440	-0,2%	441	3,3%	427
DEMANDS TOTAL	2.555	-6,6%	2.735	-6,8%	2.935

a) Refers to, mostly, to demands pertaining the performance of other public agencies or to consumer relationships between financial institutions and their clients, both outside the scope of the Ombdusmanship from Central Bank.

b) Demands related to requests for information or guidance are transferred to the Public Service Division.

Source:Banco Central do Brasil - Report on Financial Citizenship - 2018 - https://www.bcb.gov.br/content/publications/report_fincit/Report%20on%20Financial%20Citizenship%20-%202018.pdf

The 'proactive for large & reactive for small' approach applied to customer-related issues, however, was of no use to AML/CFT supervision. Money laundering and terrorism financing[233] are activities that could be infiltrated into any financial institution,

---

232. Since 2002, the BCB ranks financial institutions considering their profile of complaints regarding integrity, reliability, safety and confidentiality of performed transactions, as well as the legitimacy of the contracts and services provided — contributing to increasing the transparency of supervision actions carried out by BCB. The Ombudsman's Quality Ranking, published every quarter since late 2017, measures the performance of ombudsmans, taking into account how they deal with complaints (average time for an answer and its quality) and their compliance with regulation.

233. Up to now, only a few events concerning the financing of terrorism took place in Brazil. The most vulnerable geographic area of the country is the triple border among Brazil (Foz do Iguaçu), Argentina (Puerto Iguazu) and Paraguay (Ciudad del Leste).

regardless of its size or systemic relevance. In fact, criminal organizations prefer to use less significant entities to conduct their illicit schemes. Thus, to be effective, an approach to AML/CFT supervision had to be the same to all institutions, and this was a huge challenge!

For a long time, BCB had been putting efforts on the search for innovations that prevented personnel and budget limitations from becoming a barrier to the development of working processes focused on less systemically relevant institutions.

Finally, efforts have materialized in the form of a system, the SisCom[234], that provided tools for supervisor, to carry out inspection routines remotely[235]. Thus, travel expenses to perform on-site supervision works went down to zero, as routines were fully carried out virtually, and, as the tool permitted the replication of procedures, personnel constraints were not anymore an obstacle to abandon the sampling approach applied to the AML/CFT supervision, and go towards the coverage of the whole supervised universe.

> "The use of questionnaires and remote communication brought efficiency and effectiveness to supervisory processes. Based on the questions asked by the Authority, the institution may also improve its compliance and internal management. Besides, with the remote approach, supervision of conduct is able to cover the entire supervised universe." (Donizeti Maia)

The remote inspection methodology allows the execution of monitoring and inspection routines remotely and at a large scale, collecting information from the entire inspected universe.

---

234. SisCom - Integrated System for Supervision Support and Communication (*Sistema Integrado de Suporte e Comunicação da Supervisão*) is a system developed by the BCB, with the objective of allowing communication with the supervised entities, for most of the supervision actions carried out by the Central Bank.

235. A 'remote inspection' is characterized by the elaboration and application of electronic inspection scripts and electronic templates for requesting information and documents. This methodology allows the execution of monitoring and inspection routines remotely and at a large scale, collecting information from the entire supervised universe.

Subsequently, a similar approach was extended to non-banking prudential supervision activities and enabled the implementation of the consolidated inspection working process.

> "We send a request for information, receive the requested information, do the summaries of occurrences, forward them to the institution, that is, we manage to carry out the entire supervision process via the system. Doing the remote inspection work in 100 institutions at the same time is easy, the tricky part is dealing with the corrective actions afterwards!" (Sandra Castro)

In 2014, Congress had established an Inquiry Parliament Commission - CPI (*Comissão Parlamentar de Inquérito*) to investigate the Car-Wash Operation[236] scandal (*CPI da Lava-Jato*), and the BCB had been appointed to supply the CPI with information on the involvement of the financial system in illicit activities[237]. Upon identifying that foreign exchange brokers were being heavily used to launder illicit money, a thorough inspection work on these institutions was chosen for the debut of SisCom's remote inspection tools.

Remote inspections allowed for the identification of institutions with breaches in formal documentation, such as policies, procedures and manualization. At the same time, the monitoring area reported suspicions of improper FX operations, such as financial transactions with deceased counterparties. Thus, by crossing information, supervisors could identify and take action against institutions with irregular activities[238].

---

236. 'Car Wash Operation' (*Operação Lava-Jato*) was the largest corruption investigation in Brazil's history. It has resulted in more than a thousand warrants of various types and has involved administrative members of the state-owned oil company Petrobrás, politicians from Brazil's largest parties, presidents of the House of Representatives and the Federal Senate, state governors, and businessmen from large Brazilian companies.
237. CPIs' demands for information were excessively time-consuming to supervisors. The segregation of supervision of conduct activities in one specific department came to solve this problem, as they became responsible for this agenda.
238. The work involved the remote inspection of 60 foreign exchange brokers, simultaneously. Several of them were liquidated. In a single day, BCB liquidated 10 of them.

Figure: SisCom Workflow

Source: Banco Central do Brasil[239]

"In the early 2000s, FATF[240] had rated as insufficient the supervision practiced in non-banking financial institutions regarding AML/CFT issues. Today, we can say that we have carried out a complete inspection cycle in the 1600 institutions of the Financial System and, for those with higher risk, we are already in the second cycle." (Andreia Lais Vargas)

When BCB incorporated the responsibility of ensuring a competitive financial system in its institutional mission in 2019, the

---

239. The workflow was elaborated based on information provided by the BCB.

240. The Financial Action Task Force (FATF-GAFI) is the global money laundering and terrorist financing watchdog. It sets international standards that aim to prevent these illegal activities and the harm they cause to society. (https://www.fatf-gafi.org/en/home.html)

supervision of conduct was transferred to the area created to deal with issues related to competitiveness. Its hierarchical segregation of the supervision area came to reinforce its independence and alignment with the 'Twin Peaks' model. Operationally, however, its work processes continue to maintain a strong link with the supervision area, especially monitoring, where the warnings received are essential inputs for the supervision of AML/CFT issues.

> "The mission of the Banco Central do Brasil is to ensure the stability of the currency purchasing power, to foster a sound, efficient and competitive financial system, and to promote the economic well-being of society."(BCB website - https://www.bcb.gov.br/en/about)

CHAPTER 6

Macro Prudential Monitoring

"It is now widely recognized that a key missing ingredient was an overarching policy framework responsible for systemic financial stability in the run-up to the recent crisis and thus authorities in many countries are exploring a systemic approach, which is called macro prudential policy. Brazil has been one of the early adopters in this policy area and its experience has received much attention from the international community."

(IMF/FSAP - Brazil: Technical Note on Macroprudential Policy Framework – June/2013)

"Brazil stands out among its FSB peers for the pioneering work it has carried out on trade reporting and its use in systemic risk monitoring."

(FSB Peer Review of Brazil – April/2017)

This chapter details the activities of the macro prudential monitoring model and its importance in the management of financial stability in Brazil: the peculiar Brazilian macro prudential monitoring model, micro-based on supervisory databases and tools, allows a more intrusive and accurate performance in the identification and measurement of vulnerabilities of the financial system. The chapter describes the involvement of the supervisory area in the trajectory for the structuring of a financial stability framework at the BCB, as well as its participation in relevant pillars of the process, such as the Financial Stability Report (REF) and the Financial Stability Committee (Comef). The chapter also presents the testimony of then-Governor Henrique Meirelles regarding BCB's strategies and actions to mitigate the effects of the great financial crisis of 2007-2008.

6.1 THE GLOBAL FINANCIAL CRISIS

"On the left side, there is nothing right, on the right side there is nothing left." (Unknown author)

In 2008, BCB's macro prudential monitoring area was in its early stage. Data infrastructure was segmented and databases could not 'talk to each other' easily. There was still too much to explore and innovate in the development of tools and data quality processes.

The GFC contributed to accelerate and guide that evolution. At the time, monitoring was the only BCB area that could provide certain answers to the Board, as they were able to monitor banks' liquidity on a daily basis and to perform simulations to assess the impact of measures drawn to mitigate the crisis effects.

> "The 2008 crisis raised the need for macro prudential monitoring." (Caio Ferreira)
>
> "The whole idea that the financial system could be left free, that any vulnerability could be fixed by the very action of economic agents, that failures were part of a capitalist economy, was taken apart by the cost of the 2008 crisis." (Alexandre Tombini)

Report of Dr. Henrique Meirelles[241] on the role of the BCB during the GFC:

"In September 2008, I was in the United States to attend IMF and World Bank's meetings, when the BCB's head of supervision called me to report that a relevant bank was being subject to very large deposit withdrawals. There were many rumors in the market, due to what had happened in the United States, and a huge concern about the volume of withdrawals. He expected the bank to fail in a few days ("at this rate, by next Friday, the bank won't be open anymore").

In the morning when I arrived back in Brazil, I called a meeting with the presidents of the largest banks to warn them about these issues and to demand for absolute transparency. In the evening of the same day, I had a meeting with the BCB Board, and by that time, we had already mapped out the problems. First, it was the obvious bank run in some banks[242]. To mitigate that, we announced, in the next morning, a special credit line, where BCB permitted the big

---

241. Henrique Meirelles was the BCB Governor from January/2003 to December/2010.
242. Banks that were highly dependent on institutional investors had the maturity of deposits from these clients closely monitored by supervision. From inside the banks, on-site supervisors collected data of the actual cash flow, while the liquidity monitoring team estimated the expected contractual cash flow, based on information daily reported to the BCB by the trade repositories. Both information were daily compared and reported to the Board.

banks to use resources from the reserves requirements at the BCB, for granting loans to small and medium banks, at a certain rate. As a result, we injected liquidity into small and medium-sized banks, which were the ones more exposed to the risk of bank runs[243].

Figure: Bank's Time Deposits Fluctuation (Jun/2008 - Dec/2009)

Jun/2008 = 100

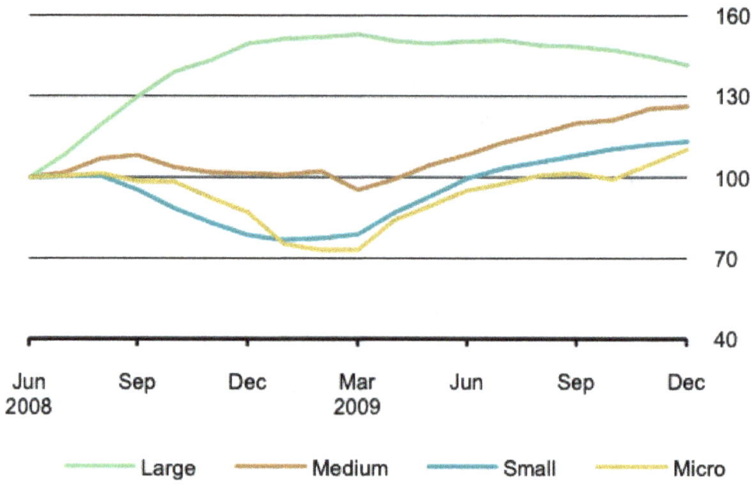

Source:Financial Stability Report - April/2010 -https://www.bcb.gov.br/en/publications/financialstabilityreport/201004

A relevant issue regarding a stockbroker from the south of the country was also on our radar. Supervision had identified concerns regarding the exchange rate applied to operations with a well-known industrial company. In fact, the company was the one in trouble. The broker was a mere intermediary of a FX operation at rates of R\$1.50-R\$1.60 per USD, with a leverage rule in the event of loss: if the dollar reached R\$1.70, it should be paid at least twice for the loss. Afterwards, these operations were known in the market

---

243. The liquidity monitoring tools permitted timely reporting to the Board about the effectiveness of the measures taken. They could verify, for example, that interbank deposit operations, although also allowed by the measure, had not been carried out, as large banks did not want to take the risk from small ones without calling for a collateral. Information from the Payment System was used to verify the settlement of credit operations to small and medium size banks.

as 'toxic derivatives' or 'exotic derivatives'. We were able to timely identify them because of the monitoring data[244]. That was the secret!

> "In 2008, we structured a very comprehensive process to monitor exotic derivatives, including asking Cetip to improve its records. We did micro and macro assessments. We looked at them on a case-by-case basis and, in the end, we aggregated the exposures to estimate the overall impact and to identify the companies that would have problems. We reported the information to the Board, so that they could make more accurate and assertive decisions during the crisis. We were also able to verify whether the measures had been effective or not. It was a totally innovative working process. It has changed the form of derivatives registry. It had even changed the market's opinion about the need for registration." (João André Calvino)

> "Market participants used to complain a lot about the mandatory registration of derivatives. They said that we were the only country in the world that required such registration. However, after the crisis, it became clear the need for information and complaints have decreased." (Simone Acioli – CETIP)

We did a complete assessment of the financial system. Thanks to prudential rules, domestic banks were ok, but non-financial companies had huge FX derivatives exposures through foreign banks. Operations were settled like this: the branch of a Brazilian company in Warsaw sold short dollars on the futures market to a London hedge fund, for example. This London hedge fund hedged its exposure through another New York fund which, in turn, hedged its exposure at the BM&F, in São Paulo. So, it was not possible for us to identify the Brazilian company's exposure, because everything

---

244. When the problem of companies exposed to toxic derivatives was identified, the information received from Cetip was not sufficient for its assessment. Monitoring had not established a work process for this data yet, as the lack of standardization of contracts hampered the organization of a structured database. Thus, it was necessary to quickly draw a reporting template and require information directly from the contract holders, in order to produce timely information to the Board. Analyzes were carried out at the micro and macro prudential levels. After all, it was necessary to estimate the total impact of exposures and to identify which companies would face the biggest problems, as well.

was abroad. They had operations in Poland, in Germany, in the United States… and most of them contracted with foreign banks, of course.

We had access to exposures overseas of Brazilian banks' branches, but not of the parent company, in which portfolio, in this case, were most of the operations. So, I talked to the central bank governors of the main jurisdictions to explain to them our need for information, and they required banks involved with relevant operations to inform us of the exposure of Brazilian companies. That's how we could estimate the total exposure of Brazilian companies: 40 billion dollars.

The entire consolidated market was short and this position tended to increase, because the American hedge funds, which had noticed the deal, were taking the opposite position to make money from the crash. Fortunately, we had accumulated 200 billion dollars in international reserves during the last years, another prudential measure we had implemented in Brazil. That amount would be enough.

Figure: Evolution of Brazil's International Reserves (2000-2021)

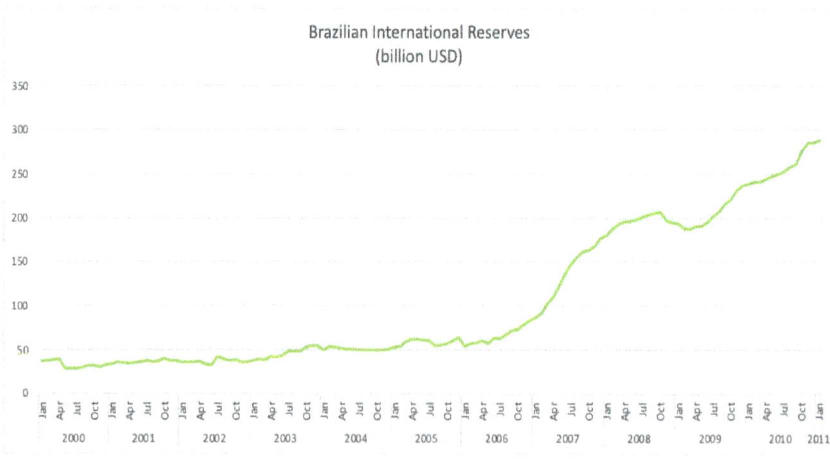

Source: Banco Central do Brasil - https://www.bcb.gov.br/en/financialstability/internationalreserves

I estimated the scale of the problem on a Sunday, returned to Brazil, and, by Monday morning, called a press conference to inform them that BCB was going to trade dollar futures, starting that same day, selling dollars. A journalist asked me 'how much?', and I replied: 'we are willing to go up to 50 billion dollars on the first day'.

Done! The dollar rate that had already reached R$ 2.50, with companies all leveraged, broken, huge companies broken, just melted and went down backwards. We really traded selling, because when you say you're gonna do it, you have to do it! We sold US$ 32 billion on the first day. Then, the FX market stabilized.

Another issue that has demanded mitigating actions regards the difficulty of Brazilian companies to roll over foreign funding: a company had, for example, a maturing bond of 1 billion dollar. As the whole system was broken, it was not possible to roll over it. So, the company had to take out a loan in domestic currency from a bank in Brazil, equivalent to 1 billion dollars, in order to purchase 1 billion dollars on the FX market and pay the bond. This type of operation was provoking such a liquidity squeeze in domestic currency that the available credit lines were not sufficient. So, we applied another mitigating measure, by announcing the following: 'we are going to start lending dollars to banks, to replace the loans from international banks'[245]. And, anticipating the questions, I added: 'we are prepared to replace the entire international financial system with regards to loans to Brazil for 1 year'. The end.

These measures have healed a very complex economic situation. Brazil's economic sector was collapsing: 800,000 jobs had been lost in the first 25 days of the crisis. By January, it started to recover and soon emerged from the crisis. In 2010, the Brazilian economy grew 7.5% and the financial system was clean, without any relevant problems. We had the shortest recession in the world and we were the first country to emerge from the crisis.

---

245. Cross border loans operations, credit lines for banks in dollars.

At the central bank governors' meeting in Basel, we were all heading to dinner at the end of the session, when one of them, my friend, asked me to wait. In fact, they had organized a surprise for me. When I walked into the room, all 33 governors stood up and gave me a standing ovation. Brazil had taught them a valuable lesson of supervision and prudential defense strategies, which led to some positive reactions in the international system as a whole.

In another meeting with European and American central banks, the governor of a major European central bank said: 'Henrique taught us a lesson. While we remained discussing, arguing, he did what had to be done. So, let's learn from Brazil and start taking strong, tough prudential measures.' That's when groups were created to reinforce prudential regulation etc.

What do we get out of it? First, good regulation, second, intense supervision."

> "When we presented our supervision process to foreign central banks and supervision visitors, many of them revealed that they were impressed with our capacity to act in order to mitigate the impacts of the 2008 global financial crisis." (Ricardo Almeida)

> "The increased quality and higher levels of capital and liquidity held by banks have helped them absorb the sizable impact of the Covid-19 pandemic thus far, suggesting that the Basel reforms have achieved their broad objective of strengthening the resiliency of the banking system. Banks and the banking system would have faced greater stress had the Basel reforms not been adopted." (BCBS - Early lessons from the Covid-19 pandemic on the Basel reforms -July/2021[246])

6.2 THE PECULIAR APPROACH OF THE BRAZILIAN MACRO PRUDENTIAL MONITORING FRAMEWORK

Until the GFC, it was believed that well-calibrated prudential regulation and well-adjusted risk models were sufficient to prevent

---

246. See the entire document at https://www.bis.org/bcbs/publ/d521.pdf.

crises of systemic proportions. Problems might arise in the event of excess or non-compliance. The best policy was to let the market operate freely, making occasional adjustments. Proactive actions to avoid or to mitigate the accumulation of imbalances were out of question.

The crisis, however, has proved the need of acting proactively to ensure financial stability, as there was a very high cost to pay if the bubble burst. The accumulation of reserves and a well-defined macroeconomic policy, with inflation targets, international reserves and access to external financing lines were no longer sufficient safeguards to manage a systemic crisis. It was necessary to integrate economic and prudential policies and assess the cross-effects between them[247], as they both were applied simultaneously during a crisis.

In this context, macro prudential monitoring activities began to play a fundamental role for central banks to fulfill their mission of ensuring the stability of the financial system.

> "Understanding the international and national scenarios has become a mandatory element for the performance of regulators and supervisors in conducting financial stability as an asset to society."
> (Donizeti Maia)

The BCB is one of the few central banks, if not the only one in the world, that has established macro prudential monitoring activities within the supervision area. The origin of this unusual framework dates back to the turn of the century, with the birth

---

247. Currently, there is a consensus formed in international financial bodies that a multi-faceted approach is desirable to deal with the volatility of capital flows. For this purpose, IMF has developed conceptual and quantitative models taking greater account of real-life frictions and vulnerabilities to guide how these tools should be used in an integrated way. The modeling effort is also being complemented by extensive empirical analysis and country case studies. The combined work aims to provide useful insights to policy makers on when and how to deploy multiple tools with special attention to their interactions, country-specific characteristics, initial conditions and the nature of the shocks. The policy paper was published in October 2020 and summarizes key analytical findings under the Integrated Policy Framework umbrella. (https://www.imf.org/en/Publications/Policy-Papers/Issues/2020/10/08/Toward-an- Integrated-Policy-Framework-49813)

of off-site supervision to subsidize BCB's Board with information from the financial system in an aggregate perspective. In fact, being supervision inside BCB[248] has helped the area to become a 'natural candidate' to this role.

> "I think the 'macro prudential' idea was raised before I joined the Central Bank[249]. It was a project led by Andrew Crockett, Bill White and others at the BIS. I bought the idea. I always thought that the Central Bank had to have a deep understanding of the credit mechanisms in the economy and know how to deal with them." (Armínio Fraga)

But what would have led the BCB to perpetuate this model?

When supervision activities were segregated into on-site and off-site, three off-site processes started simultaneously and evolved together, complementing each other: micro prudential monitoring, information management and macro prudential monitoring. While micro monitoring profited from the macro prudential demands raised by the Board to build its metrics, the perception of what was happening system-wide had its roots in the micro monitoring detailed information on large banks, that together represented over 85% of SFN's total assets.

Over time, something that was born out of unconventional reasons proved to be stronger and more appropriate. Macro prudential monitoring teams are anchored in tools with granular information and have the perspective of supervision, as they are familiar with the business model of each bank, their strategies and how they interact among themselves. Such a background enables them to act with high accuracy in the identification of a wide spectrum of potential vulnerabilities, since issues related to the domestic market, such as the credit and other financial markets'

---

248. In Brazil, supervision is within the central bank, not a separate agency, with connection or independent of the central bank. Over the course of this century, other central banks have assumed supervisory functions, mainly for systemic institutions, or even incorporated the entire supervision of the financial system.

249. Armínio Fraga was the BCB Governor from March/1999 to December/2002.

evolution and the volatility of asset prices, up to the assessment of international capital flows.

> "Having a department at the Central Bank dedicated exclusively to off-site supervision, which does not only look at the firm level, but also at the aggregate perspective, was a great advance in understanding the formation of potential vulnerabilities that lead to systemic risk." (Alexandre Tombini)

> "Microdata permits us to answer very sophisticated and varied questions. I could testify this in practice when I participated in an FSB[250] working group aimed at assessing the effects of Basel rules implementation. The vast majority of the group's participants provided very generic information, while Brazil was able to say, with high precision, which group of banks was or was not affected by the rules." (Theo Cotrim)

Macro prudential measures are typically used for two purposes: to increase the system's resilience to shock absorption and, more proactively, to prevent or contain bubble formation. An additional capital buffer during the 'good times', for example, strengthens the system's capital base so that it can more safely absorb a shock in the future. Regarding the second objective, the intelligence and granularity of macro monitoring tools improve the regulator's and supervisor's responsiveness to contain the expansion of bubbles or to prevent the formation of vulnerabilities that could lead to financial bubbles with systemic risk.

> "In the Covid-19 crisis, the issuance of LFGs[251] was a funding source largely used, as BCB accepted them as collateral to provide

---

250. Financial Stability Board.

251. In order to face the adverse impacts of the Covid-19 pandemic crisis on the Brazilian economy, the BCB announced a package of measures to increase the liquidity of the SFN. Specifically, two Special Temporary Liquidity Facility (LTEL) were temporarily available to financial institutions: LTEL – Guaranteed Financial Letters (LTEL-LFG) and Special LTEL – Debentures. In this sense, the LTEL-LFG housed loan operations against a basket of collateral, represented by Bills Payable issued by the FIs. This basket could contain private financial assets, such as: debentures, and credit portfolios with a risk rating equal to AA, A and B registered in the SCR. See (https://www.bcb.gov.br/en/financialstability/liquidityfacilities)

liquidity assistance to banks. Around R$100 billion [US$ 25 billion] LFGs were issued. The information reported by banks to the SCR enabled the operationalization of this liquidity facility. This is a positive return to the cost of providing information to the regulator." (Everton Gonçalves – ABBC)

"Circular No. 3,515, of December 3, 2010, raised to 150% the risk weighting factor applied to exposures related to credit and financial leasing operations contracted with natural persons, for the calculation of the PRE[252] . The prudential measure was a consequence of the identification of the significant expansion of long-term credit operations contracted with natural persons, whose guarantees were incompatible with the operation's structure." (Financial Stability Report - April/2011[253])

"We keep a very close eye on market conditions, whatever they may be. We need to have tools capable of monitoring the problem that is occurring right now." (André Caccavo)

Macro monitoring area assumed the responsibility of carrying out stress tests to assess the SFN's resilience to shocks and, consequently, to assist in the design of specific macro prudential measures that, combined with the relevant macroeconomic policies, would strengthen its resilience. The breadth and depth of information achieved with microdata were essential for the development of more accurate measures to mitigate systemic risk (macro prudential measures), as well as to assess their effectiveness, both at the macro and micro perspectives.

"Macro prudential monitoring was able to provide increasingly accurate answers. Thus, the decision-making process gradually became more specific and caused less 'damage'. New BCB deputy

---

for more details.

252. Required Reference Equity - PRE (*Patrimônio de Referência Exigido*). Financial institutions must keep a Reference Equity level not lower than the PRE. Resolution CMN 4,955 of Oct 21, 2021 has established the methodology for the estimation of Reference Equity. (https://www.bcb.gov.br/estabilidadefinanceira/exibenormativo?tipo=RESOLUÇÃO%20CMN&numero=4955)

253. https://www.bcb.gov.br/publicacoes/ref/201104.

governors usually get impressed with BCB's ability to know what is happening in the market. In my time[254], we didn't have information, so we started this journey with the creation of off-site supervision." (Tereza Grossi)

6.3. THE EVOLUTION OF MACRO MONITORING PROCESSES

Although the macro perspective has been present in monitoring since its inception, the area started gaining ground in 2006, with the signing of the Armistice, which led to a shift in the monitoring focus towards this approach. At that time, there were no references to the development of macro monitoring activities. However, the teams responsible for micro monitoring routines were required to develop macro prudential working processes in their areas of expertise, and a specific team was created to monitor systemic risk. In fact, the GFC marked the introduction of financial stability concerns in the international agenda, and, in Brazil, that was also the point in time at which macro monitoring issues became more relevant in the BCB agenda and started to follow the evolution of international discussions.

> "In 2006, our rationale to create a systemic risk monitoring team already stated that risks could be accumulating and a crisis could arise." (André Caccavo)

Before 2006, macro analyses were produced as a by-product of micro monitoring, that is, individual values were added to form the consolidated information. It was necessary to make the teams aware that monitoring financial stability was not limited to understanding the sum of everything, but how to aggregate them and how parts were related to each other. Then, in 2008, a project [MESF Project][255]

---

254. Tereza Grossi was the BCB Deputy Governor for Supervision from March/2000 to March/2003.

255. The MESF project lasted 4 years and one of its goals was to structure the monitoring of the BCB's financial stability for the 2012 FSAP. Thus, it has contributed with the implementation of important macro-prudential monitoring processes and products, such as the implementation of routines to calculate and publish the Brazilian Financial Stability

was developed with the purpose of structuring the macro prudential monitoring process, at the time still called 'monitoring of financial stability'.

> "It is not enough to have a sound isolated institution, the sum of the parts can have a different result than the total of the system." (Rodrigo Lara)

Incorporating the macro perspective was an arduous and exploratory process to the risk specialists [micro prudential] teams. First of all, they were supervisors by nature, with a deep-rooted focus on the soundness of each financial institution. Secondly, no one knew exactly what had to be done. There were sparse and often divergent concepts. In fact, nobody knew what was expected not even from the BCB[256] regarding financial stability oversight.

> "MESF Project's target was to lay the groundwork for what would ultimately be our financial stability monitoring process. It was very hard to 'sell the idea'. The teams were not trained, they had no skills in statistics, there was no report group catalog... Today, there are a lot of people interested in this business, but at the time, it was a disaster!" (Gilneu Vivan)

Indicators (FSI) and the modernization of the Financial Stability Report contents, as well. The proposal of creating a Financial Stability Committee in the BCB has also emerged from the project staff's discussions.

256. The concepts of 'Broad Financial System', which includes institutions regulated by the CVM, and 'Restricted Financial System', with only comprehends institutions under the responsibility of the BCB, were created in an attempt to set boundaries to BCB and the macro monitoring, as well, regarding financial stability management.

Figure: Work Breakdown Structure (WBS) of the MESF Project

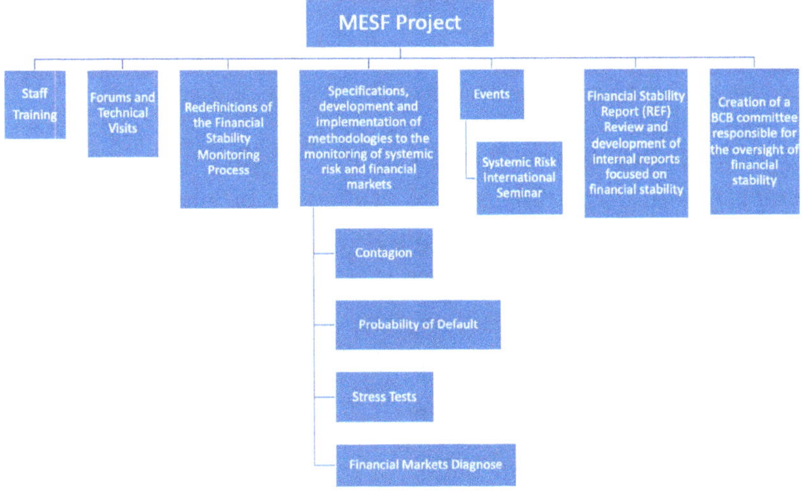

Source: Banco Central do Brasil

"I remember me complaining a lot about the sudden shift to the macro prudential approach. I used to say things like: 'Now that we've just set up the system to monitor the bank's liquidity risk, you tell me we don't do that anymore?" (Paula Oliveira)

Both the monitoring databases and tools had been designed and developed within the perspective of 'off-site' supervision, by each monitoring team, separately. Although there was still no integration of processes or products, from 2001 onwards, the databases began to migrate to the same repository, the SQL Server. This was the first step towards data integration, a central pillar of the macro-prudential monitoring framework.

"In the beginning, there was no SQL Server for users in the BCB. Then, I discovered a tool called Microsoft Data Engine (MSDE) available for Microsoft Access users, which was a compact version of SQL Server. This tool permitted us to start downloading Cosif[257] data

---

257. Cosif is the template for reporting information on financial statements. Se more details about Cosif in Chapter 4 - 4.1 Trajectory of Information Management at the BCB.

> from the mainframe. As our server's capacity was very limited, we could get data only from banks, within a 24 months moving window." (André Maurício)

> "All divisions started to bring information to SQL Server. To each its own, but everybody to the same place." (Nizam Pfeilsticker)

Nevertheless, the transformation of the 'micro-aggregate' perspective into an actual macro prudential monitoring approach required a major change of mindset: it was necessary to abandon the focus on each financial institution to focus on the market as a whole. This process took place over the years, as the monitoring team gradually realized that issues not relevant to the micro perspective could become important in a macro prudential approach.

> "The breadth and depth of available TR[258] data enable the BCB to undertake extensive systemic risk monitoring using a broad range of analytical tools, such as automated early warning indicators, contagion analysis and top-down macroeconomic stress tests." (FSB Peer Review of Brazil – April/2017)

Credit risk macro monitoring:

Regarding credit risk, implementing routines to provide aggregate information on the risk of financial institutions' portfolio (the lender perspective) was not sufficient. The macro approach needed to gather the whole panorama of the credit market. Thus, routines should also assess credit risk from the point of view of the customer, the borrower's perspective[259].

---

258. Trade Repository.

259. The credit risk macro approach has developed monitoring processes to natural person borrowers - PF (*Pessoas Físicas*) and to legal entity borrowers - PJ (*Pessoas Jurídicas*). Natural persons are classified by occupation or income range, while legal entities are classified by size: micro, small, medium and large. Procedures to assess natural persons' portfolios cover concerns like how the portfolios are evolving, how the risk is evolving or which are the main risk factors, with data aggregated for each credit type: mortgage, auto loans, payroll loans etc. Credit exposures from micro up to medium-sized companies are also assessed in aggregate by credit type, similar to the methodologies applied to natural persons. For large companies, however, monitoring procedures also comprehend the assessment of credit risk at the economic group's level, taking into account its large

Data needs for implementing monitoring processes with the new perspective went beyond the boundaries of SCR information, as it was limited to credits taken out from financial institutions. SCR was a very granular information of risks assumed by financial institutions, which was adequate to credit risk micro supervision, but for financial stability purposes, it could only tell part of the story. In order to assess the levels of indebtedness and profitability of individuals and companies, it was necessary to better understand their characteristics and their exposure to other sources of funds, such as the capital market and the foreign credit market.

> "In order to analyze the exposure to foreign exchange risk of credit borrowers, we rely on data from the foreign exchange market and the derivatives market monitoring teams. Our goal is to gather all their exposure on foreign currency and monitor their currency risk, at the economic group level. For example, if the dollar FX rate 'jumps' from R$5.00 to R$7.00, which ones would fail or be at greater risk? Then, we take a close look at them." (Theo Cotrim)

Monitoring of derivatives, securities and funding market:

Databases from the financial market infrastructures, which were the main source of micro monitoring processes of market and liquidity risks, have become extremely granular data sources (at the transaction level) for the monitoring of domestic trading markets of derivatives, securities and bank funding instruments. Metrics were developed to monitor the markets' evolution, such as trading volume, rates ranges and maturity of each traded financial instrument, as well as to identify the exposure of each market participant, their interconnectedness and the main players.

> "We started to monitor all information received, we checked the operations' rates, maturities, amounts... If anything seemed odd to us, the next step was a communication to the trade repository: 'Please

---

exposures, main counterparties, debts at risk etc.

ask the participant to check whether the information is correct."
(Edson Teixeira)

Monitoring of foreign exchange market:

The foreign exchange rate is a quite sensitive issue for the Brazilian economy. Therefore, different areas of BCB monitor the FX market from different perspectives[260]. Macro monitoring is focused on the financial flow of FX operations. Its approach consists of monitoring volumes, rates, spreads, counterparties (including the investment grade level of foreign credit borrowers[261] and its impact on the operation's costs), terms, destination, imports, exports and financial transfers overseas, as well as interbank transactions for the purchase and sale of foreign currency. Another important monitoring topic is the offer of foreign credit lines to Brazilian banks, where availability, usage, costs and deadlines, among other characteristics, are monitored.

'When I worked at Decam[262], our off-site and on-site teams performed the supervision of FIs' FX portfolios following a classic supervision model. When we were transferred to the BCB's supervision area, our team had to encompass the macro monitoring perspective. The development of methodologies under this new approach was very challenging to us." (Ademir Schenatto)

"In addition to providing information to Comef, REF and REB[263], the FX macro monitoring team is responsible for the

---

260. The Department of Foreign Reserves (Depin) is responsible for the management of Brazilian international reserves; the Department of Economics (Depec) produces studies and publishes export/import data series; the Prudential and Foreign Exchange Regulation Department (Dereg) is responsible for foreign exchange regulation; the Department of Conduct Supervision (Decon) supervises foreign exchange operations; and the Department of Statistics (Dstat) monitors the exchange rate from a Balance of Payments perspective.

261. 'Foreign credit borrowers' are those Brazilian financial institutions and non-financial corporate that operate in the foreign credit market as borrowers.

262. The Foreign Exchange Department (Decam) is a former BCB department, responsible for FX rate control.

263. The Banking Economy Report (REB) is published annually by the BCB and addresses a broad range of issues related to the National Financial System and the relationship be-

production of four monthly reports and one daily FX bulletin, used for monitoring purposes." (Nilo Tezzari)

Macro monitoring approach to financial statements information:

The team responsible for the individual economic-financial analysis of financial institutions and conglomerates developed the macro perspective by carrying out cross-sectional analysis work[264], aimed at the need to understand specific characteristics at the whole system or specific peers' perspective, such as assessing banks' profitability, for example.

They have also developed a group of indicators capable of flagging the need for a cross-sectional analysis, whenever the same problem is identified simultaneously in several financial institutions. After all, although individually covered, banks' reaction to excessive risk exposures or to changes in regulation, for example, may face problems to be executed according to the plan, when the whole system/peer is impacted.

> "Our analyses are generally surveys on issues that top management is concerned about or is requiring additional information on. We indicate whether there is a problem or impacts should not be taken as relevant. A recent example regards customers' overdrafts. BCB wanted to put a ceiling on the banks' overdraft rate charged to customers. Thus, we carried out a series of studies to size the ceiling according to its impact on banks' profitability." (Marcelo Bicalho)

Systemic risk monitoring:

The team responsible for systemic risk analysis was the first monitoring team with a macro prudential focus since its inception.

---

tween institutions and their clients and users. REB can be accessed through the link https://www.bcb.gov.br/en/publications/bankingreport.

264. A cross-section analysis is the assessment of the same issue in all or a group of financial institutions.

Without the micro bias and supported by information mostly at the level of financial operations, it began its activities by mapping the positions of all financial institutions, with the objective of identifying the interconnectedness among market participants. As the final counterparties of each operation were identified in databases, including those of derivative contracts, the interconnectedness map was designed based on the actual exposures of financial institutions. Such a map laid the groundwork for the development of BCB's contagion risk model[265].

> "In 2007, Deputy Governor [for Regulation] Tombini[266] asked us to map the SFN interconnectedness. We used the Pajek software[267] to draw the map and presented it to the Board. They liked it a lot. Then, as we already had mapped all FI's exposures, it was very easy to run a contagion simulation." (André Caccavo)

Figure: SFN interconnectedness - September/2010

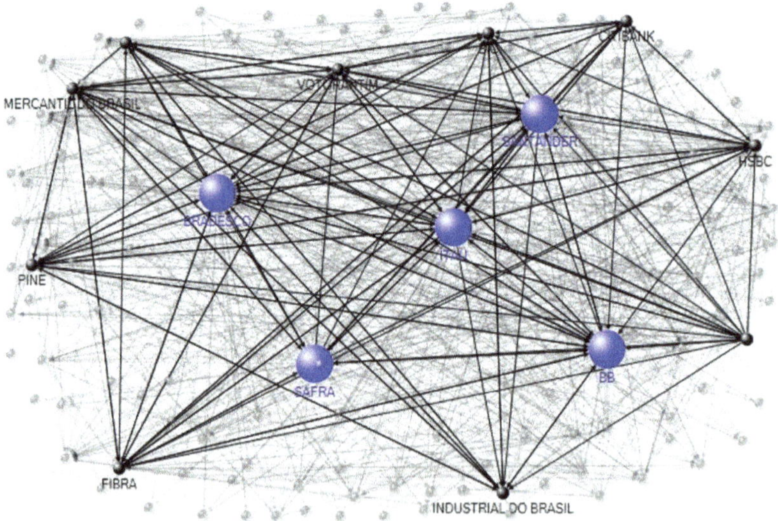

Source:Banco Central do Brasil

---

265. The contagion risk model consists of a stress test routine to estimate the domino effect due to contagion, in the event of the failure of one institution.
266. Alexandre Tombini was the BCB Governor from January/2011 to June/2016.
267. Pajek is an open source program for Windows, developed for analysis and visualization of large networks that have thousands or even millions of nodes.

The systemic risk monitoring team has also developed macroeconomic stress tests, sensitivity analysis of key market parameters[268] and financial flows' analysis. They are currently developing a prototype to integrate the contagion analysis with the macroeconomic stress testing.

Step-in risk monitoring:

As of 2013, analysts of macro prudential monitoring teams began to represent the BCB in international working groups, focused on financial stability[269]. In those forums, they realized that some of the issues on discussion had not yet been addressed by the BCB, such as the relevance of shadow banking[270] for the assessment of step-in risk.

> "The GFC provided evidence that banks sometimes have incentives beyond contractual obligation or equity ties to 'step in' to support unconsolidated entities to which they are connected. This happened in the form of credit or liquidity support that banks provided to, among others, securitisation conduits, structured investment vehicles and money market funds." (BCBS – Guidelines on the Identification and management of step-in risk[271] – October/2017)

---

268. A sensitivity analysis consists of the identification of which institutions would go into default due to the variation of the parameter in analysis, within a range. The parameters analyzed are: interest rate, FX rate and the credit default rates, both of total credit operations and of real estate financing operations.

269. The Deputy Governor for Supervision is the BCB representative on the FSB's Standing Committee on Assessment of Vulnerabilities (SCAV) and analysts from the macro prudential monitoring teams participate in several SCAV's working groups, FSB task forces and peer reviews, as well as in BCBS' working groups focused on shadow banking and interconnectedness.

270. "The term 'shadow banking' has been attributed in 2007 by the economist and money manager Paul McCulley to describe a large segment of financial intermediation that is routed outside the balance sheets of regulated commercial banks and other depository institutions. Shadow banks are defined as financial intermediaries that conduct functions of banking without access to central bank liquidity or public sector credit guarantees." (Bryan J Noeth and Rajdeep Sengupta, Is Shadow Banking Really Banking?, 2011)

271. Link to access the document: https://www.bis.org/bcbs/publ/d423.htm.

Figure: Participation of BCB supervision members in international working groups (May/2023)

BIS/BCBS	BISIN	BIS Innovation Network Suptech and Regtech Working Group
	FTG	Financial Technology Group
	GAT	G-Sibs Assessment Team
	LIQ	Liquidity Group
	P2EG	Pillar 2 Expert Group
	SCG	Supervisory Cooperation Group
	TFCR	Task Force on Climate-related Financial Risks
	TFFSRC	Task Force on financial stability Risks of Cryptoassets
World Bank	ICCR	International Committee on Credit Reporting
BRICS	RISC	Rapid Information Security Channel
G20/OCDE	GAFI/FATF	Financial Action Task Force
	TFFCP	Task Force on Financial Consumer Protection
FinCoNet		The Governing Council
Mercosul	SGT-4	Mercosul Financeiro
NBB	SOF	Swift Oversight Forum
FSB	AGV	Analytical Group on Vulnerabilities
	SCAV/CVD	Climate Vulnerabilities and Data Group
	CMCG	Compensation Monitoring Contact Group
	SRC/CWG	Crypto Working Group
	CIR	Cyber Incident Reporting
	FIN	Financial Innovation Network
	NMEG	Non-bank Monitoring Experts Group
	SCG	Experts on supervisory Issues related to Benchmark Transition
	SRC	Workstream on Unwinding of COVID-19 Support Measures
	SRC	Working Group on Regulatory and Supervisory Approaches to Climate Risk
	SRC/RIS	Working Group on Regulatory Issues of Stablecoins
	TPRWS	Workstream on third-party Risk and Outsourcing
NGFS	TF B&NR	Task Force Nature-related Risk
	WSSp	Workstream Supervision
	WS2	Workstream Scenarios

Source: Banco Central do Brasil

Although the investment funds are the most relevant shadow banking entities in Brazil, they are not under the BCB's umbrella. The legal obligations of regulating and supervising them lies with the Securities and Exchange Commission - CVM (*Comissão de Valores Mobiliários*). Thus, BCB and CVM have signed a data sharing agreement, in order to permit bilateral access to the information needed to support working processes of both entities: the market operations' micro data existing in the BCB databases, combined with the funds' registry data provided by the CVM, allowed the mapping of the funds' portfolios.

For the BCB's macro prudential purposes, the information allowed the measurement of step-in risk and the estimation of its potential impact on the liquidity buffer of banks exposed[272] to investment funds.

> "We started to have more and more interaction with the CVM, in order to monitor investment funds. In the end, we have established an intensive and continued exchange of information." (Frederico Torres)

Alignment of working processes:

The macro prudential monitoring area has developed itself to provide the BCB Board with information on the SFN's resilience to shocks, as well as to warn them about its vulnerabilities. In 2011, the newly created Financial Stability Committee - Comef (*Comitê de Estabilidade Financeira*) became the BCB's forum for discussions of this nature. In consequence, the macro prudential monitoring working processes needed to be aligned with the committee's agenda.

'Pre-Comef' meetings were established to foster internal discussions among the monitoring teams regarding their main findings and concerns. During the pre-meetings, each team opened the results of its monitoring process for discussion among all participants. The dynamics made the teams realize the existence of interconnections among the individual issues brought up for discussion, and move towards a more integrated assessment. Besides, as it contributed to strengthening the analysts' holistic perception, the integrated approach was also gradually being applied to the development of macro monitoring tools.

> "When we started holding pre-Comef meetings, the biggest challenge was to make people focus on the message. Everyone wanted to show everything they had done!" (Rodrigo Lara)
>
> "We use the pre-Comef meetings to align ourselves, because the other teams can also contribute to one's analysis. Integrated works,

---

272. The microdata of market operations also permitted BCB to measure the banks' direct and indirect (by name or brand) exposures to investment funds.

where the cause is the same, but the consequences can be observed by several teams, such as profitability, credit and liquidity, for example, are usually the most interesting ones." (Marcelo Bicalho)

In 2014, the Car-Wash Operation provoked the bankruptcy of numerous non-financial companies, which, in consequence, led their workers to unemployment. Since monitoring data had the identification of credit borrowers and market participants at the operation level, the risk of default of a financial institution (as well as its contagion effect in the financial system[273]) due to the default of a client or counterparty impacted by the Car-Wash scheme could be estimated, as soon as the monitoring analysts were able to identify who these companies and employees were. Part of the problem was solved: the access to microdata from the Ministry of Labor and Welfare[274] permitted BCB to identify the employees of a non-financial company. Therefore, the missing piece in the jigsaw puzzle was the list of the companies impacted by the Car-Wash Operation.

Thus, the bridge between the real sector of the economy and the financial sector microdata was modeled based on the Payment System's information[275]. Macro analysts mapped the companies with financial dependency of Petrobrás[276], and those with financial dependency of them, repeatedly, until the complete list of companies with high probability of default due to the Car-Wash Operation was mapped, by identifying the large relevance of money transfers to them, when compared to their total cash inflow, regularly received

---

273. REF – October/2015 describes in detail BCB's contagion model and its application to address the impact of Car-Wash Operation in the financial sector (https://www.bcb.gov.br/publicacoes/ref/201510).

274. Statistical data of the Social Information Annual Report RAIS database is available to the public (http://acesso.mte.gov.br/portal-pdet/o-pdet/portifolio-de-produtos/bases--de-dados.htm).

275. Liquidity risk's micro prudential monitoring process uses the Payment System database since 2000 to map the Reserves Account Profile of banks (see Chapter 3). Currently, the non-financial companies' money transfers are also mapped in other data sources, such as bank bills, payment of credit and debit cards, import/export operations and PIX.

276. Petrobrás is a state-owned Brazilian multinational corporation in the petroleum industry.

before the Car-Wash Operation event. The jigsaw puzzle was finally completed.

> "One of the main developments in systemic risk analysis since the 2012 FSAP has been contagion analysis based on the development of a real economy network model using Brazilian Payments System data." (IMF/FSAP - Brazil: Financial Sector Assessment Program – November/2018[277])

> "If a non-financial company defaulted, we were able to identify which companies were directly exposed to it, which companies were indirectly exposed to it, and even who were the employees of all these companies (who would be dismissed). And we could assess what would happen to the credit operations of all of them. I've never seen anyone doing that." (Rodrigo Lara)

---

277. See the full document at https://www.imf.org/-/media/Files/Publications/CR/2018/cr18339.ashx.

Figure: Interconnectedness of the real sector of the economy

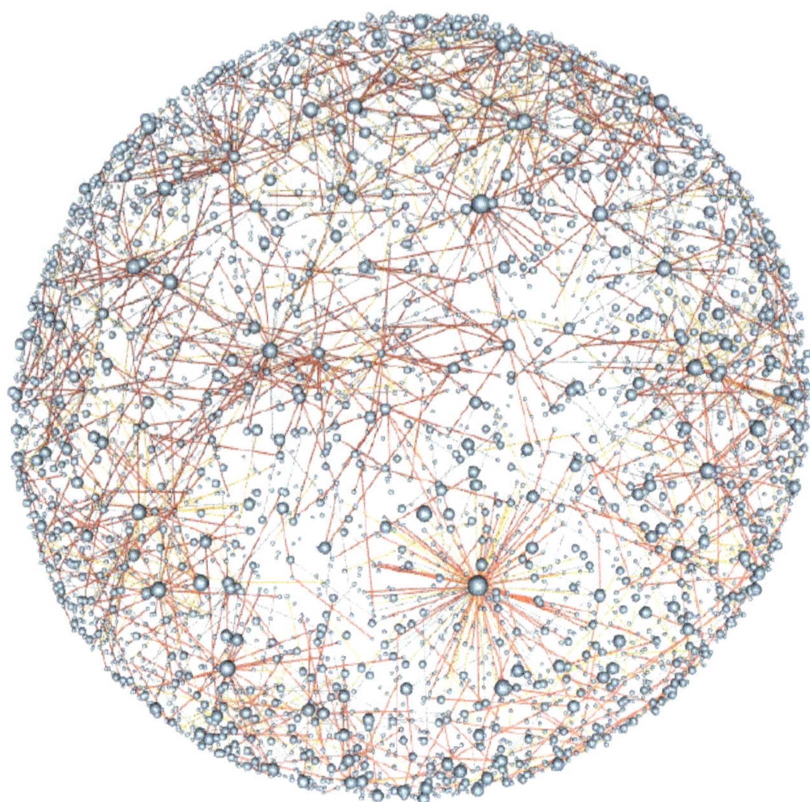

Each sphere represents an economic group. Their size is proportional to their participation in the SPB financial flow. The colors of the edges reflect the financial flow importance level to the receiving company – the darker the red, the greater its importance and the chances of contagion. Not all groups are represented.

Source:Banco Central do Brasil - REF October/2015 - *https://www.bcb.gov.br/publicacoes/ref/201510*

"The challenge of structuring the interconnectedness of the real sector of the economy and estimating the probability of default in the financial system that one or more defaulting companies can provoke is not limited to identifying their direct and relevant connections with suppliers and service providers, but also the connections of these suppliers and service providers with their own suppliers and service providers, and so on." (REF - October/2015)

Figure: Interconnectedness of the financial sector - Interfinancial Network

Blue = multiple and commercial banks

Green = development banks

Red = investment banks

Orange = credit unions

Yellow = brokers and leasing companies

Source:Banco Central do Brasil - REF October/2015 - https://www.bcb.gov.br/publicacoes/ref/201510

"In general, people work with theoretical or partial networks to understand contagion. We work with the real network: how companies, people and banks relate to each other. At first, we were not ready to process the analysis, but we knew, theoretically, that micro data could be integrated to get the job done. So, we stopped the regular activities of the whole department for one month. Each team was made responsible for its part of the work, and, in the end, we brought everything together. It was awesome!" (Gilneu Vivan)

Figure: Contagion Model

Source:Banco Central do Brasil - REF May/2023 - https://www.bcb.gov.br/publicacoes/ref

"In macroeconomic stress tests, we seek to understand the possible effects on the financial system caused by drastic but plausible changes in macroeconomic variables. In a real sector contagion analysis, our goal is to map the effects caused by a default of some non-financial company in other companies also from the real sector, based on the financial interrelationship among them. In this case, we do not take as a basis the behavior of macrofinancial variables, given that the nature of the contagion is idiosyncratic and localized." (Robert Nygaard)

The BCB contagion model was one of the pioneers in the world and, for Brazil, it represented the starting point of a new macro prudential monitoring approach. From that event onwards, database integration permitted successive evolutions in the macro prudential monitoring tools, enhancing more and more their capacity to explain causes and consequences of an issue under investigation.

Consequently, in a short time, SQL Server reached its processing limit and became an obsolete technology, unable to respond satisfactorily to the growing demand for information crossing. Thus, in 2015, supervision started a databases migration process to a more robust and scalable platform, the Teradata[278].

> "When we brought an appliance with a huge processing capacity, all users realized the advantage of migrating to this new environment. As it is a flexible platform, you can create specific 'datalabs', where the analyst is free to develop his/her analyses. The implementation of this Big Data appliance was a turning point for BCB's analytics and monitoring capacities." (Haroldo Cruz)

The timeliness and detailed information that supports the Board's decisions on financial stability issues allowed the BCB to take a very innovative step regarding the accountability of measures to mitigate the Covid 19 pandemic crisis effects to its control agency, the Federal Court of Auditors – TCU (*Tribunal de Contas da União*).

Central banks usually account for the measures taken during a crisis, after the crisis. After all, during the crisis, there is no time left for such formalities. Nevertheless, the retrospective assessment of the facts brings uncertainties regarding the information available to support decisions taken during the crisis and the central bank capacity to predict adverse effects. Consequently, the control agency may apply penalties to the decision makers for omissions or acts which results did not go as expected. In order to avoid this risk, BCB decided to report to TCU in real time very comprehensive information regarding each Covid-19 crisis mitigating measure, i.e., just after its issuance. The innovation brought good results, as all reported measures were approved by the TCU.

---

278. Teradata is a platform from Teradata Corporation that consists of specialized servers and a relational database management system to support solutions involving data analysis. Its architecture basically consists of a data warehouse area, which allows the integration of corporate data, and 'data labs' (spaces for developing and prototyping departmental solutions). The solution is scalable, which allows the evolution of processing and storage capacity. It also allows for a centralized and optimized management of corporate data.

Figure: TCU's assessment of measures to mitigate the effects of the COVID-19 Pandemic on the Financial System (09/09/2021)

BCB has achieved institutional objectives in managing the crisis caused by the pandemic

TCU's monitoring to verify the performance of the BCB during the crisis caused by the covid-19 pandemic concluded that the monetary authority was successful in achieving its institutional objectives and that the measures adopted have had the expected effect of increasing liquidity and stimulating credit.

SUMMARY

· TCU's monitoring to verify the performance of the BCB in its regulation of the SFN, in the face of the crisis caused by the covid-19 pandemic, concluded that the measures adopted have had the expected effect of expanding liquidity and stimulating credit.

· The action of the monetary authority has created a favorable environment for the evolution of the volume of credit granted under the SFN. By adopting the various measures to confront the current crisis, the BCB has so far been successful in achieving its institutional objectives.

· This is because it was possible, among other measures, to keep the banking system liquid and stable, to guarantee a capitalized system and to offer special conditions so that the banks could roll over the debts of the sectors affected by the crisis.

Source:TCU - Process: TC 016.028/2020-1, Session: 9/01/2021 - https://portal.tcu.gov.br/imprensa/noticias/banco-central-atingiu-objetivos-institucionais-no-enfrentamento-da-crise-provocada-pela-pandemia.htm

"This experience was very interesting. First, it allowed TCU to better understand how a crisis is managed, as the auditors could experience the same uncertainties as the decision maker's. Thus, their real-time evaluation of BCB measures was more reliable. And we could do that because we had information. Otherwise, we wouldn't be able to justify why we were taking those measures." (Enrico Vasconcelos)

"BCB's macro monitoring process is a case of success. We started with simple aggregated 'elevator' analysis[279] and now we support Comef's decisions, with consequences for macro prudential policies!" (Rodrigo Lara)

6.4 FINANCIAL STABILITY REPORT – REF (*RELATÓRIO DE ESTABILIDADE FINANCEIRA*)

"It's important to know what's going on. Looking at the history of financial crises, often and almost always, market participants were not actually realizing the global exposure of the economy." (Armínio Fraga)

"In 2002, I was BCB's deputy governor for economic policy.[280] We saw the financial stability report as a good international practice and decided to implement it in Brazil." (Ilan Goldfajn)

The BCB's Financial Stability Report was published for the first time in November/2002 and it already had a chapter dedicated to stress tests! Nevertheless, although BCB was one of the pioneers in disclosing stress tests results in such reports, the real purpose of a financial stability report and what it should consist of was still unclear at that time. Besides, everyone at the BCB wanted to talk about financial stability. As a result, the report looked like a compendium of disconnected information about the financial system[281].

---

279. 'Elevator analysis' are those limited to describing indicators' ups and downs along the time, such as: 'the liquidity ratio dropped 10% in the period'.

280. Ilan Goldfajn was the BCB Governor from June/2016 to February/2019.

281. Initially, REF consisted of six chapters: 1. Evolution of Financial Markets - assessment of the recent behavior of the international and domestic financial markets; 2. National Financial System - composition and evolution of assets, liabilities and shareholders' equity, analysis of results, adequacy to international minimum standards, credit and market risks; 3. Payment System – analysis of measures adopted to adapt the payment system to international best practices and recommendations for safety and efficiency; 4. Stress Scenarios – analysis of impacts on banks' compliance with the Basel capital standards, considering fluctuations in the foreign exchange rate and interest rates, as well as the deterioration in

> "The report was the communication vehicle of everyone, even if the message didn't have too much connection with financial stability. For example, people talked about changes in the quantity of credit unions along the time, how many transactions were settled through the Payment System during the day etc... Later, a lot of those statistics migrated to the REB[282]." (Rodrigo Lara)

Initially, REF was practically unknown to the public. On one hand, BCB did not put efforts to enhance its disclosure, on the other hand, the financial market did not express any interest in the report. Nevertheless, its simple existence contributed to recognize the central role of BCB in the oversight of financial stability in Brazil.

In terms of content, REF still has a long way to go. Analyses were generally limited to simple descriptions of the variations presented in the charts. Although everyone criticized the 'elevator' analysis, no one dared to go further, fearing the consequences of publicly exposing a BCB's opinion. Thus, the report lacked discussions on the rationale of the issues presented, as well as on eventual impacts to the financial stability.

> "After much discussion among all REF authors, we finally agreed that the report needed structural changes. Then, we researched the best practices around the world[283] to prove that some contents of our REF were not part of any other financial stability report taken as a

---

credit quality; 5. Rules Relating to Prudential Regulation - evolution of the implementation of prudential regulation in Brazil, in line with the Basel core principles for effective bank supervision; and 6. Selected Studies – working papers related to the conduct of monetary and supervisory policies. Off-site supervision was responsible for writing chapters 2 and 4 and for the consolidation of the whole report.

282. Between 1999 and 2015, the BCB published, annually, the Banking Economy and Credit Report - REBC (*Relatório de Economia Bancária e Crédito*), focused on the credit market, such as volume, interest rates and the spread's decomposition. The Banking Economy Report - REB (*Relatório de Economia Bancária*) replaced REBC in 2017, with a broader scope, covering a wide spectrum of issues related to the SFN.

283. The off-site team responsible to propose a new format to the REF took as a reference the reports of other central banks, such as the Bank of England, Reserve Bank of Australia, Bank of Korea, Bank of Japan, European Central Bank, as well as that of the International Monetary Fund.

benchmark. That's how we convinced people to remove contributions out of context from the report." (Rodrigo Lara)

Finally, a comprehensive review process undertaken in 2008 improved REF's focus[284], timeliness and usefulness. The disclosure of the BCB's prospective vision in the report, however, did not evolve at the same pace. It was feared that the BCB could exacerbate the system's vulnerabilities, should it express its expectations to the market, especially if those expectations were not promising. Nevertheless, the path to transparency was gradually being paved, which reinforced BCB's confidence to evolve in its analysis, as long as the market got used to know and react to the REF's messages.

> "Analysts were very reticent to expose their opinion to the public. Over time, they felt more comfortable with it, but this process is still evolving." (Rodrigo Lara)
>
> "Some people say that the market may get scared with our statement on what we expect to happen in the future, but this is a gradual process. As the market is getting used to our messages, fear gradually disappears. REF's approach is increasingly forward looking." (Enrico Vasconcelos)

---

284. The contributions from the regulation area focused on regulations aimed at financial stability; Payment System and Financial Market Infrastructure (FMI) contributions focused on the systemic relevance of FMI participants; and the area of Economic Research started to contribute to the REF with the results of its Financial Stability survey. Regarding the contents under the responsibility of the monitoring area, the evolution of macro prudential monitoring tools enhanced the teams' skills to explain rationals and impacts on issues raised as concerns. Stress tests and contagion analysis models, for example, allowed for the identification of the institutions most vulnerable to an adverse event and and the estimation of the impact on their liquidity and capital levels.

Figure: Presentation of REF's main messages on the BCB webpage

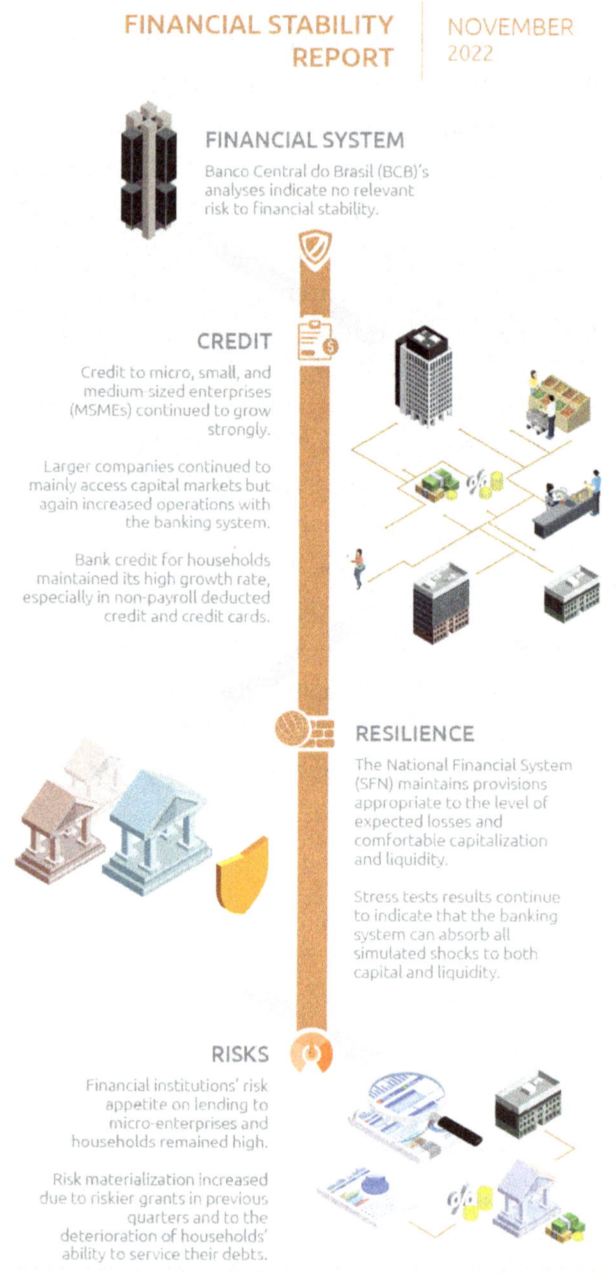

Source:Banco Central do Brasil - REF November/2022 - https://www.bcb.gov.br/en/publications/financialstabilityreport

Since April/2010, REF comes with a Statistic Annex, consisting of data of all charts and tables existent in the report, also available for download at the BCB website. Since September/2011, the Deputy Governor for Supervision formally presents the REF in a collective press release, simultaneously with its publication on the BCB website. All combined efforts to improve REF's focus, accessibility and disclosure have strengthened the BCB's commitment to the oversight of financial stability and finally led to the desired effects in the report's usefulness to the financial market and the general public.

In 2021, Complementary Law 179 designated the BCB as responsible for ensuring the stability and efficiency of the SFN[285]. Besides, article 11 of the same law has raised the REF to the status of an accountability document, to formally report to the Federal Senate, BCB's performance in terms of financial stability oversight[286].

6.5 FINANCIAL STABILITY COMMITTEE - COMEF (*COMITÊ DE ESTABILIDADE FINANCEIRA*)

In the early 2000s, there was a great deal of international debate: one group defended that monetary policy instruments should also be used for the purpose of financial stability, while another saw them as very raw instruments, which could create distortions. A rise in interest rates, for example, affected the entire economy; it was not possible to isolate the problem to specific sectors, like the car financing market, 'subprime' or real estate. For those issues, macro prudential measures were the best option.

---

285. The sole paragraph of Art. 1 of Complementary Law No. 179 of February 24, 2021 (LC 179/2021) establishes that the BCB, without prejudice to its fundamental objective of ensuring price stability, aims to ensure the stability and efficiency of the system financial sector, smoothing fluctuations in the level of economic activity and promoting full employment. (https://www.in.gov.br/en/web/dou/-/lei-complementar-n-179-de-24-de-fevereiro--de-2021-305277273)

286. LC 179/2021, Art. 11. The President of the Banco Central do Brasil must present, in the Federal Senate, in public hearing, in the first and second semesters of each year, an inflation report and a financial stability report, explaining the decisions taken in the previous semester.

> "I believe that monetary stability must be pursued through monetary policy and financial stability through macro prudential policy and, eventually, the use of specific measures to contain capital flows. The IMF and the BIS have been studying an integrated macroeconomic policy framework, which includes not only fiscal and monetary policies, but also macro prudential policy and interventions in the foreign exchange market. All this to improve the monetary policy dilemmas." (Alexandre Tombini)

In the BCB Board, there was an imbalance between the functions of ensuring monetary stability and financial stability. While Copom, the monetary policy committee, existed since 1996, the first initiative to create a financial stability committee in the BCB emerged 10 years later, as an initiative from the supervision area.

At that time, macro prudential monitoring activities were still incipient and, therefore, not a supervision priority. Thus, the proposal to create a financial stability committee in the BCB was shelved[287]. Nevertheless, the Board's interest in discussions regarding financial stability issues had been triggered. As a result, the monitoring area started to present an overview of the financial system's risks and vulnerabilities to the Board, at regular meetings[288].

> "Our presentations to the Board raised discussions regarding non-performing loans in an aggregate approach, or a more specific concern in one financial institution, but it lacked a governance, a pre-established objectives or a mandate. It was a relevant step towards financial stability management, but still a learning process. In fact, the whole world was structuring itself at that time. Financial Stability Committees were starting to be formally established in some jurisdictions." (Rodrigo Lara)

---

287. In 2006, the monitoring area proposed to the then Deputy Governor for Regulation Alexandre Tombini the creation of a financial stability committee at the BCB. The proposal was motivated by the new monitoring horizons established by the Armistice, and supported by international best practices.

288. Although informal, those meetings with the Board always counted with the participation of Deputy Governors for Supervision, Regulation and Economic Policy, among others. Meetings were held regularly, every 4 months.

In 2008, the GFC triggered the need for greater coordination among BCB Board members, for the conduction of measures to mitigate the crisis' effects. The Deputy Governors for Regulation, Monetary Policy, Supervision and Economic Policy carried out all discussions regarding emerging problems, as well as the design of measures to mitigate them. In practice, they had organized themselves as a committee, albeit an informal one.

It was only in 2011 that BCB has finally formalized its Financial Stability Committee (Comef), composed of all members of the BCB Board[289]. Comef's first official meeting was held on July 14 of that year.

> "Governor Alexandre Tombini stated that one of Comef's objectives is to promote greater integration of the economic and market areas with the areas of regulation and supervision. He determined that in the next meetings there will [also] be presentations: i) from the economic area, regarding the current situation of the economy and the credit; ii) from the market area, regarding potential risks to financial stability, such as, for example, the possible transmission of current external crises to the domestic market; and iii) from the regulation area, regarding the prospects for prudential regulation."
> (BCB/Minutes of the first Comef meeting – 07/14/2011)

Comef's mission consists of defining BCB's strategies and guidelines for the conduct of processes related to financial stability management, from risk prevention mechanisms, such as the activation of the Countercyclical Capital Buffer (CCyB)[290], to contingency plans

---

289. Comef is composed of the BCB Governor and 8 Deputy Governors. Decisions are taken by simple majority, and the chairman (BCB Governor) has the casting vote. BCB Resolution No. 173, of December 9, 2021 establishes the responsibilities of each Comef participant, and gives to the Deputy Governor for Supervision the role of organizing the committee's meetings, as well as REF's elaboration. See the full Comef regulation at   https://www.bcb.gov.br/estabilidadefinanceira/exibenormativo?tipo=Resolução%20 BCB&numero=173.

290. The Basel III CCyB requirement aims to ensure that banking sector capital requirements take account of the macro-financial environment in which banks operate. It is calculated as the weighted average of the buffers in effect in the jurisdictions to which banks have a credit exposure. It is implemented as an extension of the capital conservation buffer. Comef is responsible for CCyB activation and deactivation in Brazil, as well as for establishing its requirement level.

for dealing with crises. Meetings take place quarterly[291] and are held in two sessions on the same day. In the morning session, BCB areas provide an overview of the main aspects regarding financial stability to the Committee members, and raise for discussion those issues of concern. Decisions regarding strategies and guidelines to preserve financial stability and to mitigate systemic risk, such as the CCyB requirement[292], are taken during the afternoon session, which is restricted to the committee's members and a few BCB participants, directly involved in the issues on discussion.

"Comef filled the gap that existed in the BCB's approach to manage financial stability. The supervision area took on the role of providing Comef with information on the soundness of the SFN, as well as its main vulnerabilities." (Anthero Meirelles)

Figure: Responsibilities of BCB areas before Comef[293]

Deputy Governor for Supervision (Difis) *Comef meeting organization* *REF elaboration*	Head-office (Difis)	- Organization of the Committee's meetings
	Financial System Monitoring Department (Desig)	- SFN overview - Assessment of risks to financial stability - Prospective assessment of credit
Deputy Governor for International Affairs and Corporate Risk Management (Direx)	International Affairs Department (Derin)	- Identification and assessment of risks of foreign origin
Deputy Governor for Monetary Policy (Dipom)	Department of Banking Operations and Payment System (Deban)	- Overview of systemically important financial market infrastructures
Deputy Governor for Economic Policy (Dipec)	Research Department (Depep)	- Perception of regulated entities on risks to financial stability - Long-term prospective assessment of credit
	Economic Department (Depec)	- Short-term prospective assessment of credit
Deputy Governor for Regulation (Dinor) *elaboration of CCyB's disclosure note*	Prudential and Foreign Exchange Regulation Department (Dereg)	- Assessment of regulatory policy - Communication strategies aimed at maintaining financial stability
Deputy Governor for Licensing and Reolution (Diorf)	Department of Resolution and Sanctioning Actions (Derad)	- Assessment of risks to the resolvability of systemically important financial institutions.

Source:BCB Resolution No. 173, of December 9, 2021
https://www.bcb.gov.br/estabilidadefinanceira/exibenormativo?tipo=Resolução%20BCB&numero=173

---

291. In addition to the regular quarterly meetings, extraordinary meetings may be held, in case of need. For example, when Brazil was downgraded below the investment grade level in September/2015, an extraordinary Comef meeting was held to define an action plan to deal with possible capital outflows.

292. BCB publishes the CCyB requirement level after each ordinary Comef meeting. Regulation and supervision (macro-prudential monitoring) areas are responsible for conducting studies and proposing the CCyB ratio to Comef. The decision-making process takes into account aspects associated with credit growth and asset prices, as well as the use, cumulatively or alternatively, of other instruments aimed at maintaining financial stability.

293. The Secretary of Comef is responsible to coordinate and integrate works from the various BCB areas, involved with financial stability issues.

"Comef has decisively contributed to BCB's achievement of a comprehensive and integrated approach, given that financial stability activities permeate several BCB's areas and requires a direct relationship with all involved teams." (Lucio Capelletto)

The macro prudential monitoring area is responsible for presenting the panorama of the SFN, the assessment of risks to financial stability and the prospective assessment of the credit market in every Comef meeting. To fulfill its role, it has developed a set of indicators capable of covering the various perspectives of financial stability (or the lack of it) and presents them as a heatmap, named the Financial Stability Map[294] - MEF (*Mapa de Estabilidade Financeira*).

MEP indicators are grouped into three dimensions: Risk Appetite, Payment Capacity and Broad Financial System. The 'Risk Appetite' dimension intends to capture the economic agents overconfidence level, which could lead to unsustainable credit growth or poor asset pricing[295]. The 'Payment Capacity' dimension aims to assess vulnerabilities arising from the level of indebtedness of different sectors of the economy[296]. The 'Broad Financial System' dimension aims to assess the economic-financial conditions and risk exposures of institution belonging to the financial system, as well as other agents outside the regulatory perimeter of the BCB, that carry out some type of financial intermediation[297].

---

294. The October/2019 REF presents MEF's methodology in detail: https://www.bcb.gov. br/content/publications/financialstabilityreport/201910/FSR201910-fsrSection2_1.pdf.

295. The Risk Appetite dimension includes the broad credit growth rate, 79 indicators for the valuation of the stock and real estate markets and measures of persistence of low volatility (interest rate and exchange rate markets). Its purpose is to answer questions such as: is the credit gap moving away from its long-term trend? Is risk spread among non-financial companies [borrowers] falling? Is the dollar FX rate too stable? Is the interest rate too stable? etc.

296. The Payment Capacity dimension includes payment capacity's indicators of households, companies and the government, as well as payment capacity measures of these domestic sectors in relation to the rest of the world.

297. The Broad Financial System dimension comprises different metrics of bank resilience and vulnerabilities, as well as indicators related to entities outside the regulatory perimeter of the BCB, but relevant to financial stability.

"We open the Comef meetings with the financial stability map and discuss the different perspectives: risk accumulation, agents' ability to pay and the SFN resilience." (André Caccavo)

Figure: Financial Stability Map

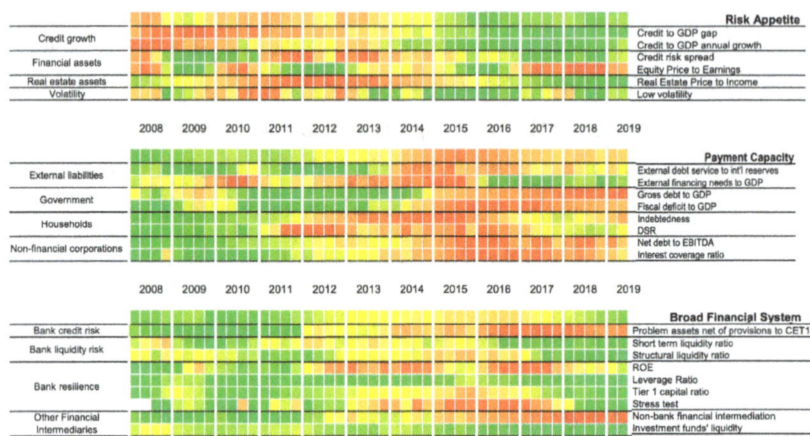

Source:Banco Central do Brasil - REF outubro/2019 - https://www.bcb.gov.br/content/publications/financialstabilityreport/201910/FSR201910-fsrSection2_1.pdf.

The improvement of methodologies and skill of the areas involved with financial stability resulted in important evolutions for the dynamics of Comef. The stress tests presented during the meetings, for example, were initially focused on the supervised entities, even though the approach was already systemic. The monitoring area could map the financial system interconnectedness and simulate contagion, but the scenarios applied in those tests lacked economic basis.

In fact, the monitoring area had already tried to expand its analysis towards a macroeconomic approach, but Comef opted to encourage integration among the areas involved with financial stability, instead. Thus, a partnership between the monitoring and economic research areas was established to develop the BCB's macroeconomic stress test model. Additionally, a Scenario Committee coordinated by the Secretary of Comef and composed of representatives of 4 BCB's departments[298] was specially created

---

298. Research, Economics, International Affairs and Financial System Monitoring departments.

to calibrate the scenarios' parameters, every time the stress test was performed. As a result, Comef meetings that previously dealt with past events started to discuss expectations for the future.

"The Research Department has elaborated the scenarios we apply in the macroeconomic tests." (Robert Nygaard)

Figure: Macroeconomic Stress Test Scenarios (REF November/2022)

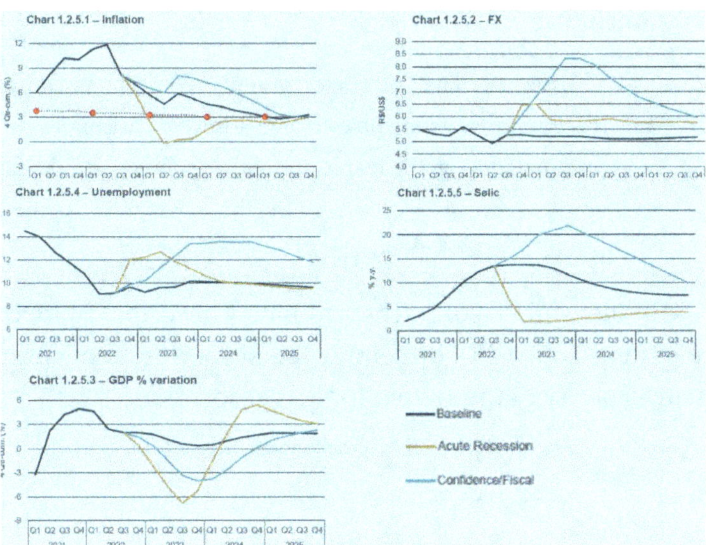

Stress Scenario 'Acute Recession': significant drop in domestic demand, together with an acute GDP decline of the global economy from Q4 2022 onwards.

Stress Scenario 'Confidence/Fiscal': significant increase in uncertainty in the economy starting in 2022 Q4 due to fiscal deterioration, leading to increased risk premiums, sharp exchange rate depreciation, an increase in the economy's neutral interest rate, and a contraction in economic activity.

Source:Banco Central do Brasil - REF (November/2022) - https://www.bcb.gov.br/en/publications/financialstabilityreport/202211

The trajectories of macroeconomic variables calibrated in the stress scenarios generate risk factors for the financial system. These factors impact the balance sheet of each financial institution. Those that eventually go into default, impact other financial institutions by contagion, which may also go into default and spread the contagion to other institutions. The contagion effect is estimated until the entire impact is absorbed. The absorption of this impact, however, causes changes in the ability of the financial sector to grant credit or to keep minimum levels of capital and liquidity. These changes may affect the real sector of the economy, which, in turn, impacts the financial system again. This cycle is repeated until the entire system is in equilibrium.

> "Due to data coverage, granularity and timeliness, our macroeconomic tests are able to assess impacts arising from action and reaction between the real sector of the economy and the financial system in successive cycles, until the contagion is completely dissipated." (Enrico Vasconcelos)

REF November/2022: The estimated need for capitalization of the system is low in both simulated scenarios, confirming the adequate capacity of the system for loss absorption.

Figure: Results of Macroeconomic Stress Tests

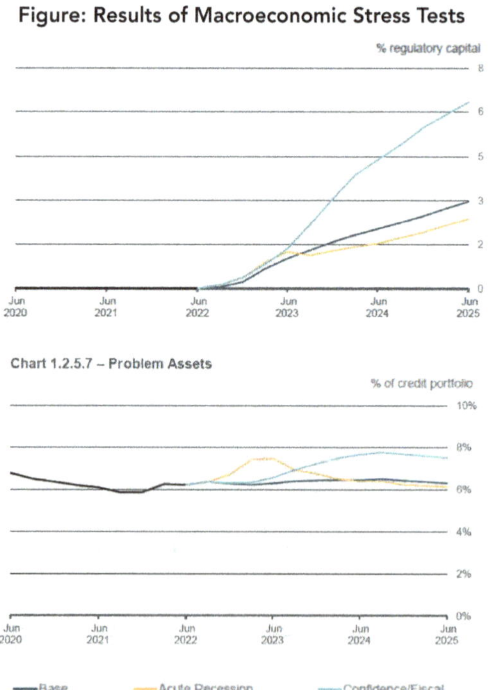

Stress Scenario 'Acute Recession': significant drop in domestic demand, together with an acute GDP decline of the global economy from Q4 2022 onwards.
Stress Scenario 'Confidence/Fiscal': significant increase in uncertainty in the economy starting in 2022 Q4 due to fiscal deterioration, leading to increased risk premiums, sharp exchange rate depreciation, an increase in the economy's neutral interest rate, and a contraction in economic activity.

Source:Banco Central do Brasil - REF (November/2022) -https://www.bcb.gov.br/en/publications/financialstabilityreport/202211

The partnership approach brought great advances to the improvement of models. However, sometimes teams are faced with unavoidable barriers, such as structural breaks in data series. Although the available data allow the quick and accurate assessment of vulnerabilities, in the temporal dimension, however, records are still too short. Thus, dating of financial cycles is not yet possible, which hinders the analysis of past regularities that might be predictive of systemic crises.

> "It's like if we had a TV screen with a lot of pixels, but the movie it shows is very short. Data has to tell us a longer story, so that we can seek for regularities in the past that would be a good guide to the future. I agree we have the 'feeling' of our history, but I still don't see the possibility of doing data-based analysis of financial cycles. We are on a good path, but we need to bide our time." (Enrico Vasconcelos)

Comef was created in the same year as the Law on Access to Public Information was enacted, but, at that time, transparency was not on the Committee's agenda. Besides, it was believed that the secrecy of Comef's minutes was supported by the LAI itself[299]. Thus, the REF was the BCB's communication vehicle to society, regarding financial stability.

Internally, however, despite the great synergy, the processes for the elaboration of REF and the presentations to the Comef had separate and independent agendas. The trigger to align both

---

299. Art. 23 of Law 12,527, of November 18, 2011: "Information whose disclosure or unrestricted access may... IV – offer a high risk to the country's financial, economic or monetary stability... are considered essential to the security of society or the State and, therefore, subject to [secrecy level] classification." (https://www.planalto.gov.br/ccivil_03/_ato2011-2014/2011/lei/l12527.htm).

processes was the matching of agendas: it was established that the semiannual REF elaboration process should start just after the second and fourth Comef's quarterly meetings. From that moment on, REF could effectively mirror Comef's vision to society.

Additionally, as long as the worldwide movement for transparency gained in strength, concerns about maintaining the secrecy of Comef's minutes were dissipating. Thus, since March/2021, the minutes are being published just after each Comef meeting[300].

> "My contribution to Comef was to systematize, communicate, organize the topics and disclose the decision on the countercyclical capital buffer. We didn't need to give different information to the public. The information that supported Comef's discussions could also be used to write the REF." (Ilan Goldfajn)

In the following year[301], a new mandate was added to Comef's agenda: to address issues related to the efficiency and the competitiveness of the financial system. The purpose of allocating these topics together with financial stability issues was that eventual trade-offs among them could be mediated by Comef itself[302].

> "Bringing the themes of efficiency and competitiveness into Comef was a very welcome innovation, as it responds to the demands of society. And we can do that now because we have already solved the soundness issue. When compared to a soccer game, financial soundness is the referee, who is only noticed if he is missing. Efficiency, on the other hand, has a more evident effect on price and the public is more reactive to it." (Enrico Vasconcelos)

Despite all Comef's efforts to lead the management of financial stability, it is important to remember that BCB is not the

---

300. Comef minutes are disclosed at https://www.BC.gov.br/publicacoes/atascomef.

301. BCB Resolution 173/2021, Art.5: "Comef is responsible for: .... X - evaluating the efficiency of the SFN (Included as of 3/1/2021, by BCB Resolution 68/2021).

302. In terms of communication to society, the issues of stability and efficiency/competitiveness are dealt with in different vehicles, the Financial Stability Report and the Banking Economy Report, respectively.

sole regulatory and supervisory agency of the Brazilian financial system, and other agencies should join the discussions on financial stability at the national level. For this purpose, a project for the creation of a Brazilian Financial Stability Council, in which all regulatory and supervisory financial authorities will have a seat, is already in progress.

CHAPTER 7

Suptech in Process

"Gathering all data and transforming it into information is the biggest challenge."

(Marcelo Fernandes)

"Today, one single supervisor can do what it took 100 people to do in an IGC."

(Belline Santana)

The challenges for the use of machine learning for supervisory purposes, as well as the new risks to the financial system arising from externalities that affect the planet as a whole, such as climate risk and cyber risk, are addressed in this chapter. It also discusses how the expansion of data collection beyond the boundaries of supervised entities has enabled the cross-referencing of data and the expansion of micro and macro prudential analyses' capacity.

improvements, in order to expand the supervision's boundaries on data requirements.

> "The ACTs have increased over time. We've signed agreements with the INSS[305], with C3[306], we've expanded the agreement with the Federal Revenue Service, we've negotiated with the MDIC[307] to access the data of companies registered in notaries..." (Elvira Schulz)

> "Previc[308] exchanges information with the BCB, but there is no database integration yet. It would be interesting if we had a common database for the use of all supervisory entities of the financial system." (Lucio Capelletto – Previc)

Expanding data boundaries beyond supervisory and regulatory powers brought some challenges to quality control processes, as the BCB could not demand adjustments or improvements in the process of collecting information from sources out of its scope, even when the reporting entity had committed itself in the ACT to report the information in a certain structure and frequency. Besides, the continuous increase in data volume also raised concerns on its maintenance and the consequent continuity of processes and tools associated with it.

> "Data cleaning and curation requirements are extraordinarily complex for the formation of so-called 'data lakes'. Otherwise, if not cleaned and organized in a logical way, gathering data can give rise not to lakes, but to useless 'data swamps'. It is necessary to have the appropriate personnel and the necessary investment in infrastructure.

---

305. INSS (*Instituto Nacional de Seguridade Social*) is the Brazilian social security federal entity, responsible for the payment of the pensioners. The Brazilian government allows for a special credit line for them, with payments direct from the INSS. INSS data provides information regarding the undrawn portion of the pensioners' credit limit.
306. C3 Registradora is a financial market infrastructure that provides registration services for credit operations intended to be used in the market as collateral of funding instruments. (https://www.cip-bancos.org.br/Paginas/C3.aspx)
307. Ministry of Development, Industry, Foreign Trade and Services.
308. The National Superintendency of Complementary Social Security - Previc (*Superintendência Nacional de Previdência Complementar) is* the supervisory body of pension funds in Brazil.

7.1 EXPANDING DATA COLLECTION BEYOND SUPERVISED ENTITIES

Looking beyond borders is a characteristic that has always been present in the BCB monitoring area. Since its creation, when off-site supervisors around the world were structured to collect and analyze the information sent by their supervised entities, Brazil started to collect microdata, both from independent sources, such as trade repositories and the payment system, as well as those provided by institutions, such as microdata on credit operations. Over time, these bases have proven to be cheaper, more detailed, more timely and more reliable. Most importantly, analysts have learned to look at the problems from other perspectives, even when the focus of analysis was still off-site supervision.

When the monitoring area expanded its performance to the macro prudential dimension, it also expanded the need for information beyond the supervised universe. After all, vulnerabilities and risks to financial stability did not arise exclusively from the internal dynamics of the financial system. During the last two decades, events from outside the regulatory perimeter of the BCB have had relevant impact in the financial institutions, such as the Car-Wash [303] scandal, the Covid-19 pandemic and concerns regarding climate risk.

Monitoring teams needed to go deeper in information of customers, guarantees, collaterals… They wanted to know who were the non-financial players in the market, how they interacted with the financial system and how they impacted it. Thus, they started to sign data sharing agreements with other regulatory and governmental entities, named Technical Cooperation Agreements – ACT (*Acordos de Cooperação Técnica*), to access databases directly from websites[304], and even to make legal and regulatory

---

303. See Chapter 6 - 6.3 The evolution of macro monitoring processes, for more details on BCB's role regarding the assessm of Car-Wash operation impacts to the SFN.
304. The 'Web Scraping' technique is used to extract data from websites of unsupervised institutions or other regulators, such as the CVM, due to the agility of this process.

> Discussions on this issue are part of the BIS agenda." (Alexandre Tombini)

> "There is nothing more important in this whole process than having data organized. How we are going to use it comes later." (Marcelo Fernandes)

Currently, the cost of storing data is relatively cheap and new technologies also allow handling data more efficiently. There is, however, the need to maintain each developed tool, and, with it, the risk of dependency on the tool's developer to guarantee its continuity. Thus, to mitigate this risk, the monitoring area established an IT management policy, with the obligation of transferring the tools that have already reached a certain degree of stability and maturity to the corporate dimension. In this new status, BCB's IT area assumes the responsibility for their maintenance.

> "In 2020, we switched off the Central Bank's mainframe. Our migration to the low platform was a gradual and studied process. New technologies are better suited to BCB's size and IT needs, with a better cost/benefit ratio. PIX[309], for example, currently processes around 55 million transfers/day, while the platform's capacity exceeds 300 million transfers/day. On the mainframe, the cost of storing this data would be much higher. In parallel, we made other improvements, such as investing in increasing BCB's analytical capacity, with the implementation of a specific appliance of high capacity and performance." (Haroldo Cruz)

Despite limitations and new challenges, monitoring analyses have grown in breadth and depth with the arrival of new structured information. In 2010, monitoring teams were able to identify that the maturity of cars financing operations was increasing and, with it, the risk that the depreciation of the purchased car could impact

---

309. PIX is the Brazilian payment scheme managed by the BCB that enables its users — people, companies and governmental entities — to send or receive payment transfers in few seconds at any time, including non-business days. (https://www.bcb.gov.br/en/financialstability/pix_en)

its coverage capacity as collateral along the time[310]. Structured information allowed analysts to know who were the people that could lose their jobs with the bankruptcy of their employer, and to estimate the impact on banks in the event of the employers' and respective employees' default.

> "Anyone who offers us data, we accept. CIP[311] reported us data on credit assignments. One day, they asked me if we also wanted data on credit portability. I accepted. Now, we are able to analyze the effectiveness of credit portability in Brazil." (Marcelo Fernandes)

The combat against money laundering has brought new challenges to the monitoring teams. The strategies used so far for risk analysis were too time-consuming and limited to keep up with the frantic and random dynamics of the search for evidence, fraud and suspicious situations. For this purpose, the data universe needed to expand beyond the boundaries of structured data. Thus, BCB invested in technology, expertise and new data sources, to enter the world of information crossing with the use of unstructured data[312]. This evolution allowed AML analyses to be carried out across the entire database, no longer by sampling.

From then on, each technology developed or new database captured and organized was no longer limited to its initial purpose, but quickly incorporated by other perspectives of monitoring & supervision: data on bank bills payment, for example, initially collected for AML monitoring purposes, improved the contagion model, as it became one additional source for the identification of the the real sector interconnectedness; the natural-language processing (NLP) tool, created to read investment fund deeds and identify their characteristics for purposes of step-in risk assessment,

---

310. The April/2011 REF published an analysis of this credit market vulnerability. https://www.bcb.gov.br/publicacoes/ref/201104.

311. Interbank Payments Chamber (*Câmara Interbancária de Pagamentos*) https://www.cip-bancos.org.br.

312. Unstructured data are those without a well-defined, aligned and standardized structure. The unstructured data collected by supervision is gathered in a large database for multiple uses.

also started to be used in on-site supervision routines, in order to optimize the reading of audit reports and other non-digitized documents reported to the supervisor by the financial institutions.

> "I am increasingly involved in obtaining information, systematizing it and carrying out multiple crossings. And we are able to find a use for data because we are able to systematize and process it." (Marcelo Fernandes)

7.2 THE USE OF MACHINE LEARNING TECHNIQUES IN SUPERVISION AND ITS CHALLENGES

> "Looking back, we've come a long way. We went from Excel spreadsheets to artificial intelligence." (Helton Maciel)

After the migration of databases and monitoring tools to Teradata and the completion of the database integration process[313], applications using machine learning technologies began to emerge. The world had already entered the age of artificial intelligence (AI), machine learning, and data science, but until 2018, they were still not very widespread in the BCB.

Furthermore, it was not enough to simply train people to use those technologies. First, it was necessary to create infrastructure support and a governance process for the validation of applications developed with the use of artificial intelligence.

That was the appropriate moment to move supervision towards a great technological leap. Thus, a project named S-Lab Project was designed with a scope range comprehending since training staff in data science, up to the creation of a support and management infrastructure, for the development of machine learning solutions to the BCB supervisory activities.

In fact, interests in exploring those new horizons at the BCB went beyond supervision and demands for AI skills were rising

---

313. Database integration process was carried out by the I2M Project (Integration of Monitoring Information), specially designed for this purpose.

everywhere, which led to a IT restructuring at the corporate level. As a result, BCB implemented an Analytical Intelligence Laboratory - LIA (*Laboratório de Inteligência Analítica*) for IT users, as well as a specific data science training program. In terms of infrastructure, the IT area implemented the Machine Learning as a Service (MLAS), a platform that transforms the applications developed by users and validated by their business areas into corporate AI solutions[314].

> "LIA provides an experimental environment for the development of AI tools. When a solution proves to be adequate, it can be added to the corporate process. This allows not only the use of artificial intelligence in a variety of working processes of the BCB, but also the experimentation of several possible algorithms to arrive at the best algorithm, the best possibility. Many areas of BCB are interested in this technology. We are all heading in that direction." (Helton Maciel)

This new environment, where sometimes users feel they have reached the unachievable, in practice, brings great challenges to users' training and management. In fact, users' training is essential to the leap in performance. After all, if algorithms learn, they need someone to teach them.

> "The natural-language tool transforms a text into a structured database, but we cannot forget that it is necessary to teach the machine each letter, each word: 'when you find a certain set of text, bring me the information'. It's the evolution of the keyword." (Gilneu Vivan)

In the past, the mixed teams framework was established to bring the information manager closer to the monitoring analyst. The interaction of people with different expertises has been the

---

314. First, the developing area carries out the application's validation through proofs of concept, verifying the possibility of using the analytical intelligence solution as a working tool. If possible, tests are carried out and the tool is put into production by the business area. When the working process is mature, it is migrated from the departmental environment to the corporate environment, through the MLAS platform. The process of maintaining applications in this new environment consists of periodically retraining the machine learning analytics solution to ensure its performance. Good performance is one of the success indicators of that solution.

key to eliminate the communication barriers between these two worlds. 'Speaking the same language' contributed to the evolution and integration of working processes. Similarly, the data scientist needed to be part of the teams, to be in direct contact with the environment they wanted to model, just as the analysts needed to be familiar with the developed solutions, in order to interpret outputs. However, recruiting and retaining people with data science skills to the monitoring teams is still a major challenge.

Initially, it was necessary to invest in data science training, respecting individual abilities and needs of trainees. Although all analysts needed to know at least the basic concepts of machine learning processes, so that they could identify the need and usefulness of solutions to their own activities, few people had skills to become a top-level data scientist.

> "BCB carried out an interesting process to introduce its employees to the AI world, as it established agreements with international training companies. Online training licenses are offered according to a rotation scheme among the teams. Many people are being trained with this approach." (Helton Maciel)

Unfortunately, not all monitoring teams had people with the skill-set needed to become data scientists. To fill this gap, the IT-Experts team formed a group of developers for the development of AI-based solutions for these monitoring teams without the expertise to do that by themselves. This group has also become responsible to provide support and guidance to the teams able to develop their own tools.

Training, however, was not the sole nor the major obstacle. Along the S-Lab Project's research phase, it was observed that other central banks and supervisory entities that already shared the same interest in technological advances of this nature were very cautious about applying technologies whose rules might not be clear enough to support a decision based on their results. After all, supervision implied capitulating problems based on evidence.

Although smart algorithms were revolutionizing econometric modeling, the intensive use of granular data combined with the growing ability to interconnect data led machines to often exceed the human capacity to justify and even to understand outputs. However, supervisors needed to justify why those outputs denoted a problem. If the process that came to a conclusion were a black box, it could hamper the use of artificial intelligence for supervisory activities.

So, what could supervision really get out of this new technology?

Investing in the improvement of working processes' performance - in other words, optimizing the workforce to identify evidence - was how BCB chose to incorporate the new technologies to the improvement of supervision and monitoring actions.

> "The forecast can be accurate, precise, but if it has little ability to explain and interpret the data, its use for the design of macro prudential measures is compromised." (Alexandre Tombini)

Following this approach, the development of solutions based in Natural Language Processing[315] (NLP), for example, has been extensively explored by the monitoring and supervision areas, producing good results in various activities. Systems with specific objectives have also been developed, such as SAMOA[316], for fraud detection, and ADAM[317], for selecting the best sample of credit operations to be inspected in an on-site work.

---

315. Natural-language processing is a subfield of computer science, artificial intelligence, and linguistics that studies the problems of automatic generation and understanding of natural human languages. Applications for natural language generation convert information from databases into human-understandable language and applications for natural language comprehension convert human language messages into more formal representations, more easily manipulated by computer programs.

316. The System for the Automatic Monitoring of Atypical Operations - SAMOA (*Sistema Automático de Monitoramento de Operações Atípicas*) has three functionalities: textual classification, outlier detection and an AML tool, which flags suspicious operations involving individuals and companies listed in the input table, throughout the whole database universe.

317. The ADAM (Machine Learning Sampling Selection) algorithm analyzes the institution's entire loan portfolio and selects suspicious operations. It investigates, for example,

"Using NLP to analyze banks' reports will give supervisors more time to analyze their business models." (Belline Santana)

"We spent a lot of time getting the United Nations terrorist list and making a system that could match names. For now, I use it to try to identify who are the Brazilians who have names similar to the ones on the list. The chance of them being terrorists is very low, but it is a flag to my list of atypical operations. Then, we check whether there are operations of large amounts involving them as natural persons or as owners of the involved company." (Marcelo Fernandes)

"The number of hits we have with the use of artificial intelligence is very high. We have used ADAM to select suspicious credit operations of credit unions of the same confederation and asked the respective auditor to check them. We hit the jackpot!" (Sandra Castro)

In a short period of time, the 'smart' tools and the use of granular data have revolutionized the working processes. Ongoing routines[318] with algorithms capable of analyzing the entire data universe were achieving more and better results. As a result, they gradually replaced some actions previously recognized as classic supervision, like the on-site inspection of credit portfolios, for example. After all, what is the purpose of applying such a procedure to credit operations that were born digital and whose information is monthly reported in detail to the SCR?

"Everyday people ask me questions about tools they're developing. IT skills are evolving very fast in the BCB. Naïve people do not exist anymore. Rarely, I meet people not doing their job in the best way they should." (Nizam Pfeilsticker)

"This is another way of doing supervision. We became more focused and more assertive. Those were the main changes we had with the application of AI technologies." (Sandra Castro)

---

whether the operation is a hedging or speculative strategy, whether the client is facing difficulties in paying principal or whether interest and principal are already threatened.
318. Ongoing routines are those automatically processed with each new data entry.

Nevertheless, it's important to highlight that although the world is moving towards doing more and more in terms of technology, the supervision process will always need people to assess the business model, the governance, and the technological infrastructure of supervised entities. Thus, the focus of inspections tends to be increasingly directed towards those issues, while the monitoring area automates data-based procedures. Finding the balance between human and machine resources is the secret to the success of a modern and efficient supervision model.

> "The great support of those who work in the assessment of the FI's strategy are the teams that check the numbers reported by them. If the supervisor doesn't properly understand what numbers mean, he/she may let him/herself be taken by false words. Understanding the business and understanding the numbers have to walk together."
> (Álvaro Freitas)

7.3 FINTECHS & SUPTECHS

The financial system is under an ongoing evolutionary process. With an increasingly complex ecosystem, the participation of new non-bank financial players has completely changed competition. Fintechs[319] are taking credit risk[320] and shrinking the market share of big banks. The new financial conglomerates that are challenging the classic banking conglomerates are emerging from the payment system environment.

> "The performance of payment institutions (IP) in the payments market seeks to fill gaps that are in many cases neglected by traditional

---

319. According to the FSB, FinTech is defined as technologically enabled innovation in financial services that could result in new business models, applications, processes or products with an associated material effect on financial markets and institutions and the provision of financial services. (https://www.fsb.org/work-of-the-fsb/financial-innovation-and-structural-change/fintech/)

320. Two types of fintechs may be authorized by BCB to grant credit to the public: direct credit company - SCD (*Sociedade de Crédito Direto*) and peer-to-peer loan company - SEP (*Sociedades de Empréstimo a Pessoas*). Both of them are required to provide information to the SCR.

banking institutions. They work focused on the customer experience, providing specific services and with differentiated prices and benefits. In this context, many entities start with payment facilities, and gradually achieve a wider range of products and services, either through partnerships with other institutions or even through the transformation or incorporation of new types of entities into the economic group." (Gustavo Santos)

Relationship between Fintechs, open banking[321] or open finance with supervision is, therefore, a little different. There are issues associated with the consumer, such as data protection or customer relationships, for example, that become part of the supervisor's agenda. On the other hand, Fintechs are more like a new business model than a new risk at the supervisory perspective. Besides, they come from the same environment that central banks have entered as Suptechs: both make massive use of microdata with highly technologic tools.

"Suptech is the use of innovative technology by supervisory agencies to support supervision." (Dirk Broeders and Jermy Prenio – FSI/Innovative technology in financial supervision (suptech) – the experience of early users[322])

---

321. Open Banking or open financial system is the possibility for customers of financial products and services to allow the sharing of their information between different financial institutions and the movement of their bank accounts from different platforms, and not just through the bank's application or website, in a safe, agile and convenient way. The BCB and the CMN define the Brazilian Open Finance environment as the sharing of data, products and services among regulated entities — financial institutions, payment institutions and other entities licensed by BCB — at the customers' discretion, as far as their own data as individuals or legal entities is concerned. (https://www.bcb.gov.br/en/financialstability/open_finance)
322. https://www.bis.org/fsi/publ/insights9.pdf.

Figure: Brazilian Open Finance environment

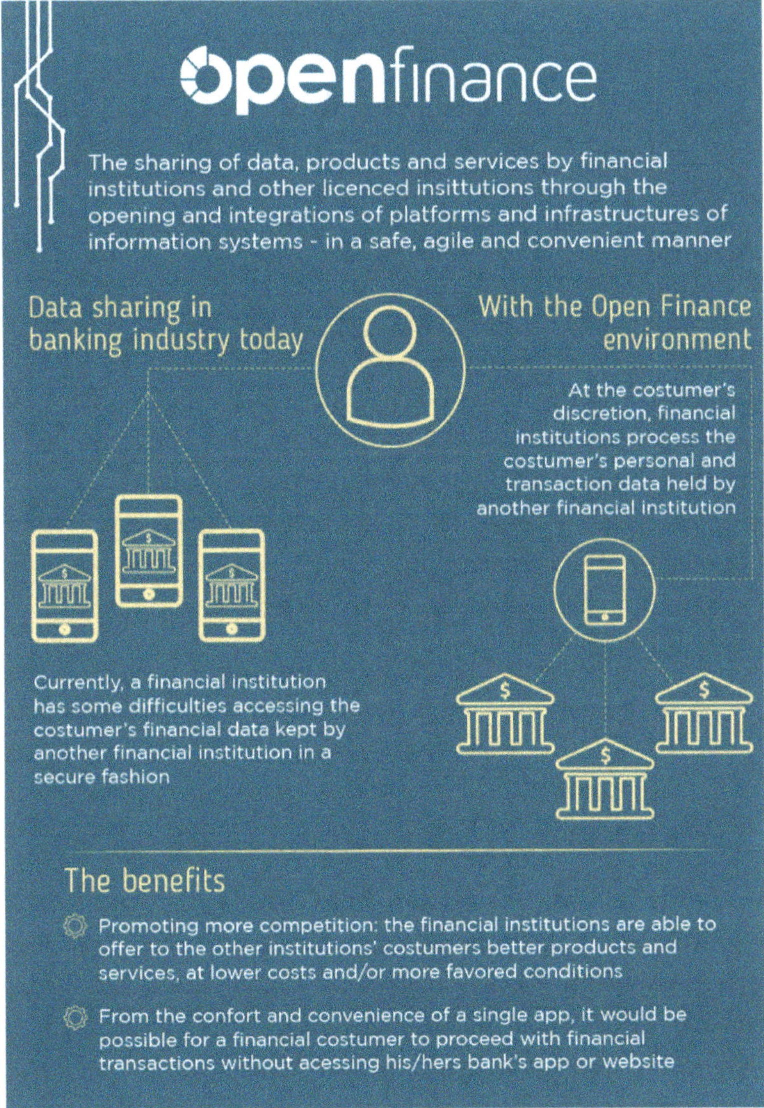

Source:Banco Central do Brasil - https://www.bcb.gov.br/en/financialstability/open_finance

The interaction between Fintechs and Suptechs is still under construction, both from the industry and the supervisory sides. BCB's 20 years of experience in developing microdata-intensive analysis tools that extrapolate the information reported by supervised entities put Brazil some steps ahead in understanding this new environment and how to face its challenges.

7.4 CHALLENGES OF A GLOBAL ENVIRONMENT

Supervision needs to deal with an increasingly globalized world. Previously, concerns about globalization were linked to challenges in assessing the impacts of cross-border capital flows. It was necessary to be attentive not only to the inflow of foreign capital, for example, but to the financial system's capacity of absorbing it, as well as the market players' protection level to do so: the currency mismatch risk should be covered by capital requirement and the market risk of the non-financial sector would be converted into credit risk for the financial system, also covered by capital requirements.

Nevertheless, there are risks emerging from environments still unexplored by supervision, such as cyber, climate and socio-environmental risks. Those are borderless risks.

> "In the past, we thought we were able to protect our country with appropriate regulation: we mitigated risks by requiring minimum risk protection standards for financial operations. Now, we've figured out that a flood comes and takes away the borrower and the collateral!" (Gilneu Vivan)

Borderless risks have two highly challenging characteristics. The first one is that its analysis demands a universe of microdata that is totally new to the supervisor. Climate risk, for example, needs to be addressed from two perspectives: the physical risk itself (drought, flood, cyclone etc.), and the transition risk, that is, the risk of companies not sustaining themselves as a result of eventual changes in legislation to contain carbon emissions, for example.

Modeling of both perspectives requires information beyond the supervisory universe, such as: the identification of the companies' physical location; how much they are water resources' dependent; how much carbon they produce; how much they demand energy power; which are their suppliers chains; how much their physical location will be climatically affected; how vulnerable are they to regulation requirements to reduce carbon emissions etc.

To follow the steps of international discussions, supervisors are being expected to estimate the companies' exposure and to assess their ability to survive in the new physical and regulatory environment, in order to estimate the impacts of climate changes in the credit market. Then, they need to assess how companies will survive (or not) in the market's new credit offer level and how this whole new environment shall affect the financial system in 2050!

> "We are committed to the assessment of the impact of climate events on the banking sector. To this end, in April 2021[323], we have published in REF our first study on this topic, where we have addressed exposures and impact on banks' deposits and credit portfolios of weather fluctuations, droughts, floods and climate change. We have also addressed exposures and impacts of transition risk. Other studies are already planned to be regularly published every REF." (Gilneu Vivan)

The second characteristic, and the most challenging, is that the mitigation of those risks will not be effective with isolated initiatives. There is a great effort of central banks and international organizations to find out how the financial system can collaborate with this agenda. In this sense, for example, CEMLA has held its first Course on Environmental Risks and Financial Stability[324] in July/2022, which covered fundamental topics, such as: the understanding and management of environmental risk by financial The participants comprehend institutions, climate scenario analysis and stress testing, the development of definitions and standards

---

323. https://www.bcb.gov.br/en/publications/financialstabilityreport/202104.

324. The course was held in a digital format and was attended by 26 representatives from 22 institutions and associates of CEMLA, representing 19 countries from Latin America and the Caribbean, 2 European countries, and 1 Asian country. (https://www.cemla.org/activi-dades/2022-final/2022-07-course-on-climate-risk-and-financial-stability-i.html)

to identify green assets, and the adaptation of macro prudential frameworks to climate-related risks.

In 2020, BCB has joined the Network for Greening the Financial System (NGFS)[325], created in 2017 and which has become the international focal point for supervisors and central banks to discuss risks related to climate change and the environment, as well as to foster green finance[326]. BCB has contributed to the publication of the NGFS Progress report on the Guide for Supervisors in October/2021, where its regulation on socio-environmental risk was used as a reference of good practices.

Figure: BCB comtribution to the NGFS Progress Report on the Guide for Supervisors - October 2021

Box 3

Including social-environmental and climate-related risks as a supervisory priority

For the past three years, social-environmental (S&E) risks ranked among Supervision's top five priorities in the **Banco Central do Brasil** (BCB)'s Supervision Area Annual Plan (SAP). The SAP is a cyclical process that results in a detailed set of activities to be performed throughout the year, as well as its monitoring and evaluation rules and targets. Several of BCB's areas collaborate at different stages of such strategic planning, using as inputs data from a large range of sources.

In 2021, as a result of the incorporation of the new 'Sustainability Dimension' to the Agenda *BC#* (BCB's overall institutional strategic agenda), climate-related risks were specifically included in the set of supervisory priorities. Up to that point, climate-related risks were addressed to the extent of their overlap with environmental ones. Deforestation is an example of an environmental issue deeply interconnected with climate-related risks, which has already been included at SAP's list of actions. The four main premises to include S&E and climate-related risks in the supervisory activities were: (i) the necessity to improve BCB's ability to assess and monitor these risks, including the development of new tools, such as stress tests; (ii) the importance to improve continuously the on-site supervision process; (iii) the added value from information exchange and collaboration in national and international fora; and (iv) the importance to include all financial institutions in the analysis, but considering relevance and proportionality, thus focusing on the institutions most exposed to risk and/or with risk management deficiencies. In order to determine which financial institutions will be subject to supervisory actions, BCB uses a Residual Risk Matrix (SERM), which is described in **Box 14**.

---

325. The Network for Greening the Financial System is a coalition of central banks and supervisory authorities from all continents that are committed within their mandates to concretely contribute to greening the financial system.
326. Green finance are structured financial activities, such as loans, debt mechanisms and investments, used to encourage the development of ecologically correct projects and/or minimize the impact on the climate of conventional projects.

Box 14

Using a Socio-Environmental Residual Risk Matrix

Since 2016, **Banco Central do Brasil** (BCB) has been employing a socio-environmental (S&E) risk matrix – based on the exposures of Brazilian financial institutions to S&E risks – to prioritise its supervisory activities. In 2020, a new dimension, which uses the information of the supervised institutions' risk management practices, was included, leading to the creation of what was called 'social and environmental residual risk matrix' (SERM).

From then on, the SERM has been used not only to support the supervisory planning process, but also to identify topics that should receive greater attention from the supervision. This new matrix is composed by the aggregation of two different scores, the first associated with each financial institution's S&E credit exposures (S_{SA}) to risky activities, and the second linked to the adequacy of the FI's S&E governance and risk management (S_{GRM}).

The S_{SA} is built as an application of the S&E sectoral risk criteria developed by the International Finance Corporation (IFC),[1] which assigns, to each industry sector, a grade (high, medium, or low) to different environmental and social risks. The BCB calculates the S_{SA} score as a weighted average of the financial institution's credit exposures to these industries, assigning a weight of 3, 2 and 1 to the exposures marked as high, medium or low risk, respectively. Using the data from its Credit Information System (a database, updated monthly, in which credit providers report detailed information, including data regarding obligors' economic activity, of all credit assignments greater than BRL 200.00) the BCB is able to map the entire credit portfolio, of every financial institution, according to the IFC's criteria.

The S_{GRM} is calculated as a weighted average of several themes within the assessment of the following seven broad S&E topics: (i) governance; (ii) risk management; (iii) credit risk; (iv) specific rural credit procedures; (v) operational risk, including legal risk; (vi) market risk; and (vii) reputational risk. The weights are given according to the importance of each theme, with the highest importance being given to issues related to regulatory requirements. The first round of assessment was based on responses to a questionnaire sent to the largest Brazilian financial institutions (which collectively hold more than 95% of all credit exposures in Brazil). Since then, the SGRM has been updated through several supervisory actions, such as: (i) follow up of deficiencies identified in the financial institutions; (ii) on-site supervision work at specific financial institutions;

(iii) assessments of specific supervisory concerns, related to significantly high S&E risks; and (iv) the Risks and Controls Assessment System (a regular risk assessment applied to Brazil's largest banks). Updated questionnaires could also be applied again in the future.

Finally, as the BCB has been continuously improving its S&E supervisory process, the SERM has also been refined.

Recent work focused on the creation of new S&E exposure metrics, and on incorporating individual borrowers' specific information. As an example of this last point, the BCB has been able to refine credit exposures to the power generation sector, distinguishing each company from the sector according to the cleanliness of the energy it produces, thus identifying with greater accuracy credit exposures associated with clean and dirty energy generation.

1 See *https://firstforsustainability.org/risk-management/risk-by-industry-sector/*

Source: NGFS Progress report on the Guide for Supervisors - October 2021 - https://www.ngfs.net/sites/default/files/media/2021/11/08/progress_report_on_the_guide_for_supervisors.pdf

"We're talking about financial microdata from institutions, geographic data, climate projections... It's a huge worldwide effort! It is necessary to have information not only on the companies' financial situation, but on the environmental impact they and their suppliers chain may provoke. We discuss how to map risks and how to make projections. And all of it has to do with the financial system!" (Gilneu Vivan)

Figure: Origin of NGFS

Origin of the NGFS

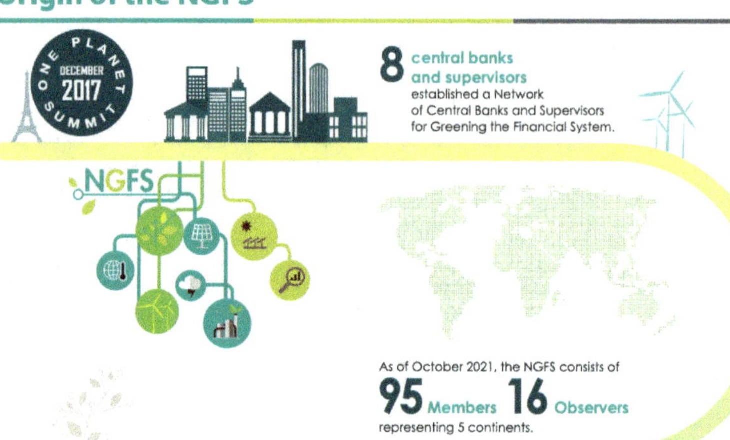

Central banks and supervisors

Recommendations		Main actions undertaken by the NGFS
1.	Integrating climate-related risks into financial stability monitoring and micro-supervision.	Publication of several deliverables, including (i) various reports on supervisory practices (May 2020, October 2021) and the use of climate scenarios (June 2020, October 2021); and (ii) the NGFS climate scenarios (see NGFS Scenarios Portal).
2.	Integrating sustainability factors into own-portfolio management.	Publication of two reports: *A sustainable and responsible investment guide for central banks' portfolio management* (October 2019) and a *Progress report on the implementation of sustainable and responsible investment practices in central banks' portfolio management* (December 2020).
3.	Bridging the data gaps.	Publication of (i) a *Dashboard on scaling up green finance* (March 2021) and (ii) a *Progress report on bridging data gaps* (May 2021).
4.	Building awareness and intellectual capacity and encouraging technical assistance and knowledge-sharing.	The NGFS is one of the four founding partners of the Climate Training Alliance (CTA), launched in July 2021. Also, the NGFS Secretariat frequently organises internal workshops and outreach sessions with its members. On top of that, NGFS members and the NGFS Secretariat are very active in sharing experiences beyond the NGFS membership, by organising and participating in conferences/events.

Policy makers

Recommendations		Main actions undertaken by the NGFS
5.	Achieving robust and internationally consistent climate and environment-related disclosure.	Although there are many aspects of reporting that fall outside the remit of central banks and supervisors, disclosure of climate and environment-related risk is an instrumental element for better management of these risks and for the scaling up of green finance. Therefore, several NGFS workstreams are working on the topic from various perspectives. For instance, the NGFS published a *Guide on climate-related disclosure for central banks* (December 2021).
6.	Supporting the development of a taxonomy of economic activities.	The NGFS is an observer of the International Platform on Sustainable Finance (IPSF) and of the Platform on Sustainable Finance (PSF).

In November 2021, the NGFS published the *NGFS Glasgow Declaration*, no longer being just a coalition of the willing but also a coalition of the committed.

Source: NGFS Annual Report 2021 - March 2022 https://www.ngfs.net/sites/default/files/medias/documents/ngfs_annual_report_2021.pdf

7.5 CYBER RISK AND THE NATIONAL SIMULATION EXERCISE ON CYBER-SECURITY

"In recent years, it is noticeable the digital transformation process experienced by financial institutions, culminating in the development of financial services, which are increasingly digital. This technological dependency and inter-connection between systems and processes brings vulnerabilities to financial stability, since the risk of failures or cyber-attacks to The processes can have systemic proportions.

This risk is amplified to the extent that some services providers, such as cloud computing and data processing and storage services, become systemically relevant due to the potential concentration on certain companies. A cyber-attack targeted at a provider can affect all financial institutions that use its services. This concern is majorly affected by the fact that the services providers are not subject to financial markets regulation.

Figure: Cyber interconnectedness with the financial system

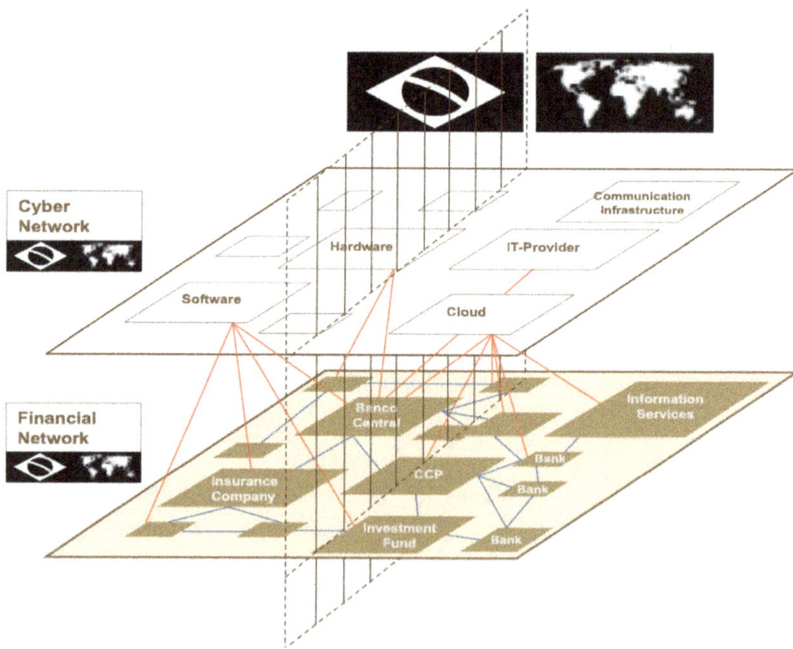

Source: Thilo Liebig, Deutsche Bundesbank, edited by BCB.

The unpredictability, the immediate materialization and the growing complexity of cyber-attacks leverage the concern of regulators from different jurisdictions with cyber risk. Furthermore, as the attacks are not limited to physical borders and economies are increasingly interconnected, it is necessary to enhance articulation among supervisors, both at domestic and international level, aiming at information sharing and the development of joint actions, as well.

In the context of the SFN, issues related to technological risks, including aspects related to information security, have always been part of the BCB agenda[327]. Recently, following the evolution of cyber-attacks, BCB has intensified technical contact with other central banks, for experience exchange on the treatment of cyber threats, and started the exchange of information on threats and cyber-attacks among the SFN entities.

In the regulatory spectrum, issues related to cyber security used to be treated under the operational risk scope. In 2018, CMN and BCB issued regulation[328] with the objective of disciplining the use of important services for the innovation of the SFN technological framework, without despising cybersecurity issues[329]. Institutions are also required to report to BCB information on the contracts related to relevant data processing and storage services, and cloud computing, as well[330]. This information allows BCB to

---

327. In 1996, BCB established a supervisory team specialized on the FI's technological infrastructure supervision, the IT-Systems Auditor Team. Since then, the BCB has continuously developed various initiatives related to cyber security, as a response for the accelerated digital transformation observed in the financial system. The initiatives include the improvement of financial crisis management procedures for dealing with cyber-attacks that could affect the financial system; the review of MoUs established with supervisory entities from other jurisdictions, for the inclusion of specific agreements related to cybersecurity; and the revision of its own supervisory procedures and routines, as well. Since 2001, BCB coordinates the Subgroup for the SFN Security, whose mission is to develop, consolidate and implement security standards for the electronic exchange of information among the SFN entities.

328. Resolution No. 4,658, for financial institutions, and Circular No. 3,909, for payment institutions.

329. Both documents require institutions to implement cyber security policy and to report cyber incidents to the supervisor. They have also established minimum requirements to be followed by regulated institutions, whenever hiring services on data processing and storing, and cloud computing.

330. This includes the identification of where those services are physically located, speci-

map the SFN cloud services network and to identify any existing systemically important dependency on IT services providers." (Source: REF – October/2018 - https://www.bcb.gov.br/en/publications/financialstabilityreport/201810)

In 2018, the National Command for Cyber Defense (ComDCiber) of the Ministry of Defense developed a national simulation exercise on cyber incidents: the Cyber Guardian Exercise.

> "Companies need three pillars to ensure cybersecurity: people, processes and technologies. It's a big challenge, as at the same time we have many technologies being disseminated and transforming the industry, we have a gap of specialized professionals" (Felipe Morgado - SENAI[331])

The exercise consisted of the application of scenarios[332] in a virtual simulator, with the objective of disclosing and disseminating best practices in the treatment of cyber incidents, and tabletop simulations, to train and integrate the high decision level of the participants[333] with the cyber security national entities. Participants[334] were encouraged to act in cooperation and integrated,

---

fying the countries and respective regions of each country.

331. Text extracted from 'Portal da Indústria' webpage: https://imprensa.portaldaindustria.com.br/releases/setores-estrategicos-participam-de-simulacao-para-aprimorar-seguranca-cibernetica-no-pais/.

332. The scenarios comprehended denial-of-service attacks, sabotage, informational leakage, fraudulent modification of systems and web pages, fake news, commitment to integrity of databases, among others.

333. The first exercise comprehended representatives of the following entities: Ministries of Defence, Justice and Foreign Affairs; Presidency Institutional Security Cabinet (GSI); Navy, Army and Air Force; Federal Government agencies; BCB; Banco do Brasil; Caixa; Itaú; Bradesco; [B]3; companies from the nuclear sector; academic community and entities linked to the cyber sector.

334. The teams comprised representatives from different hierarchical levels within each organization: (i) representatives from decision-making staff (Crisis Committee): top managerial level, from the following areas: IT, communication, legal support and senior management. They were responsible for deliberating actions and measures to address the cyber events; (ii) representatives from technical-operational staff: experts from the IT security area, responsible for responding to incidents at the virtual simulator; and (iii) remote support team: experts from IT security and crisis monitoring areas, located at the headquarters of each participant entity, responsible for responding to the demands for information and executing the actions and measures commanded by their respective Crisis Committee.

with efforts focused on preventing and resolving incidents not only regarding direct impacts on its informational assets, but also eventual indirect reputational and/or legal impacts.

BCB's role at the exercise consisted of coordinating the actions and reactions of participants from the financial sector, including the BCB itself, directly impacted by the attacks, as well as taking the appropriate measures to mitigate their effects and contagion to the society and to the financial system.

The exercise happens annually and encompasses more and more participants each year. Since 2021, a public call invites volunteer entities of the private sector to participate[335].

Figure: Evolution of the Cyber Guardian Exercise

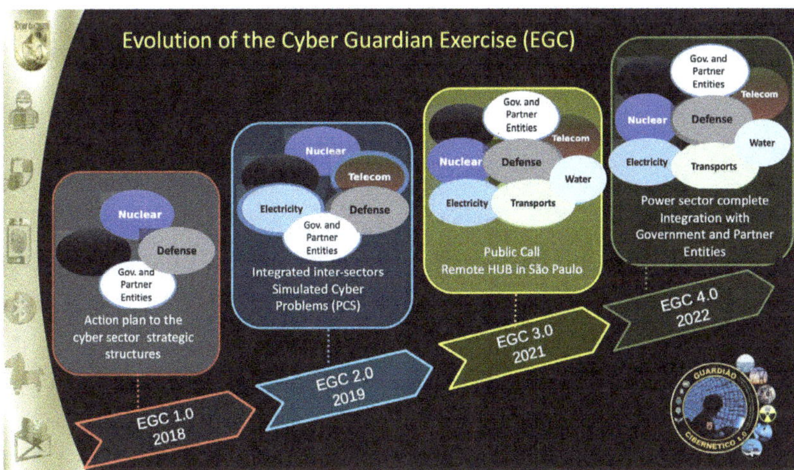

Source:Centro de Estudos Político-Estratégicos da Escola de Guerra Naval (Navy's School of War - Center of Politic and Strategic Studies) - https://www.marinha.mil.br/cepe/sites/www.marinha.mil.br.cepe/files/a_defesa_cibernetica_no_brasil.pdf

---

335. In August/2022, the 4th Cyber Guardian reunited 120 public and private entities in a 4-days simulation exercise and comprehended 450 civil and military participants.

Epilogue

**"The Brazil of the past mirrored itself in
foreign supervisors and followed the steps
of what was being done overseas. Today,
we are much more of a paradigm than
apprentices."**

(Cláudio Mauch)

A well-regulated and well-supervised financial system allows for better levels of capitalization, liquidity and security to stakeholders. The Brazilian supervisory model has raised the reputation of its financial institutions and the financial system as a whole with domestic clients and institutions, as well as with financial systems of other countries.

> "Banks are not interested in an inappropriate functioning of the financial system and lack of discipline. Every banker is very aware that the biggest enemy is the bad banker, the one who operates outside the rules." (Sidney Marques)

The high adaptability of the Brazilian financial system and the framework Monitoring & Supervision based on granular and timely data were not exactly planned. The circumstances of the country led to this. Today, BCB's supervisory model is an asset that allows for very well-supported decision-making in the early stages of a problem. However, all this collective effort cannot be taken as an accomplished task. It is always necessary to continue in the search for improvements for the modernization of the SFN and society welfare. Thus, it is necessary to maintain a regulation that moves forward, a BCB that modernizes itself, with qualified staff, well trained and in sufficient numbers.

All these advances are now materialized in the Agenda BC#[336], a work agenda of the Brazilian Central Bank focused on technological evolution to develop structural issues of the financial system.

Figure: Agenda BC#

INCLUSION: Facilitate the overall access to financial markets

COMPETITIVENESS: Promote the competition within the SFN and the Brazilian Payment System

---

336. In 2016, to promote easy access to financial markets, long-term low interest rates and better financial services in the Brazilian economy, the BCB implemented a strategic work agenda, denominated the Agenda BC+, focused on tackling structural issues of the SFN through fostering technological innovation. In 2019, the Agenda BC# added new dimensions and strengthened the so-called Pillars of the Agenda BC+. In addition to pursuing the reduction of cost of credit, the enhancement of the banking regulation, and the efficiency and the competitiveness of the SFN, the Agenda BC# started to focus on three news dimensions: 'Inclusion', 'Competitiveness', and 'Transparency'.

TRANSPARENCY: Increase the transparency, quality, and flow of information originated from markets and the BCB

EDUCATION: Stimulate savings and the conscious participation in the financial market

SUSTAINABILITY: Promote sustainable finance and contribute to the reduction of socio-environmental and climate-related risks in the economy and in the SFN

Source:Banco Central do Brasil -https://www.bcb.gov.br/en/about/bcbhashtag?modalAberto=about_agenda

> "The Sustainability dimension was included in the Agenda BC# in 2020, reflecting the importance given by the BCB to the topic, within the scope of the financial system. In this context, the work we have carried out in prudential regulation has contributed in several ways not only to improve the management of social, environmental and climate risks by financial institutions, but also to a better alignment between the promotion of financial stability and financial efficiency." (Kathleen Krause)

Each step of its history has contributed to pave a path of efficiency and excellence. Today, BCB supervision is a reference not only for other central banks but also for other regulatory and supervisory entities of the SFN and even outside it. After all, every monitoring and supervision process has structural similarities, regardless of the object being inspected. Information quality, process automation, use of microdata, individual and systemic perspectives, as well as information disclosure are common steps to any well-structured process.

> "Everything I have implemented at the Ministry of Economy to assess state-owned companies is similar to what we have developed at the BCB: segmentation, creation of indicators, processes to improve data quality, individual and aggregate analysis, overview through consolidated data, assessment inspired by the rating/score methodology..." (Elvira Schulz)

Along a 20-year trajectory, BCB supervision has become recognized as an international reference of best practices. Recently, its supervisory model has been qualified as Suptech. But, in fact, it has been a Suptech in process since the beginning of the century, has it not?

> "Suptech is what we do. In fact, what we have always done, we just didn't know it had that name!" (Andre Maurício)

Afterword

When I joined the BCB in 1992, I didn't imagine the great adventure my professional life would become. I initially worked for eight years in the banking operations' area, which later also took on the role of Payment System oversight. There, I discovered my gift for automating working processes through Excel macros, a true revolution for the 1990s. As a result, I have performed Excel training classes for 10 years at BCB, which gave me the nickname 'Paulinha Excel', a title I carry to this day with great pride!

I moved to supervision in 1999, attracted by the 'international area', that is, to work in the division responsible for producing information about branches of Brazilian banks overseas. I was very excited about the idea of working with something that would go beyond our borders.

Unfortunately, my tasks were much more bureaucratic and less interesting than I had imagined, but an unexpected (for me) event was about to change my life forever: the 'mitosis' of the supervision department into on-site and off-site supervision occurred six months after my arrival. Luckily, I was assigned to the off-site area that would develop the first works based on daily databases from trade repositories[337]. A new way of doing supervision was being born and I was there since day 1!

---

337. Selic, Cetip and BM&F. See more details in Chapter 3 - 3.1 The Off-site Supervision Implementation.

The days of boredom were gone! Certainly, nothing would have happened without the engagement and the innovative skills of those involved. In fact, we were irreverent and always complaining about the shortage of all sorts of resources, but deep down, we loved challenges!

The next 19 years of my career were full of transformations, debates, new ideas, some failures and many successes: I have had the chance of actively participating in innovative projects, such as the implementation of the new Brazilian Payment System (SPB), the development of the System for the Monitoring of Liquidity and Market Risks (SMM) and the creation of the Monitored Issues process; I have experienced the dilemmas between on-site and off-site supervisors for the design and implementation of the Monitoring & Supervision model; I have fought the battles for adequate software and hardware to deal with gigantic databases; I have followed the birth of all macro-prudential monitoring processes and I could verify in practice their importance for the management of financial stability by the Central Bank; with great pride, I realized that my past at the banking operations area has contributed to the construction of our unique contagion model, as I was the responsible for establishing the monitoring of the banks' Reserves Accounts and for organizing the payment system databases for supervisory purposes; and, finally, I was able to realize my dream of working beyond the borders, as a representative of the BCB in the BCBS Working Group on Liquidity for 7 years (2009 to 2016), in the elaboration of the Basel III liquidity standards.

I have always believed that great capacities and great opportunities are followed by great responsibilities. That was our case, and we got the job done! Nevertheless, something was missing: we needed to record our history. After all, the past can act as a springboard for new evolutions and help people to avoid recurring errors. Thus, not only our successors in the BCB supervision, but everyone who experiences challenges similar to those we have gone through could in some way benefit from our experience.

This, however, was not the only and perhaps not the main reason that led me to dedicate two-and-a-half years of my life to this project. I was proud of my history, my institution, and my co-workers. I had been part of a unique and important process for the improvement of the Brazilian financial system and for the worldwide recognition of Brazil's technical excellence. It was then up to me (and why not?) to register it. After all, great opportunities bring great responsibilities.

But how could I tell a collective story being just a brick in the wall? I needed to go directly to the source, that is, to the authors of the history. Then, I first invited Gilneu Vivan, my 20-years working partner, to build the structure of the book together. It took us many hours of brainstorms and debates to organize 25 years of history in 7 chapters!

The second step was to conduct interviews with those people who have lived this trajectory with us. Our most optimistic expectation was to get in touch with 15 people, but just when we started the interviews, we could realize the true dimension of the project. What we once thought was a 'crazy idea of two freaks' was greeted by everyone with surprise and admiration. Each interviewee became an ally of the project and provided information, reference material and new contacts for further interviews. Thus, the project grew far beyond our preliminary expectations: by the end of 15 months, 66 people had kindly shared their memories with me, and we had almost 80 hours of recorded video conferences! Many thanks to CEMLA and to Victor Salazar and Ricardo Jiménez who have provided me operational support to perform all interviews.

Well, we definitely needed help to put all that number of testimonials into paper. It was then that we added a phantastic group of collaborators to the project: Clara Rizel, my sisters Iassanã and Patrícia and my husband Weslley helped us transforming all records into 520 pages of interviews. Me and Gilneu are eternally grateful to them for that!

The next step was the most challenging: organizing the material within the themes and then transforming it into a narrative that followed the original plan of the book's structure and held the reader's attention, without losing faithfulness to the testimonials. Gilneu, Clara and Weslley were tirelessly dedicated to revise the various versions that I produced incessantly, until the achievement of a proper text. The comings and goings of this process transformed the first version with a 'technical report' style, according to Gilneu's opinion (he was right!), into this book. How did we get there? The moment I read the same 'technical report' chapter to my daughter Maria Clara (biomedical) and she asked me, really interested: 'So, what happened next?', I realized we had got it. My friends Josiana Aguiar (architect), Rodrigo Lara (FSI) and Cláudio Ferreira (journalist) have also made valuable contributions at this stage. I'm very grateful for that.

Special thanks to the BCB team responsible for responding to citizen demands and to the colleagues who have interrupted their tasks to provide graphs, tables, infographics and information not available on the website, in response to my specific requests. Excellent work! Thanks to you, we could illustrate our history with a wealth of details compatible with its importance.

By September 2022, the manuscript achieved its first full version. It was ready to be translated into English, which took us five months and the help of two specialists, Regina Coeli Machado and Patrícia Stall Cordeiro. Afterwards, Carola Müller (CEMLA) performed the arduous task of revising the book. Her comments and suggestions were so relevant that they were also incorporated in the Portuguese version, such as the Appendix[338]. To all of them, my sincere thanks.

Finally, three curiosities deserve to be highlighted in this trajectory. First, I am a person of an itinerant nature. Traveling around the world is part of my soul. Thus, because the project lasted

---

338. The Appendix provides basic information about the SFN, the Central Bank, and supervision, for readers unfamiliar with the structure of Brazil's financial system.

a considerable time period, it has literally followed my steps, in a total of 41 cities, from 13 countries of 5 continents[339]!

The second, and more exciting, is that I had my computer stolen the day after concluding the revision of this English version. Someone just entered our apartment (in Salvador, Bahia) and stole the computer with the manuscripts!!!! Fortunately, my husband could track its location through the mobile app. The computer had been taken to the outskirts of the city. With the help of armed police officers, they managed to surrender the thief and recover the stolen material on the same day! If today this book is a reality, it is due in part to the insane courage of my husband and the bravery and diligence of Lieutenant Luana, corporal Cândido and soldiers Fredson and Bastos, of the 81st CIPM Itinga from Lauro de Freitas[340]. To all of them, and to the Apple app, our deepest thanks!

After this heroic adventure, me and Gilneu could finally complete the final adjustments and continue the work for the book's publication, with the very valuable sponsorship of IREE[341], in the figure of our dear Marcel Mascarenhas. We thank you from the bottom of our hearts.

The third curiosity? Well, I don't want to look like a doting mom, but the cover art and the cartoon from Chapter 2, which are beautiful, by the way, are authored by my son Arthur[342].

Paulinha Excel

---

339. Belize: Ambergris Caye; Brazil: Brasília, Cabo Frio, Cambuci, Campos dos Goytacazes, Goiânia, Guarapari, Lumiar, Pedra Azul, Rio de Janeiro, Salvador; Cape Verde: Praia; Denmark: Kopenhagen; France: Annecy, Colombier-Saugnieu, Lyon; Germany: Hamburg; Ireland: Dublin, Kilkenny; Italy: Milano, Torino; Mexico: Cancún, Ciudad del México, Isla Mujeres, Playa del Carmen; Portugal: Almada, Lisboa, Paço de Arcos; Spain: Madrid; Sweden: Sölvesborg; United States: Anchorage, Dallas, Denali, Denver, Fargo, Fenix, Hershey, Miami, New York, Portland, Washington.

340. Lieutenant PM Luana Queiroz Braga, corporal PM Cláudio Cândido Bispo dos Santos, soldier PM Fredson Andrade da Silva and soldier PM Paulo Maciel de Melo Bastos.

341. IREE, the Institute for the Reform of State-Business Relations, is an organization whose mission is to promote democratic and pluralistic debate in order to improve the the interaction between the public and private sectors in Brazil. (https://iree.org.br/)

342. Arthur Camanho is graphic designer and illustrator.

The Interviewees

"One swallow does not make a spring."

(Aristotle)

To all interviewed[343] BCB governors, deputy-governors, consultants, Comef secretaries, department heads and deputy heads, data managers, IT specialists, monitoring analysts and supervisors, as well as financial market representatives, our sincere thanks for your time and relevant contribution. You represent the voice of hundreds of people who have worked to change the trajectory of BCB supervision. Looking at history from all your perspectives was a great privilege.

Figure: Historic evolution of Difis infrastructure

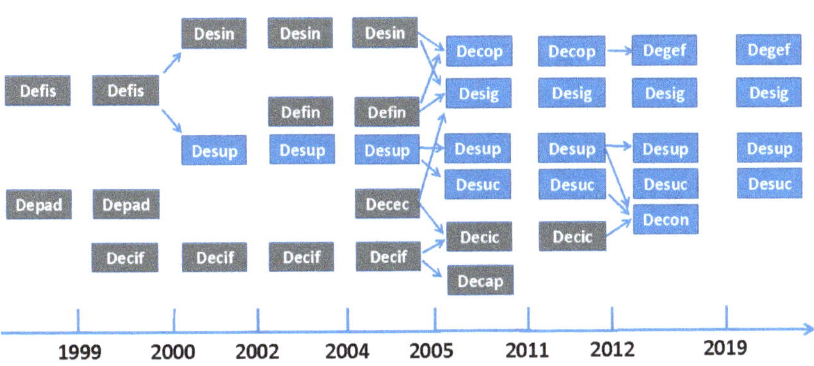

---

343. The information on the current activity developed by the interviewees presented in this book refers to July/2023.

Current Departments:

Decon[344] – Department of Conduct Supervision

Degef – Strategic Management and Specialized Supervision Department

Desig – Financial System Monitoring Department

Desuc – Credit Unions and Non-Banking Financial Institutions Supervision Department

Desup – Banking Supervision Department

Former Departments:

Decap – Department of Control and Analysis of Punitive Administrative Proceedings

Decec – Department of Foreign Capital and Foreign Exchange

Decic – Department for Preventing Illicit Financial Activities and Responding to Demands for Information from the Financial System

Decif – Department for Combating Foreign Exchange and Financial Illicits

Decop – Department of Supervision Management and Planning

Defin – Financial System Information Management Department

Defis – Supervision Department

Depad – Department of Control of Administrative Proceedings and Special Regimes

Desin – Off-site Supervision Department

Source: Banco Central do Brasil

⚘ ADALBERTO FELINTO da Cruz Junior

PhD in Information Science and Master in Administration – Universidade de Brasília (UnB); Graduated in History – Universidade Estadual do Ceará (UECE)

Head of Department - Degef

Adalberto joined the BCB in 2000 and made his career in the Planning area. Although he did not work in supervision, he always kept very close contacts with the people in this area. He took over as head of Degef in 2021.

---

344. Currently, Decon is under the umbrella of the Deputy-Governor for Institutional Relations, Citizenship and Conduct Supervision.

"I feel like I came to supervision at a time when
things are more structured and people more mature."

↗ **ADEMIR Júlio SCHENATTO**

Graduated in Public and Business Administration – Universidade Federal
do Rio Grande do Sul (UFRGS)
Foreign Exchange Director - Banco Topázio S.A.

BCB employee from 1977 to 2015, Ademir has always worked in the foreign exchange area. He joined Decec when the BCB's Foreign Exchange Department was extinct in 2004 and took over as head of the foreign exchange market monitoring team at Desig in 2005, with the extinction of Decec. At Desig, he structured foreign exchange rate's micro and macro prudential monitoring processes.

"Over the years, foreign exchange supervision
took different approaches and the issues related to
conduct has migrated to Decon."

↗ **AILTON de AQUINO Santos**

Postgraduated in International Accounting – Fucape Business School;
Postgraduated in State Law and Constitution – Faculdade Integrada
Planalto Central (FIPLAC); Graduated in Accounting – Universidade do
Estado da Bahia (UNEB) ; Graduated in Law - Centro Universitário do
Distrito Federal (UDF)
Deputy-Governor for Supervision

Ailton joined the BCB in 1998 and has worked in the supervision area for over 15 years , where he held various leadership positions, both at the on-site supervision and monitoring areas. He left supervision to assume as BCB's Chief Auditor. He was named Deputy-Governor for supervision in July/2023.

"The micro and macro monitoring areas must
coexist harmoniously, without supremacy. People
must understand the processes and the importance

of each side. It's important to attach value to the
teams responsible for data management. It's a very
hard and essential work."

⚹ ALEXANDRE Antônio TOMBINI

PhD in Economics – University of Illinois (USA); Graduated in Economics
– Universidade de Brasília (UnB)
Head of the BIS Representation for the Americas

Tombini joined the BCB in 1998. He worked as the consultant of
the Deputy-Governor for Supervision (1998-1999), head of the Research
Department - Depep (1999-2001), senior advisor to the Brazilian board
of directors (2001-2005) and Director of Standards (2006-2011) at the
IMF. In his return to Brazil as the BCB Governor (2011-2016), he created
the Financial Stability Committee (Comef). He has represented Brazil at
the IMF and the World Bank as Alternate Governor of both institutions.
He left BCB in 2016 to take over as Executive Director at the IMF[345] and
leads the BIS Representation for the Americas since 2019.

"Central banks of emerging countries have always
been more concerned about financial stability, due to
the intensity and frequency of the crises faced. Any
macroeconomic policy cannot be sustained within
an environment of financial instability."

⚹ ÁLVARO Lima FREITAS Júnior

Postgraduated in Economics – Universidade federal da Bahia (UFBA);
Postgraduated in Corporate Finance and MBA in Contemporary
Management – Fundação Getúlio Vargas (FGV); MBA in International
Accounting – Universidade de São Paulo (FUCAPE/USP); Graduated in
Business Administration – Universidade Católica de Salvador (UCSAL)
Head of Division - Decon

---

345. Alexandre Tombini was the Executive Director for Brazil, Cabo Verde, Dominican Republic, Ecuador, Guyana, Suriname, Timor-Leste, Trinidad and Tobago at the International Monetary Fund from 2016 to 2019.

Álvaro joined the BCB in 1992 and the supervision area in 1994. He worked at Defis, Desup and Desig prior to joining Decon. At Desig, he developed economic-financial analysis routines and tools for banking institutions' monitoring. He has also coordinated the structuring of the monitoring process of payment institutions, which was the prototype of the Monitored Issues Framework. At Decon, he works in the supervision of AML/CFT.

> "The Monitored Issues Framework is a formalization of what Desig usually does and delivers, but the supervisor needed to understand what we were delivering and if he was 'OK' with it."

⚲ ALVIR Alberto HOFFMANN

MBA in Finance – IBMEC; Postgraduate in Internal and External Auditing - Centro Universitário de Brasília (ICAT/UniCeub); Graduated in Accounting - Universidade Federal do Paraná (UFPR)
Independent Consultant and member of audit committees of publicly traded financial entities

BCB employee from 1978 to 2011, Alvir was the Difis' representative in the working group responsible for the creation of Cosif. Alvir, Tereza Grossi and other colleagues carried out the first inspections of Brazilian banks abroad in the late 1990s, an event considered the trigger for the modernization of supervision in Brazil. In this line, he contributed to the realization of the first IGC and to the proposal of Resolution 2682/1999[346]. He has joined various working groups at BCBS/BIS along his career. He was Deputy-Governor for Supervision from 2007 to 2011, and left BCB to take over at the IMF, where he worked for 3 years.

> "Prior to Cosif, Coban was the financial statement template for commercial banks, Codes, for development banks and there was no standardized template for credit unions."

---

346. This Resolution establishes parameter for credit provisions. See Chapter 1 - 1.5 First steps towards the Supervisory Model modernization.

⚡ **ANDRÉ BARBOSA Costa**

Master in Finance - Fundação Getúlio Vargas (FGV); Postgraduated in Business Administration and Graduated in Advertising - Universidade Presbiteriana Mackenzie; Graduated in Economics – Universidade de São Paulo (USP)
Head of Division - Desig

André joined the BCB in 2006 and, after two years, the supervision area. At Desup, he worked for 3 years in banking supervision. In 2010, he took over in Desig's credit risk monitoring area. Currently, he leads the team responsible for the monitoring of credit borrowers.

> "In the credit risk macro monitoring approach, there is a specific process to assess borrowers, by verifying which peers or portfolios could bring greater risks to the financial system."

⚡ **ANDRÉ Luiz CACCAVO Miguel**

Specialization in Finance and Capital Markets - Universidade Cândido Mendes (UCAM); Graduated in Chemical Engineering - Universidade Federal do Rio de Janeiro (UFRJ)
Deputy Head of Department - Desig

Founding member of monitoring activities, André joined the BCB in 2000 directly at Desin. In the early days of Desin, he consolidated the FI registry database for the monitoring processes, which gave him the nickname 'Capitain Registry'. He has also participated in the development of the 'Analisador' monitoring tool[347]. He has worked in the team for monitoring systemic risk since its formation. In 2015, he took over as Desig's deputy head, responsible for leading macro-prudential monitoring activities.

> "It is very difficult to summarize such a broad subject as financial stability to a few indicators. The Financial Stability Map gives us the 'Big Picture', but

---

347. Chapter 3 – 3.1 The Offsite Supervision Implementation.

we are always looking for new indicators. We have to
be aware of the accumulation of risk. A market may
be doing well, but it may be relaxing controls and
accumulating risk."

⚹ ANDRÉ MAURÍCIO Trindade da Rocha

Specialization in Finance, Financial System, and Investments –
Universidade de Brasília (UnB); Graduated in Chemical Engineering –
Universidade Federal do Rio de Janeiro (UFRJ)
Deputy Head of Department - Desig

André Maurício joined the BCB in 1998, at Defis. He has worked at
Desin and Defin before joining Desig, where he is currently deputy head.
He started his career in the development of monitoring tools. He has had
an important role on the design and implementation of SMM, the system
developed for the monitoring of liquidity and market risks[348]. He led the
team responsible for the monitoring of those risks from 2012 to 2016.

"A tool's flexibility has a cost: you become responsible
for its performance. Ideally, we should leave the
most operational and stable processing steps under
the responsibility of the IT area, as they are better
able to handle that than we do. Processes that allow
for a flexible access to information or to meet more
specific demands should remain under our control."

⚹ ANDREI Cardoso VANDERLEI

PhD in Microelectronics - Université Paris-XI (France); Graduated in
Electrical Engineer – Universidade de Brasília - UnB
Head of Division - Desig

Andrei joined the BCB in 2010, at Desig, more specifically in
the team responsible for monitoring tools' development and database
management. He had an important role in the development of key tools,

---

348. Chapter 3 – 3.1 The Offsite Supervision Implementation.

such as the Monitor and the Calculadora, as well as the Monitored Issues Framework. He has coordinated the project developed to disseminate data science technology to supervision activities. Currently, he leads the IT-Experts team.

> "At least the basic AI concepts should be provided for
> all analysts. They don't need to know how to apply or
> program with machine learning techniques, but they
> need to become able to identify the needs and uses of
> AI in their tasks."

⭷ ANDREIA LAÍS de Melo Silva VARGAS

Postgraduated in Economic Law - Fundação Getúlio Vargas (FGV); Graduated in Civil Engineering Universidade de Brasília (UnB)
Retired since 2022

Andreia joined the BCB in 1991 and Defis in 1999, to work with international issues related to financial institutions. She was consultant of the Deputy-Governor for Supervision from 2010 to 2013, when she was designated to head the newly-created department of conduct supervision (Decon). Andreia headed Decon up to her retirement in 2022.

> "The need for a department of conduct supervision
> was raised in 2008, during the subprime crisis.
> At the heart of that crisis, there was a very large
> consumer relationship issue, because those banks
> offered inappropriate products to a huge range of
> customers."

⭷ ANTHERO de Moraes MEIRELLES

PhD and Master in Administration, Graduated in Communication and in Mathematics - Universidade Federal de Minas Gerais - UFMG
Director of Benefits - Fundação Banco Central de Previdência Privada (Centrus)

A BCB employee since 1994, Anthero was Deputy-Governor for Supervision (2011-2017), Deputy Governor for Regulation (February to April 2015) and Deputy-Governor for Administration (2007-2011) at the BCB's Board. He was vice chairman of the Association of Banking Supervisors of the Americas (ASBA), from 2013 to 2015, and director for the Southern Cone at ASBA, from 2015 to 2017. During his tenure at the supervision area, he created Decon, promoted the integration of supervision departments and implemented the Monitoring&Supervision model.

> "I asked Cofis[349] to design the supervision model we wanted to achieve in the future, our target. Then we would define a strategy to achieve it."

⅄ ARMÍNIO FRAGA Neto

PhD in Economics – Princeton University (USA); Master and Graduated in Economics - Pontifícia Universidade Católica do Rio de Janeiro (PUC-Rio) **Founding Partner - Gávea Investimentos; Board Chairman - IEPS and IMDS[350]; Member - Group of Thirty[351]**

Between July 1991 and November 1992, Armínio was BCB's Deputy-Governor for International Affairs. In March 1999, he returned to BCB as the Governor (1999-2002). During his tenure, he promoted the split of Defis into on-site and off-site supervision

---

349. Cofis is the supervision committee composed of 1 deputy head of each supervision department, which conducts discussions regarding supervision within a strategic perspective. Chapter 2 – 2.4 The strategic area: planning supervision.

350. The Institute of Studies for Health Policies - IEPS (https://ieps.org.br) aims to contribute to the improvement of public health policies in Brazil. The Mobility and Social Development Institute - IMDS (https://imdsbrasil.org) is a platform to outline, test, propose, disseminate and monitor the implementation of public policies with an impact on social mobility. Both institutes are non-profit, non-partisan and independent.

351. The Group of Thirty, established in 1978, is an independent global body of economic and financial leaders from the public and private sectors and academia. It aims to deepen understanding of global economic and financial issues, and to explore the international repercussions of decisions taken in the public and private sectors. The Group is characterized by the extensive experience of its members and open-minded, forward thinking. (https://www.group30.org).

departments (Desup and Desin), as well as the publication of the first Financial Stability Report.

> "All those works done by supervision I would classify
> as being the product of a correct and competent
> institution. I make a point of mentioning it."

⩘ BELLINE SANTANA

Graduated in Economics – Universidade São Judas Tadeu (USJT)
Head of Department - Desup

Belline joined the BCB in 1997 at Defis and, after its split, he was allocated in Desup. In the creation of the specialized teams, he joined the off-site analysis team, which evolved to internal controls analysis along the time. He participated in the implementation of supervisory procedures for the analysis of banks' internal controls and operational risk. At Desup, Bellin was Banco do Brasil supervisor, top supervision manager for large banks and, currently, is the head of department. He has also worked as Degef's consultant, for the implementation of the department's strategic vision.

> "All the challenges we went through brought us very
> positive results. We keep evolving towards efficiency
> and excellence, and we continue to be highly
> respected and very robust. I am very proud of that."

⩘ CAIO Fonseca FERREIRA

PhD in Economics, Master in Finance and Graduated in Chemical Engineering – Universidade de São Paulo (USP)
Deputy Division Chief at the Global Markets Analysis Division of the Monetary and Capital Markets Department – IMF

BCB employee from 1998 to 2015. In supervision, Caio worked at Decif and Desup. He was the head of the Prudential and Foreign Exchange Regulation Department (Dereg), where he was responsible for macro and micro prudential regulation and coordinated, among other projects, the implementation of Basel III standards in Brazil. Basel Committee member between 2011 and 2014: Task Force on Standardized Approaches (TFSA) co-chair for two years, and PDG member between 2009 and 2011. He left BCB in 2015 to join the IMF.

> "The 'Basel Project'[352] was important to strengthen
> the dialogue between regulation and supervision,
> and between the BCB and banks' associations as well,
> mainly with Febraban[353]."

⚡ CARINE Moreira de Almeida BASTOS

Master and Graduated in Business Administration - Fundação Getúlio Vargas (EAESP/FGV)
Advisor - Degef

Carine joined the BCB in 2010 as a planning and management analyst at Desig. She participated in the task force for mapping the value chain of the supervision area, as well as in the analysis of its working processes. She has been working at Degef since 2017, where she currently coordinates the RTECs' working processes[354]. She is also Team Leader of the NGFS Progress Report Group[355].

> "The RTECs aim to give equal voice to supervision
> departments. Besides, everything that is discussed
> through an RTEC, comes from the departments'
> focal points, copied to their respective deputy heads.
> Therefore, it does not matter who has produced the
> information, formally, it is the department's opinion,
> not the analyst's."

---

352. The Basel Project was conducted by the BCB with the objective of implementing international financial regulatory and supervisory standards in Brazil. It has encompassed the implementation of Basel I, II and III accords.

353. The Brazilian Federation of Banks – Febraban (*Federação Brasileira de Bancos*) is the main bank association entity in Brazil. Currently, it is composed of 119 associated financial institutions (https://www.febraban.org.br).

354. Chapter 2 - 2.4 The strategic area: planning supervision.

355. Chapter 7 - 7.4 Challenges of a Global Environment.

⚲ Carlos **DONIZETI** Macedo **MAIA**

PhD in Politics and Master in Economics - Pontifícia Universidade Católica de São Paulo (PUC-SP); MBA in Controllership and Graduation in Economics and Law – Universidade de São Paulo (USP)
Advisor certified by the Brazilian Institute of Corporate Governance (IBGC)

A BCB employee from 1977 to 2012, Donizeti was the Deputy-Governor for supervision's consultant from 2009 to 2010 and head of Desup from 2010 to 2012. He represented BCB in FSB and BCBS groups.

> "The Central Bank has an extremely robust system to address financial institutions, with an equally robust supervision manual."

⚲ **CLARA** Medeiros **RIZEL** Santana

Graduated in Civil Engineering – Universidade de Brasília – UnB
Retired since 2018

BCB employee from 1994 to 2018, Clara joined supervision when BCB's information management activities were transferred to the supervision area[356]. She joined Desig in 2007, always working with information management. Clara has collaborated intensively for the production of this book, both with the transcription of many interviews, as well as the revision of various versions of the manuscript.

> "When we moved to the supervision area, we started to have a greater contact with information users. We both have profited from the new framework, because they also had no close contact with the information management area."

---

356. Chapter 4 - 4.1 Trajectory of Information Management at the BCB.

⚘ CLÁUDIO Ness MAUCH

Graduated in Accounting – Universidade Católica de Pelotas (UCPEL)
Partner - Quantum Consultoria LTDA

A BCB employee from 1976 to 1999, Mauch began his career as an auditor, working in banking supervision. He joined the BCB Board in 1993 as Deputy-Governor for Regulation (1993-1996). He had an important role in the implementation of the Real Plan[357]. The supervision modernization process began during his term as Deputy-Governor for Supervision (1995-1999), with the creation of the supervision model based on IGCs.

> "The supervisor's purpose is to maintain the
> soundness of the financial system and, for that,
> all risks must be identified, priced and covered
> by capital, reserves requirements or provision,
> according to the nature of each one of them."

⚘ CLEYSSON Ribeiro VIEIRA

Master in Economics – Universidade Católica de Brasília (UCB); Graduated
in Business Administration – Universidade de Brasília (UnB)
Senior Advisor - Desig

Cleysson joined the BCB in 2014 at Desig's liquidity risk monitoring team. In 2015, he became the team's head. From 2017 to 2020 he was the Brazilian representative in the BCBS Working Group on Liquidity (WGL). Since April 2020 he is Senior Advisor at Desig's head office. He has actively participated in the implementation of NSFR[358] regulation and monitoring process. As senior advisor, he coordinates the consolidation of Monitored Issues Framework as the monitoring process of the Monitoring&Supervision model.

> "When I joined the BCB, I joked that the supervisor
> knew more about the risk of financial institutions

---

357. Chapter 1 - 1.1 Introduction.
358. The Net Stable Funding Ratio (NSFR) is a Basel III Liquidity minimum standard. (https://www.bis.org/bcbs/publ/d295.pdf)

than they did themselves. No wonder the BCB is
always well recognized by international assessments.
However, the environment and risks are changeable,
which makes preserving financial stability a never-
ending process."

⚹ EDSON Broxado de França TEIXEIRA

MBA in Finance - IBMEC; Specialization in Economics [Minerva Program] - George Washington University (USA); Master and Graduated in Electrical Engineering - Universidade Federal do Rio de Janeiro (UFRJ); Graduated in Law – Universidade Estadual do Rio de Janeiro (UERJ)
Supervision's Chief of Staff - BCB's Board

Edson joined the BCB in 1994 in the foreign exchange area and was transferred to supervision in 2007, when Desig incorporated FX market monitoring routines. He was Head of the Securities and Derivatives Market Monitoring Division (Dimot) and Deputy Head of Deparment from 2014 to 2018. At Dimot, he implemented monitoring processes of funding instruments and derivatives market. He has also coordinated the working group that extinguished the collection of fines for delay in reporting information to the BCB by the supervised entities[359].

"The problem we really wanted to solve by charging
fines, i.e., to have timely and quality information,
was not solved with that approach, because it was
cheaper for the institution to pay fines than to invest
in a process to improve data quality."

⚹ ELVIRA Mariane SCHULZ

Master in Auditing and Business Management (in course) - Universidad Europea Del Atlántico (Spain); Postgraduate in Accounting and Auditing – Universidade de Brasília (UnB); Postgraduated in Total Quality and Reengineering – Unopar; Postgraduated in International Accounting

---

359. Chapter 4 - 4.2 Fines, a bad strategy to ensure data quality.

- Fucape/Fipecafi; Graduated in Business Administration – Universidade Estadual de Londrina – UEL; Graduated in Mathematics – Cesulon
Investment Risk Coordinator - Funpresp-Exe

A BCB employee from 1998 to 2013, Elvira joined supervision at its regional office in Curitiba/PR and moved to Brasília in 2000, to join the offsite supervision teams. She was involved in the creation of the Analisador[360] and the methodology for banks' segmentation. At Desig, she was head of the Liquidity and Market Risk Monitoring Division (Dirim), where she worked in the development of monitoring processes to identify off-price operations in the government securities market and to check compliance of funding and liquid assets portfolios[361]. As the head of the Access Control and Information Disclosure Division (Diadi), she worked on the implementation of the methodology for controlling data collection that replaced the fines' application routines[362]. She left the BCB in 2013 to take over at the Ministry of Economy.

"To convince the heads of monitoring teams on the importance of data quality, I decided to use a 'gastronomic' example. I said: 'I have a fully equipped kitchen, I have a chef all to myself and I want to bake a cake. If the egg is spoiled, the cake is spoiled. The same occurs to data quality: bad data breeds bad products, and credibility is lost'. Everyone got it!"

⚡ ENRICO Bezerra Ximenes de VASCONCELOS

PhD and Master in Economics - Fundação Getúlio Vargas (EPGE/FGV); Graduated in Computer Science – Universidade da Bahia (UFBA)
Head of Department - Secretariat of Governance, Coordination and Strategic Monitoring (Segov)

Enrico joined BCB in 2000, at Desup. He worked as BCB Governor's advisor before taking over the Comef secretariat in 2017. At

---

360. Chapter 3 – 3.1 The Offsite Supervision Implementation.
361. The methodology consisted of cross checking the balances of certificates of deposits and federal government securities reported in the financial statements, with data from the trade repositories.
362. Chapter 4 - 4.2 Fines, a bad strategy to ensure data quality.

Comef, he promoted the integration of the areas involved with financial stability to support Comef's activities; worked to include topics related to the efficiency of the financial system on the agenda; and implemented relevant developments in the transparency of the BCB's activities with regard to financial stability, such as the regular publication of the Comef Minutes and the process of timely communication to the comptroller body (TCU) regarding the measures taken to mitigate crisis effects[363].

> "It's important to communicate. We already have a
> forward looking approach. We are now going to put
> the Comef minutes on the internet with the BCB's
> opinion of the financial system's dynamics and the
> points that deserve the financial market participants'
> attention."

⚲ EVERTON Pinheiro de Souza GONÇALVES

PhD and Master in Business Economics and Graduated in Business Administration - Fundação Getúlio Vargas (FGV/SP); Graduated in Mechanical Engineering - Escola de Engenharia Mauá (EEM)
Chief Economic and Commissions Advisor - ABBC[364]

Everton joined ABBC at the time of the discussions with the BCB for the implementation of the three pillars of Basel II. Since then, he has represented his bank association in discussions with the BCB for prudential regulation purposes and other topics of interest to ABBC.

> "In recent years, the Central Bank has aimed to
> provide conditions for an improvement in banking
> competition. Those are important issues for ABBC,
> as well as the search for greater efficiency, asymmetry
> reduction and market opportunities. Discussions
> with the Central Bank are very intense."

---

363. Chapter 6 - 6.5 Financial Stability Committee – Comef.
364. ABBC – Brazilian Association of Banks (*Associação Brasileira de Bancos*).

⚹ FÁBIO LACERDA

Master in Business Administration - Fundação Getúlio Vargas (EAESP/ FGV); Master in Business Economics[365] – Universidade de São Paulo (FEA/ USP); Graduated in Economics - Universidade Federal do Ceará (UFC)
Head of Division - Department of Resolution and Sanctioning Action (Derad)

A BCB employee since 1994, Fábio has joined supervision at its regional office in Fortaleza/CE and moved to São Paulo in 1997. He has been deputy head at Desig and Desup. At Derad, he works in the elaboration of resolution plans for the five largest banks.

"'Wearing another hat' now, I experience a complementary dimension of relevance and integration with supervision. A process of partnership and approximation with Desig is being built, with adjustments of tools for resolution planning. Our goal is to implement a reverse stress test, a type of approach not considered by financial stability."

⚹ FREDERICO TORRES de Souza

Master in Finance - Purdue University (USA); Graduated in Economics - Universidade Federal de Minas Gerais (UFMG)
Head of Division - Desig

Frederico joined the BCB in 1994, at Defis. He was a 'founding member' of monitoring activities. In 2003, he took over the coordination of REF elaboration, as well as the Desig's presentations to the Collegiate Board of Directors, which, as of 2011, started to be presented at Comef. He has also led the team responsible for implementing shadow banking monitoring.

"When we participated in the project supported by the British Embassy that organized visits to

---

365. Specialist in Economics of the Banking Sector.

the BoE[366], we brought several proposals for
improvement that we have actually implemented,
such as the Comef Minutes, the Coremec[367], the
permanent list of risks to financial stability, and the
financial stability survey."

∕ GABRIELA Gouveia Guedes Loureiro RUBERG

PhD and Master in Systems Engineering and Computers - Universidade Federal do Rio de Janeiro (COPPE/UFRJ); Graduated in Computer Science - Universidade Federal da Paraíba (UFPB)
Analyst - Information Technology Department (Deinf)

Gabriela joined BCB in 2000, at the Open Market Operations Department (Demab) and moved to Deinf in 2008. She has led the design and implementation of BCB's internationally awarded information governance framework[368].

"We can say that we are information vectors, like
the development of the PIER platform[369], which
integrates the regulators of the Financial System
and allows the exchange of information in a
decentralized and completely secure environment,
thus inspiring the European Central Bank."

---

366. Bank of England.
367. The Committee for Regulation and Supervision of Financial, Capital, Insurance, Pension and Capitalization Markets (COREMEC) aims to promote the stability of the National Financial System, through the articulation of the federal bodies responsible for regulating and supervising those segments. More information regarding Coremec's role at: https://www.bcb.gov.br/conteudo/eventos/Documents/Seminarios-Riscos-Estabilidade-Financeira-Economia-Bancaria/2017_XIISemRiscosBCB/Apresentação_Enrico.pdf
368. Chapter 4 - 4.1 Trajectory of Information Management at the BCB.
369. PIER (*Plataforma Integradora de Entidades Regulatórias*) is a blockchain platform for information exchange among Brazilian regulatory authorities. https://www.bcb.gov.br/en/pressdetail/2249/nota.

⚡ GETÚLIO Ribeiro FIALHO

Graduated in Electronic Engineering - Universidade Federal do Pará (UFPA)
Analyst - Desig

Getúlio joined the BCB in 1994, at the supervision regional office in Belém/PA. In 2000, he was transferred to Desup in São Paulo, to work in the ALM[370] specialized team, at the IGCs. In 2004, he moved to Brasília, to be part of the team responsible for the development of the SMM[371]. He was responsible for building up the system's market risk monitoring module, designing the Market Risk Report[372] (DRM) template, and implementing the market risk monitoring process.

> "In 2004, Gilneu was working on a market risk
> reporting template for his master's degree. DRM
> was inspired by that template. And based on DRM
> data, we've developed the market risk monitoring
> routines."

⚡ GILBERTO Hanssen ANDROVANDI

Master in Economics - Universidade Católica de Brasília (UCB); Specialization in Derivatives – Instituto BM&F; Specialization in Climate Risks and Sustainable Finance - University of London (England); Graduated in Computer Science - Pontifícia Universidade Católica do Rio Grande do Sul (PUCRS)
Team Coordinator - Desig

Gilberto joined BCB in 2002, at the Information Technology Department (Deinf). In 2008, he joined Desig's liquidity risk monitoring team. He has had an important role in the SMM implementation process, in monitoring liquidity risk of banks most impacted by the GFC, and in the development of plans to monitor financial crises, among others. He currently coordinates the team responsible for liquidity monitoring of

---

370. Assets and Liabilities Management.
371. Chapter 3 - 3.1 The Offsite Supervision Implementation.
372. Chapter 3 - 3.2 Monitoring & Supervision Model – a new perspective for the micro prudential teams.

non-banking institutions, and represents the BCB in the BCBS Liquidity Group (LIQ).

> "The liquidity monitoring process for credit unions and other non-banking institutions[373], such as financial companies, was improved in 2020, as it has incorporated the daily information available at SMM."

⚡ GILNEU Francisco Astolfi VIVAN (Author)

Master in Economics - Universidade de Brasília (UnB); Graduated in Economics - Universidade Federal do Rio Grande do Sul (UFRGS)
Head of Department - Desig

Gilneu joined BCB in 1994, at the supervision regional office in Porto Alegre/RS, and moved to Brasília in 1999, to help develop the use of microdata in the supervision process. He has headed Desig since 2013. He is one of the developers of the BCB's liquidity risk monitoring model, which gave rise to the SMM[374]. He has actively participated in all stages of the design and implementation of the BCB's micro and macro prudential monitoring processes.

> "Our monitoring approach was born with the use of microdata. What we did along the time was to develop ourselves within that process."

⚡ GIOVANI Antônio Silva BRITO

PhD and Master in Accounting - Universidade de São Paulo (FEA/USP); Graduated in Accounting and Postgraduate in Risk Management - Fipecafi
Head of Division - Desig

---

373. Chapter 3 - 3.2 Monitoring & Supervision Model – a new perspective for the micro prudential teams.
374. Chapter 3 - 3.1 The Offsite Supervision Implementation.

Giovani joined the BCB in 2000. He has always worked in the credit risk area, both at Desup (2000-2005) and Desig (from 2005 onwards). He currently leads the team responsible for credit risk monitoring at the micro prudential perspective, Dimic.

> "When I took over Dimic, my main mission was to
> implement the credit risk micro monitoring routines
> in line with the Monitored Issues methodology.
> We currently have almost thirty Monitored Issues
> already in place and a long waiting list..."

↗ GUSTAVO Martins dos SANTOS

Specialization in Financial Market and Investments and Graduated in Business Administration - Universidade de Brasília (UnB)
Deputy Head of Department - Desup

Gustavo joined the BCB in 2007, at Desuc, where he participated in activities related to the analysis of regulatory proposals and technical consultancy to inspectors and to the head of department. He moved to Desig in 2015, as the deputy head responsible to lead the monitoring of non-banking financial institutions. Currently, he is deputy head at Desup, and leads the on-site supervision teams of banking entities, especially those with public control.

> "In the beginning, Desig had one single monitoring
> team to monitor all non-banking institutions. Now,
> banking and non-banking monitoring processes
> are converging. For example, the credit risk micro
> prudential monitoring team has incorporated the
> non-bank financial institutions to its routines, and so
> for the other monitoring teams as well."

↗ HAROLD Paquete ESPÍNOLA Filho

Specialization in Business Administration – INPG Business School; Graduated in Mechanical Engineering – Universidade de Taubaté (Unitau)
Head of the Department – Desuc

Harold joined the BCB in 1998. He has worked as chief of staff for the Deputy-Governor for Supervision, head of department at Decop, deputy head and consultant at Desig, and, currently, he is the head of Desuc. At Desuc, he led the modernization of the supervision processes for credit unions and non-banking financial institutions.

> "We need to continually improve our supervision model. Every year the non-banking supervision framework is adjusted towards specialization."

↗ HAROLDO Jayme Martins Froés CRUZ

Specialization in Systems Analysis - Pontifícia Universidade Católica do Rio de Janeiro (PUC-Rio); Graduated in Mathematics - Universidade Estadual do Rio de Janeiro (UERJ)
Head of Department - Information Technology Department (Deinf)

Haroldo joined the BCB in 1992, at Deinf. He has worked as systems developer, project manager and team manager. In 2009, he joined Deinf's strategic team, as Deputy Head for IT solutions development. Since 2019, he has been acting as the head of department.

> "Desig has always been a differentiated department, with specific demands. We need to create specific technology niches for areas like that, because they demand more technology than just a more powerful workstation."

↗ HELTON MACIEL Fernandes de Paula

MBA in Accounting and Auditing - Universidade de Brasília (UnB); Specialization in Information Technology Analysis - Companhia de Processamento de Dados do Estado de Minas Gerais (PRODEMGE);

Graduated in Civil Engineering - Universidade Federal de Minas Gerais (UFMG)
Team Coordinator - Desig

Helton joined the BCB in 2000, at Desin. 'Founding member' of monitoring activities, he has always worked with the development of monitoring tools. He was one of the developers of the Analisador[375] and was responsible for creating the CRD and the Monitored Quality Issues process[376].

> "When people perceive a data problem, instead of living with it or creating subterfuges, as they used to do, they come after us, the quality team. We can solve the problem at its source, so that it will never occur to that institution or to any other reporting institution anymore. We are making strong progress with this new approach. It's a hard work, we have lots of meetings with users, but all that amuses me."

⁄ HENRIQUE de Campos MEIRELLES

MBA in Business Administration - Universidade Federal do Rio de Janeiro – (COPPEAD/UFRJ); Graduated in Civil Engineering - Universidade de São Paulo (Escola Politécnica/USP)
State Government Secretary - São Paulo

BCB Governor from 2003 to 2010. During his term, Henrique Meirelles raised the level of Brazil's international reserves and led the BCB's actions to face the GFC and its rapid recovery[377].

> "When I joined the BCB, Brazil had around 20 billion dollars in international reserves. We entered into a process of accumulating reserves and, when I left, we were close to 300 billion dollars."

---

375. Chapter 3 – 3.1 The Offsite Supervision Implementation.
376. Chapter 4 - 4.6 The incorporation of data quality in the Monitored Issues Framework.
377. Chapter 6 - 6.1 The Global Financial Crisis.

✶ ILAN GOLDFAJN

PhD in Economics - Massachusetts Institute of Technology (MIT - USA); Master in Economics - Pontifícia Universidade Católica do Rio de Janeiro (PUC-Rio); Graduated in Economics - Universidade Federal do Rio de Janeiro (UFRJ)

Governor – Inter-American Development Bank (IDB)

From 2000 to 2003, Ilan was the BCB's Deputy-Governor for Economic Policy. In June 2016, he returned as the BCB Governor (2016-2019). During his tenure at the economic policy area, he promoted the creation of the Financial Stability Report (REF). As Governor, he improved the dynamics of Comef, as well its alignment with REF, which transformed the report into the main vehicle to disclose to society BCB's activities related to financial stability.

> "What is the advantage of presenting Comef's information in the REF? The whole society can understand systemic risk and follow how far we are progressing to mitigate it."

✶ IRANY de Oliveira SANT'ANNA Junior

Graduated in Economics - Universidade Federal do Rio Grande do Sul (UFRGS)

Vice-President and Management Counselor - Banco do Estado do Rio Grande do Sul (Banrisul)

A BCB employee from 1994 to 2015, Irany has always worked in banking supervision: initially at Defis and after the split, at Desup. During his career at the BCB, he assumed the roles of inspector, supervisor, technical manager for supervision of banking institutions of the Brazilian southern region and, finally, Desup's deputy head (2013-2015).

> "At the time of Desin creation there were several moments of conflict with Desup due to excessive warnings, many of them not relevant. Over time, the process has improved."

⚡ ISMÁRIA de Almeida MIRANDA

MBA in Contemporary Management Fundação Getúlio Vargas (FGV); Graduated in Economics - Universidade Católica de Goiás (PUC-Goiás)
Retired since 2019

Ismária joined the BCB in 1992, at the Department of Economics (Depec). She has also worked at Defis and Desup (1994 to 2008), the Financial System organization Department - Deorf (2008-2012) and the Resolution Department - Deres (2012-2019), where she has finished her career as deputy head. During her tenure as supervisor, she had the opportunity to experience the transformations for the modernization of supervision, such as the arrival of notebooks and ACL, the IGCs, and the creation of electronic working papers[378]. She has also actively participated in the structuring of routines for the supervision of rural credit operations.

> "In 2003, supervision created a special team to address the banks' rural credit portfolio, due to its particular characteristics and regulations. This task was assigned to us, and we have conducted it until the creation of Derop[379] in 2008."

⚡ JOÃO ANDRÉ CALVINO Marques Pereira

PhD and Master in Finance - Fundação Getúlio Vargas (FGV); Graduated in Mechanical Engineering - Universidade de Brasília (UnB)

Head of Department – Financial System Regulation Department (Denor)

João André joined BCB in 2008 at Denor, and moved to supervision in 2012, as Deputy Head of Desig, responsible for leading the macro prudential monitoring teams. During the GFC, he has actively participated in identifying SFN's exposure to exotic derivatives. At Desig, he has promoted the structuring of macro prudential monitoring processes and the alignment of routines with the agendas of Comef and

---

378. Templates used by supervisors to conduct onsite inspection works.
379. Department of Regulation, Supervision and Control of Rural Credit and Proagro Operations.

REF. He has also had an important role in the development of the BCB's contagion analysis model[380].

> "Detailed and accurate information in all dimensions
> is extremely relevant both for the micro and macro
> prudential tasks. If the two monitoring processes
> disconnect from each other, macro monitoring risks
> to lose contact with the ground, which may affect its
> analysis capacity."

⚡ JORGE PAULINO Junior

MBA in International Accounting - Fundação Instituto Capixaba de Pesquisas em Contabilidade, Economia e Finanças (FUCAPE), in partnership with Fundação Instituto de Pesquisas Contábeis, Atuariais e Financeiras (FIPECAFI); Specialization in Systems Analysis - CTIS Informática e Sistemas Ltda; Graduated in Economics - Centro de Ensino Unificado de Brasília (Uniceub)

Team Coordinator - Desig

Paulino joined the BCB in 2000, at Desup, and soon moved to Desin's credit risk monitoring area, where he participated in the creation of the SCR. Afterwards, he moved to the area responsible for administrative proceedings and application of penalties. Since 2010, he has worked at the technical consulting team of Desig, providing technical advice to the department's head, mainly regarding regulation design and issuance.

> "We participate a lot in the discussions led by
> Denor and Dereg[381] on the issuance of financial
> regulation, considering that most of them involve the
> area of supervision and generally impact Desig, as
> responsible for collecting data to assess compliance."

---

380. Chapter 6 - 6.3 The evolution of macro monitoring processes.
381. Financial System Regulation Department (Denor) and Prudential and Foreign Exchange Regulation Department (Dereg).

⚡ JOSÉ LUIZ LOEBENS

Specialization in Financial System Regulation - Pontifícia Universidade Católica do Rio Grande do Sul (PUCRS); Graduated in Physical Education and in Agronomic Engineering - Universidade Federal do Rio Grande do Sul (UFRGS)

Analyst - Department of Regulation, Supervision and Control of Rural Credit and Proagro Operations - Derop

José Luiz joined the BCB in 2000, at Desin. He has also worked at Decif and Decic (2003-2007), Desup (2007-2015;) and Desig (2015-2021), always in activities related to the supervision of foreign exchange market and AML/CFT issues. At Desig, he led the foreign exchange risk monitoring team from 2015 to 2021, where he coordinated the creation and implementation of a risk matrix for the assessment of foreign exchange operations.

"We used to report suspicious transactions and those out of standards to Desig's office and Decon. However, it was a non-systematized process, with specific actions of limited scope. In 2015, we carried out a series of works with a more global perspective, cross-referencing and considering a range of indicators. This work gave rise to the Risk Matrix for Foreign Exchange Operations, which is available to Decon, Desup and Desuc. Now, the supervisor can look at the information in a vertical and/or horizontal analysis, thus gathering all the evidence."

⚡ José REYNALDO de Almeida FURLANI

Master in Accounting - Multi Institutional and Interregional Postgraduation Program at the following universities: Universidade de Brasília (UnB), Universidade Federal da Paraíba (UFPB), Universidade Federal de Pernambuco (UFPE) and Universidade Federal do Rio Grande do Norte (UFRN); Specialization in Financial Administration - Fundação Getúlio Vargas (FGV/DF); Graduated in Accounting - Universidade de Brasília (UnB)

Director of Licensing - Superintendência Nacional de Previdência Complementar (PREVIC)

BCB employee from 1992 to 2021 and 'founding member' of Desin, Reynaldo worked in the areas of regulation, including rural credit and Proagro, authorizations, monitoring, supervision, information management and resolution. He was deputy head of Desig (2009-2013), when he promoted the restructuring of the information management area[382]. After leaving supervision, he headed the Department of Extrajudicial Liquidations (Deliq), was chief of staff of the Deputy-Governor for Licensing and Resolution, and headed the Financial System Organization Department (Deorf).

> "Desig should not take care of all the information reported to BCB, but only of those used for monitoring purposes. The others should be transferred to the areas that really used them, together with the respective teams responsible for collecting them."

↗ KATHLEEN KRAUSE

Master in Economic Business Administration/Economics - Universidade de Brasília (UnB); MBA in Finance - Instituto Superior de Pós Graduação do Paraná; Graduated in Statistics - Universidade Federal do Paraná (UFPR)

Deputy Head of Department - Prudential and Foreign Exchange Regulation Department (Dereg)

Kathleen joined the BCB in 1998, at the supervision regional office in Curitiba/PR. In the split of Defis, she was allocated in Desup, but worked together with the Desin team responsible for the creation of the first credit risk register, the CRC[383]. She was the CRC's project manager. In 2002, she moved to the regulation area, where she has worked since then in the implementation of Basel standards in Brazil.

---

382. Chapter 4 - 4.1 Trajectory of Information Management at the BCB.
383. Chapter 1 - 1.6 The use of granular data.

> "The interaction between regulation and supervision
> areas went through a long and gradual trajectory
> until it reached the partnership that exists today.
> The gain in quality is unquestionable when the work
> has the active participation of those involved and
> impacted. With great satisfaction, we have seen that
> the regulatory construction process has become
> increasingly transparent and enriched."

⤴ LUCIO Rodrigues CAPELLETTO

PhD in Accounting - Universidade of São Paulo (FEA/USP); Master in Business Administration - Universidade of Brasília (UnB); Specialist in Banking and Financial Law - Boston University (USA); Specialist in Public Policies and Government Management - Escola Nacional de Administração Pública (ENAP); Graduated in Accounting and in Business Administration - Universidade Federal do Rio Grande do Sul (UFRGS)
Executive Secretary - Ministry of Labor and Welfare

A BCB employee from 1992 to 2017, Lúcio was at first allocated in Defis and joined Desin after its split. He has headed Desig (2011-2013) and Desup (2013-2015). He has also been the Executive Secretary of Comef (2015-2017) and consultant to the Board. The indicators created to monitor the economic-financial situation of financial institutions[384] were based on his master paper[385], and his PhD thesis[386] has inspired the implementation of methodologies for monitoring systemic risk[387].

> "In 2011, BCB had to address banks with liquidity
> problems. The liquidity risk area was responsible
> to monitor the effectiveness of the measures, which
> were reported to the Board every Friday."

---

384. Chapter 3 - 3.1 The Offsite Supervision Implementation.
385. "Contribution to the evaluation of the operational performance of banks, before and after the Real Plan" - 1995.
386. "Measuring Systemic Risk in the Banking Sector Using Economic Accounting Variables" - 2006. (https://www.teses.usp.br/teses/disponiveis/12/12136/tde-25112006-074910/ publico/LucioCapelleto.pdf)
387. Chapter 6 - 6.3 The evolution of macro monitoring processes.

⚲ MARCELO BICALHO Viturino de Araújo

Master in Controllership and Accounting - Universidade de São Paulo (FEA/USP); Postgraduate in Banking Finance - Pontifícia Universidade Católica de Minas Gerais (PUC-Minas); Graduated in Business Administration and Accounting - Universidade Federal de Minas Gerais (FACE/UFMG)
Head of Division - Desig

Marcelo joined the BCB in 2000, at Desup. He has worked at the Financial System Organization Department (Deorf) from 2003 to 2009, and works at Desig since 2013. Initially, he was part of the macro prudential monitoring team and dealt with liquidity monitoring of the banking system. He joined the economic-financial monitoring team in 2015. Currently, he is the team's head.

"In my opinion, to develop new areas, methodologies
and processes we have to go through a certain
amount of disorder, let the creation process flow,
and, afterwards, organize it. When everything always
goes right, without running any risk of inefficiency,
you end up staying in the same place, doing the same
thing."

⚲ MARCELO do Carmo FERNANDES

Specialization in Finance Strategic Management - Universidade Federal de Minas Gerais (UFMG); Graduated in Business Administration – Faculdade Newton Paiva
Head of Division - Desig

Marcelo joined the BCB in 1998 at Defis and was allocated in Desin after its split. 'Founding member' of the monitoring area, he had worked with liquidity and market risks monitoring, economic and financial analysis of the banking and non-banking financial institutions, macro prudential monitoring, data management, and development of methodologies to prevent money laundering . He was one of the creators of the liquidity risk monitoring model, which gave rise to the SMM[388].

---

388. Chapter 3 - 3.1 The Offsite Supervision Implementation.

> "What has changed from 1998 to today? Well,
> we didn't have the capacity to store data, now, we
> got it. We've learned to process data, integrate
> data, and give quality to data. On-site supervision
> is increasingly focused on understanding the
> institution's business, which makes sense. But
> someone else has to look at the rest. How to do this?
> We are using Desig and external monitoring, both
> internal and external auditing. All of them have to
> produce information in a uniform workflow and
> available to everyone. We are moving towards getting
> everything organized like this."

⫽ MARCO Antonio Guimarães VERRONE

Master in Business Administration - Universidade de São Paulo (FEA/USP); Graduated in Business Administration - Fundação Getúlio Vargas (EAESP/FGV)
Head of Division - Degef

Verrone joined the BCB in 1998, at Desup, and later, on two occasions, has coordinated the specialized credit risk team. He was also a bank supervisor. He moved to Desig in 2012, where he headed the credit risk macro monitoring team (2012-2016). He has participated in several stages of the evolution of supervision in Brazil. At Degef, he was the manager of the S-UP Program[389]. He currently heads Degef's planning area, responsible for the strategic planning for supervision and monitoring the supervision model.

> "Degef's planning area is responsible for a set of
> attributions, which include managing systems
> of interest of supervision, BI[390], monitoring the
> supervision model, planning, budgeting, training,
> communication and logistic support. Degef's

---

389. Chapter 2 - 2.4 The strategic area: planning supervision.
390. Business Intelligence.

specialized area, on the other hand, operates as the
technical advisory body for supervisors and provides
technical training to them, in addition to interact
with other BCB areas, such as regulation."

⚡ MAURÍCIO dos Santos SOARES

Graduated in Statistics - Universidade de Brasília (UnB)
Head of Division – Information Technology Department (Deinf)

Maurício joined the BCB in 1994, in the information management
area. In 1997, he moved to Deinf, where he participated in important
projects related to banking operations, currency, supervision and
organization of the SFN. Regarding supervision, he has participated in the
construction of important systems, such as the SCR[391], Cosif[392], Limits[393],
SMM[394], APS[395] and SisPLD[396].

"Dealing with the demands of supervision requires
a three timelines strategy, that need to be conducted
simultaneously: we have the 'urgent today'; the
'short-term improvements', which we have to carry
out within a few weeks; and the 'strategic thinking',
which is the next step towards evolution."

⚡ NÉLIO Rodrigues MAGINA Junior

Postgraduated in Business Administration - Pontifícia Universidade
Católica do Rio de Janeiro (PUC-Rio); Graduated in Metallurgical
Engineering - Universidade Federal do Rio de Janeiro (UFRJ)
Head of Division - Degef

---

391. Chapter 3 - 3.1 The Offsite Supervision Implementation.
392. Chapter 4 - 4.1 Trajectory of Information Management at the BCB.
393. Limits System allows for the monitoring of the operational limits required by regulation.
394. Chapter 3 - 3.1 The Offsite Supervision Implementation.
395. APS is the system developed to support onsite supervision activities.
396. SisPLD is the system developed to support the supervision of AML/CFT.

Nélio joined the BCB in 2003, at Desup. He has worked at the specialized market and liquidity risk team from 2013 to 2018 and is recently back in the area. He was also responsible for the implementation of the Supervision Practices Guide[397] (GPS).

> "I was the one who 'baptized' the GPS. Some people commented that in some cases GPS went beyond regulation. Yes, that was it. GPS is 'good practices', it cannot go against regulation, but it can do a lot that is not regulated. It's obvious that when the supervisor issues an inspection letter to the bank, it cannot be capitulate based on the GPS."

↗ **NILO Albino TEZZARI**

Postgraduate in Financial Administration and Graduated in Chemical Engineering, Business Administration and Law - Universidade Federal do Rio Grande do Sul (UFRGS)
Head of Division - Desig

Nilo joined the BCB in 1994, at the Foreign Exchange Department (Decam) and became supervisor in 1999, when foreign exchange supervision activities were incorporated by the supervision area. He has worked at Decif and Decic before the foreign exchange monitoring activities have been incorporated by Desig.

> "Desig, Dereg[398], Decon, Depin[399], Derin[400] and Dstat[401] are the departments that, in one way or another, deal with the foreign exchange issues within the BCB."

---

397. Chapter 2 - 2.7 The transparency of supervisory procedures.
398. Prudential and Foreign Exchange Regulation Department.
399. Department of Foreign Reserves.
400. International Affairs Department.
401. Department of Statistics.

↗ NIZAM de Abreu PFEILSTICKER

Master and Graduated in Statistics - Universidade Federal de Minas Gerais (UFMG)
Analyst - Desig

Nizam joined BCB in 2000, at the Foreign Exchange Department (Decam). He moved to Desig in 2003, where he has always worked on the development of monitoring tools. He was one of the pioneers in the use of machine learning technology at BCB. In his portfolio, the monitoring process using Benford's Law[402] and the SAMOA system[403] stand out.

> "With the natural-language reading tool, we are dealing with a lot of unstructured information. For example, we read the entire RDR[404] database and sort registries by theme. This is important because once a *'modus operandi'* is detected, we can capture all complaints that match the diagnosed problem."

↗ OSVALDO WATANABE

Specialization in Accounting – Universidade de São Paulo (FIPECAP/USP); Graduated in Accounting - Faculdade Alvares Penteado (FACESP); Graduated in Economics - Universidade de São Paulo (USP)
Partner and Responsible for the Financial, Accounting, Control, Strategy and Economic Viability Areas - Grupo Fenestro[405]

A BCB employee from 1974 to 2010, he has always worked in the on-site supervision area. He was head of Desup from 2003 to 2010.

---

402. Chapter 3 - 3.2 Monitoring & Supervision Model – a new perspective for the micro prudential teams.
403. Chapter 7 - 7.2 The use of machine learning techniques in supervision and its challenges.
404. RDR/SISCAP is the Citizen's Demand Registration System. It is through this system that financial institutions become aware of and provide clarification on citizens' complaints and denouncements. See more details at https://www.bcb.gov.br/estabilidadefinanceira/sistemaregistrodemandacidadao.
405. Grupo Fenestro consists of a holding company (Fenestro Participações Ltda) and 4 Restaurants: Fenestro Nações Restaurant, Filetto Burguer & Grill, Madô Restaurant and Janela Restaurant.

He actively participated in the modernization of supervision processes, which culminated in the implementation of the SRC model[406].

> "The court ordered us to investigate all complaints they received, but we didn't have enough people to do that. We began to respond that the complaint would be put in the schedule of the following year. People asked me if I was crazy and if I wanted to go to jail, because court orders were not to be discussed, but accomplished. But we sent them letters to explain our working process, our personnel restrictions, and we always gave them feedback when the scheduled work was completed. Thus, they understood that we were not delaying orders. Besides, during inspections, we tried to solve the root of the problems, which would serve for all other similar cases.Thus, I have never been arrested!"

PAULA Cristina Seixas de OLIVEIRA (Author)

Master in Economics - Universidade de Brasília (UnB); Specialization in Economics [Minerval Program] - George Washington University (EUA); Graduated in Civil Engineering Universidade de Brasília (UnB)
Retired since 2019

Paula joined BCB in 1992, in the foreign exchange area of the Regional Branch in Brasília (Debra). Then, she moved to the banking operations area. With the termination of Debra, she was allocated in Deban[407], where she participated in the project for the implementation of the SPB. She moved to the supervisory area in 1999, where she has worked with off-site/monitoring activities until her retirement in 2019. She has headed the Liquidity and Market Risks Monitoring Division (Dirim) from 2006 to 2012, where she participated in the implementation

406. Chapter 5 - 5.1 The implementation of a supervisory model on a continuous basis.
407. Department of Banking Operations and Payments System.

of liquidity monitoring routines and the SMM[408]. She was responsible for bringing the monitoring of Reserves Accounts to the supervision area. She was a representative of Brazil in the BCBS Working Group on Liquidity (2009-2015). At the Desig's Office, she has acted as senior advisor (2012-2017) and deputy head (2017-2019). From Oct/2020 to Jun/2021, she has worked at CEMLA as Deputy General Director.

> "I feel honored to have participated in important
> projects for the BC and the SFN, as well, such as the
> SPB[409], the SMM and the Basel Project[410]."

⚲ **PAULO Sérgio CAVALHEIRO**

Graduated in Accounting - Pontifícia Universidade Católica de São Paulo (PUC-SP)
Director - Banco Safra

A BCB employee from 1976 to 2007, Paulo has always worked in the supervision area. He was the first head of Desup (1999-2003) and acted as Deputy-Governor for Supervision from 2003 to 2007. He was the Chairman of the Association of Banking Supervisors of the Americas (ASBA) from 2005 to 2007. The implementation of the rating-based supervision methodology[411] started during his tenure at Desup. During his tenure as Deputy-Governor for Supervision, he led the creation of Desuc[412] and the merger of information management and off-site supervision departments to form Desig[413].

> "I proposed to Governor Meirelles the segregation
> of non-banking financial institutions' supervision, in
> order to improve the focus on them."

---

408. Chapter 3 – 3.1 The Offsite Supervision Implementation.
409. The Brazilian Payment System.
410. Basel Project has conducted the implementation of Basel Standards in Brazil.
411. Chapter 5 - 5.1 The implementation of a supervisory model on a continuous basis.
412. Chapter 5 - 5.3 Supervision of non-banking financial institutions.
413. Chapter 4 - 4.1 Trajectory of Information Management at the BCB.

⚡ PAULO Sérgio Neves de SOUZA

Executive MBA in Financial Risk Management - Fundação Instituto de Pesquisas Contábeis, Atuariais e Financeiras (Fipecafi); Graduated in Economics - Pontifícia Universidade Católica de São Paulo (PUC-SP)
Deputy-Governor for Supervision up to July/2023

Paulo joined BCB in 1998, at Defis and has always worked in the supervision area. He was head of Degef and Desup before being named Deputy Governor for supervision in September/2017. He has acted as the Chairman of the Association of Banking Supervisors of the Americas (ASBA) from 2018 to 2022. He has actively participated in the design and implementation of the M&S supervision model[414].

> "We have already contributed to the improvement of the supervision model in other countries, but a set of prerequisites is needed and sometimes the history of those countries does not allow for it. If there is no way to have centralized information, it is useless, as monitoring and off-site analysis would be incomplete."

⚡ REGINA Yassuyo ISHIDA Motomatsu

Graduated in Public Administration - Fundação Getúlio Vargas (EASP/FGV)
Technical Supervision Manager – Desuc

Regina joined the BCB in 1994, at the supervision regional office in São Paulo/SP. She worked with banking and non-banking supervision, such as the implementation of the partnership with the Credit Union Auditor[415], macro and micro prudential monitoring of banking and non-banking institutions, strategic management (training, institutional relationship) and supervision of conduct (customers and users of financial

---

414. Chapter 2 - 2.2 The implementation of the ongoing banking supervisory model in Brazil.
415. Chapter 5 - 5.3 Supervision of non-banking segments.

services). She is currently responsible for credit union auditing and the supervision of a three-tier credit union system[416].

> "I have loved being interviewed by my friend Paula,
> an admirable person, and collaborating with this
> incredible project."

⚡ RICARDO Augusto Matta de ALMEIDA

Postgraduated in International Accounting - Universidade do Espírito Santo (FUCAPE/UFES); Specialization in Financial Markets and Investments - Universidade de Brasília (FACE/UnB); Postgraduated in Accounting and Auditing - Fundação Getúlio Vargas (FGV); Graduated of Economics – Universidade de Brasília (UnB)
Advisor - Executive Secretariat (Secre)

BCB employee since 1992, he was first allocated at the Regional Branch in Brasília (Debra), and then moved to Deban[417] (1995-1997). At Defis, he was an inspector at the regional office in Brasilia until 1998, when he was assigned to participate in the IGC works. He was allocated at Desin when Defis was split and remained in the off-site/monitoring activities until 2017, when he was invited to join the Supervision Board staff (Secre/Difis).

> "Prudential regulation is essential for the SFN, as
> it provokes cultural changes and improvements in
> the institutions' internal controls. The new concepts
> brought by prudential regulation, such as minimum
> capital requirement, capital buffers, and liquidity
> coverage ratio, among others, became key elements
> of the supervisory process."

---

416. A three-tier credit union system comprises the confederation, the centrals and the singular ones. See more details on the structure of credit unions in Chapter 5 - 5.3 Supervision of non-banking segments.
417. Department of Banking Operations and Payments System.

↗ ROBERTO NYGAARD

Master in Finance and Graduated in Civil Engineering - Universidade Federal do Rio Grande do Sul (UFRGS)
Head of Division - Desig

Roberto joined the BCB in 1994 at the Regulation Department (Denor) and moved to Desig in 2011. He has worked in the monitoring of the liquidity and market risks team and has headed the area of economic-financial analysis of banking institutions (2012-2016) before taking over the leadership of the systemic risk monitoring team.

> "Practically all the work we carry out goes to REF and Comef[418]. We have a team responsible for macroeconomic stress tests and sensitivity analyses and another team that develops contagion analysis and analysis of financial flows."

↗ RODRIGO LARA Pinto Coelho

Master in Economics and Graduated in Electrical Engineering - Universidade Federal de Minas Gerais (UFMG)
Head of Policy Benchmarking - FSI, BIS

A BCB employee from 2003 to 2018, Rodrigo worked at Desig from 2005 up to 2015, when he left supervision to lead the Prudential and Foreign Exchange Regulation Department (Dereg). At Desig, he was deputy head and consultant from 2007 to 2015, responsible for leading macro prudential monitoring teams. He left BCB in 2015 to take over at BIS.

> "Comef has become a key process for Desig. We started to look at things that from an individual point of view were not very relevant, but from a financial stability perspective, they were important. It was an almost organic evolution, as the world was also structuring itself for this."

---

418. Financial Stability Report (REF) and Financial Stability Committee (Comef).

↗ ROGÉRIO RABELO Peixoto

MBA in Business Administration - Fundação Getúlio Vargas (FGV); Graduated in Computer Systems Analysis - Pontifícia Universidade Católica de Campinas (PUC-Campinas)
Head of Division – Desig

Rogério joined the BCB in 1998, and has always worked in the credit risk monitoring area. He is responsible for the SCR as a monitoring tool and a credit bureau[419], as well. He has led the credit information management team since 2012 and is responsible for conducting all projects aimed at SCR evolution.

> "During the Covid-19 pandemic, we have added
> to the SCR template an information requirement
> that permits us to assess credit and liquidity risks
> mitigation. We've worked during many weekends for
> that. It was a really cool job!"

↗ SANDRA Lucia de Assis CASTRO

Specialization in Controllership and Graduation in Business Administration - Pontifícia Universidade Católica de Minas Gerais (PUC-Minas)
Deputy Head of Department - Desuc

Sandra joined the BCB in 1998, and the supervision area in 1999. She has worked at Desuc since its creation in 2005, where she is currently deputy-head. She has been responsible for conducting the implementation of open finance in Brazil. She has also participated in a project to disseminate good practices of credit cooperatives from five countries: Brazil, Germany, France, The Netherlands and Canada, which resulted in the publication of the book 'Cooperativism of Credit: Good Practices in Brazil and in the World'[420].

---

419. Chapter 3 - 3.1 The Offsite Supervision Implementation.
420. *'Cooperativismo de Crédito: Boas Práticas no Brasil e no Mundo'* is a result of four years of study and research. (https://www.somoscooperativismo.coop.br/publicacao/2/cooperativismo-de-credito-boas-praticas-no-brasil-e-no-mundo)

"We need to continually improve the non-banking
supervision process to be able to handle the huge
number of institutions."

⚡ SÉRGIO Tostão TAVARES Pereira

Graduated in History and Geography - Centro de Ensino Unificado de
Brasília (UniCEUB); Graduated in Performing Arts - Faculdade de Artes
Dulcina de Moraes
Retired since 2017

A BCB employee from 1974 to 2015, Sérgio started his career in the
Department of Foreign Reserves (Depin). He moved to Desig in 2004, to
work in the management and planning area. He has headed the planning
team and acted as senior advisor for planning and management issues as
well.

"The Value Chain[421] was created to facilitate, organize
and provide transparency to the processes developed
by the BCB. It comprehends all main and supporting
processes, and respective responsible teams, of all
BCB's departments."

⚡ SIDNEI Correa MARQUES

Specialization in Auditing and Finance, and Graduated in Accounting
- Universidade de Brasília (UnB); Graduated in Economics – Centro
Universitário UDF
Audit Committee Coordinator - Banco BTG Pactual

Sidnei was a BCB employee from 1977 to 2019. In the supervision
area, he worked at Desin, Decec, Desig, Desuc, and as the chief of staff
of the Deputy-Governor for Supervision. He has been Deputy-Governor
for Licensing and Resolution from 2011 to 2019. During his tenure as
the head of Desig (from 2009 to 2011), he has started the reorganization

---

421. Chapter 2 - 2.6 Staff Capacitation.

process of monitoring activities, as well as the alignment of information management and supervisory activities.

> "For the well functioning of monitoring activities, we had to work hard on focus. We kicked off Desig's transformation and Lúcio, followed by Gilneu, kept the evolutionary process going on. They did a great job."

↗ SIMONE Lourival ACIOLI

Specialization in International Economics and Finance - Université Dauphine - Paris IX (France); Graduated in Economics - Universidade Federal do Rio de Janeiro (UFRJ)
Business Advisor

Simone was executive director of operations at Cetip[422] until its merger with [B]³ in 2017. She was responsible for Cetip's relationship with financial institutions and regulatory bodies, settlement accounts, trading platforms, registration, custody and monitoring. She has actively participated in the construction of procedures for the provision of information registered at FMIs[423] to the BCB.

> "There was an excellent partnership between BCB and Cetip teams. Our meetings were always held in a very cordial atmosphere."

↗ TEREZA Cristina GROSSI Togni

Graduated in Accounting and Business Administration - Pontifícia Universidade Católica de Minas Gerais (PUC-Minas)
Audit Committee Chair – Itausa; Audit and Risk Management Committee Coordinator - C&A Modal; Director and Audit Committee Chair - Dlocal

---

422. *Central de Custódia e Liquidação Financeira de Títulos Privados* (Cetip) was a private entity for asset registration, trading and settlement services created in 1984.
423. Financial Market Infrastructures.

A BCB employee from 1984 to 2003, Tereza has always worked in the supervision area. She was Deputy-Governor for Supervision from 2000 to 2003. She was responsible for bringing the Toronto Centre training to Brazil[424], for bringing the REF ellaboration to the supervision area[425] and for carrying out, in 1999, the supervision split into on-site and off-site[426].

> "Supervisors were lacking in exercising their power within the law. Inspection letters were not effective. Someone needed to sit down with the bank director and clearly say that the Central Bank did not accept certain things. This was shown during the Toronto Centre training: how to exercise supervisory power within what the law allows the supervisor to do."

⚡ THEO COTRIM Martins

Master in Economics - Pontifícia Universidade Católica do Rio de Janeiro (PUC-Rio); Graduated in Electrical Engineering - Universidade de Campinas (Unicamp)
PhD candidate in Finance - Universidade of São Paulo (USP)

Theo joined the BCB in 2010, in the Department of Banking Operations and Payment System (Deban). He moved to the supervision area in 2013, more specifically to the credit risk monitoring team. He was head of the team responsible for the macro prudential credit risk monitoring approach from 2016 to 2018.

> "Broadly, we may be called the 'big data of credit risk'. What do we do? We try to extract all information regarding the Brazilian credit market from all available granular data sources, not only from the SCR."

---

424. Chapter 1 - 1.5 First steps towards the Supervisory Model modernization.
425. Chapter 2 - 2.3 Micro-grounded macro monitoring process.
426. Chapter 1 - 1.7 Onsite and offsite supervision.

↗ VÂNIO Cesar Pickler AGUIAR

Graduated in Business Administration and Accounting - Fundação de Estudos Sociais do Paraná

Founding Partner - ADJUD Administradores Judiciais Ltda; Bankruptcy Trustee - Banco Santos S.A.

A BCB employee from 1984 to 2004, Aguiar has always worked in the supervision area. He was one of the creators of the IGC model[427] and the first head of Desin, as well. In the bankruptcy of Banco Santos in 2004, he was appointed as intervener by the BCB, later becoming its trustee.

> "Planning an IGC consisted of several steps. First, we had a meeting to define our target and to decide which banks would be supervised. This planning meeting was very important, as it brought in the experience of supervisors and division heads, where the target of supervision would be defined. The second step consisted of estimating the number of inspectors, coordinators and supervisors for the task. Third step: who was qualified to do the job? And then we had to search for the appropriate skills for each activity. And so on…Planning an IGC was a really complex task."

---

427. Chapter 1 - 1.4 Consolidated Global Inspection - the X-ray of the financial institution.

Appendix

This appendix was elaborated to help readers not familiar with the Brazilian financial system or the BCB Framework. It reunites some general information about the National Financial System composition, its main participants, and respective roles. It also comprehends information on the BCB organization framework, the scope of financial entities under its umbrella and some basic explanations on the supervision infrastructure and responsibilities. Most of the information presented in this appendix was extracted from the BCB website (www.bcb.org.br).

1. THE BRAZILIAN NATIONAL FINANCIAL SYSTEM FRAMEWORK

The Brazilian National Financial System (SFN) is structured in three functions: regulatory, supervisory, and operational. Regulatory entities set the policies and general rules for the proper functioning of the part of the SFN under their scope. The supervisory entities work to ensure that the operators follow the regulatory bodies' rules and may issue subsidiary regulation. The SFN's operators are intermediary institutions that provide financial services to the public and auxiliary institutions that provide services required for the SFN's activities.

The SFN's three regulatory boards are: the National Monetary Council (CMN), the National Council of Private Insurance (CNSP) and the National Council of Complementary Pension (CNPC).

The National Monetary Council (CMN) is the highest normative authority of the National Financial System (SFN). Its objective is to promote the economic and social progress of the country by setting the guidelines of monetary, credit, and exchange rate policies.

As the coordination body for the macroeconomic policies of the federal government, the CMN sets the inflation target, the guidelines for the exchange rate policy, the policy to be observed in the organization and functioning of the securities market, and the overarching regulation for the financial activities under its scope.

Two financial regulatory and supervisory authorities are linked to the CMN: the Banco Central do Brasil (BCB) and the Comissão de Valores Mobiliários (CVM), the Brazilian securities commission. The BCB must ensure the compliance with the CMN regulation, by conducting the monetary, credit and exchange rate policies, and monitoring and supervising financial institutions under its jurisdiction.

Figure: SFN Regulatory and Supervisory Framework

	Money, credit, capital and foreign exchange markets			Private insurance industry	Closed pension funds industry
Normative Boards	**CMN** National Monetary Council			**CNSP** National Council of Insurance	**CNPC** National Council for Complementary Social Security
Supervisory entities	**BCB** Banco Central do Brasil	**CVM** 'Brazilian Securities Commission'		**Susep** 'Superintendence of Private Insurance'	**Previc** 'National Superintendency of Complementary Social
Financial Operators	Banks and Saving Company	Consortium Managers	Stock exchange	Insurance and Reinsurance	Closed pension funds entities
	Credit Unions	Brokers and Dealers	Commodities and Futures Exchanges	Open private pension funds	
	Payment institution**	Non-banking financial institutions		Capitalization companies	

* There may be shared regulatory competence with the CVM, depending on its activities.

** The payment institutions are not within the SFN, but are regulated and supervised by the CMN and the Banco Central do Brasil.

Source:Banco Central do Brasil -https://www.bcb.gov.br/en/financialstability/nationalfinancialsystem

2. BCB ORGANIZATIONAL FRAMEWORK

BCB's governing body is composed by the BCB Governor and 8 Deputy-Governors (see Figure BCB Organizational Chart). All Board members are appointed by the President of the Republic after their approval by the Federal Senate, pursuant to the Federal Constitution. BCB Board is in charge of formulating public policies under the BCB's legal jurisdiction, as well as the BCB's executive management. Moreover, the BCB's three decision-making committees are composed of all 9 Board members: the Monetary Policy Committee (Copom), the Financial Stability Committee (Comef), and the Governance, Risks and Controls Committee (GRC).

Figure: BCB Organizational Chart

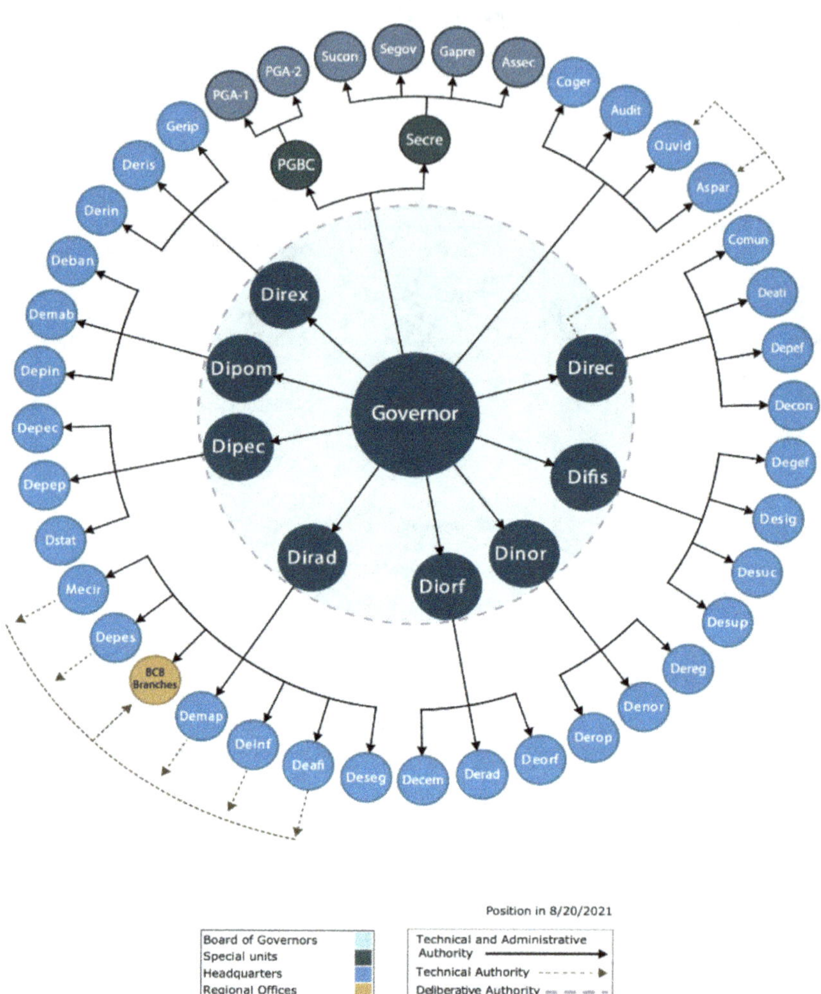

Board of Governors
Governor
Deputy Governors

Governor
Aspar – Congressional Affairs Office
Audit – Internal Auditing
Coger – Department of Professional Conduct
Ouvid – Office of the Ombudsman
PGBC – Office of the General Counsel
PGA-1 – Vice General Counsel's Office - Consulting
PGA-2 – Vice General Counsel's Office - Litigation and Management
Secre – Executive Secretariat
Assec – Office of Economic Advisors
Gapre – Governor's Office
Segov – Secretariat of Governance, Articulation and Strategic Monitoring
Sucon – Secretariat to the Board of Directors and National Monetary
Council Affairs

Dirad – Deputy Governor for Administration
Deafi – Accounting, Budget and Financial Department
Deinf – Information Technology Department
Demap – Department of Infrastructure
Depes – People, Education, Health and Organization
Management Department
Deseg – Security Department
Mecir – Currency Management Department

Regional Offices under the Deputy Governor for Administration
ADBEL – Regional Office in Belém – PA
ADBHO – Regional Office in Belo Horizonte – MG
ADCUR – Regional Office in Curitiba – PR
ADFOR – Regional Office in Fortaleza – CE
ADPAL – Regional Office in Porto Alegre – RS
ADREC – Regional Office in Recife – PE
ADRJA – Regional Office in Rio de Janeiro – RJ
ADSAL – Regional Office in Salvador – BA
ADSPA – Regional Office in São Paulo – SP

Direc – Deputy Governor for Institutional Relations, Citizenship
and Conduct Supervision
Comun – Communication Department
Deati – Department of Citizen Affairs
Decon – Department of Conduct Supervision
Depef – Department for Financial Citizenship Promotion

Direx – Deputy Governor for International Affairs and Corporate
Risk Management
Derin – International Affairs Department
Deris – Corporate Risk and Benchmarks Department
Gerip – International Portfolio Investors Unit

Difis – Deputy Governor for Supervision
Degef – Strategic Management and Specialized Supervision Departmer
Desig – Financial System Monitoring Department
Desuc – Credit Unions and Non-banking Financial Institutions
Supervision Department
Desup – Banking Supervision Department

Diorf – Deputy Governor for Licensing and Resolution
Decem – Department of Competition and Financial Market Structure
Deorf – Financial System Organization Department
Derad – Department of Resolution and Sanctioning Action

Dipec – Deputy Governor for Economic Policy
Depec – Department of Economics
Depep – Research Department
DSTAT – Department of Statistics

Dipom – Deputy Governor for Monetary Policy
Deban – Department of Banking Operations and Payments System
Demab – Open Market Operations Department
Depin – Department of Foreign Reserves

Dinor – Deputy Governor for Regulation
Denor – Financial System Regulation Department
Dereg – Prudential and Foreign Exchange Regulation Department
Derop – Department of Regulation, Supervision and Control of
Farm Credit Operations and Proagro

Source:Banco Central do Brasil - https://www.bcb.gov.br/en/about/orgchart

3. BCB SUPERVISION FRAMEWORK

The BCB is responsible for assuring the soundness and efficiency of the SFN, pursuant to its institutional mission. According to the CMN guidelines, the BCB regulates and supervises financial institutions and other entities licensed by it (Supervised Entities - SEs), by monitoring their capitalization, regulatory compliance and their conduct towards the financial consumers and users.

The supervisory review process is underpinned at the assessment of risks and controls, which is enrolled as an integrated and continuous process that can be broken down into two main macro processes: monitoring and supervision. Monitoring aims at identifying threats both to SFN's stability, from a macro prudential perspective, and to individual financial institutions, from a micro prudential perspective, as well as the compliance to operational and prudential limits. The Financial System Monitoring Department (Desig) is responsible for conducting macro and micro prudential monitoring activities. Supervisory activities are currently segregated into two main sectors: banking institutions, conducted by the Banking Supervision Department (Desup), and credit unions and non-banking institutions, conducted by the Credit Unions and Non-Banking Financial Institutions Supervision Department (Desuc).

Micro prudential monitoring is responsible for assessing several issues such as credit and liquidity risks in the banks' balance sheets, as well as their resilience and solvency positions. It also monitors recent developments in the financial markets, e.g. capital, monetary and derivatives markets.

Macro prudential monitoring processes encompass the assessment of vulnerabilities to financial stability; risks arising outside the BCB jurisdiction, which emerge from investment funds, insurance companies and pension funds; and systemic risk assessment, through stress testing, sensitivity, and contagion analysis.

The supervisory function is organized into a "twin peaks" model: prudential and conduct. Prudential supervision focuses on solvency, liquidity, business model analysis and viability of each supervised entity in the Financial System. Considering institutions have different sizes and complexity, the prudential supervision is adjusted to fit relevance, thus allowing proportional treatment by segmenting the SEs. Supervisory efforts are expended accordingly to size, international presence, and risk profile. Conduct supervision is performed by the Department of Conduct Supervision (Decon) and focuses on client and consumer protection issues, as well as Anti-Money Laundering and Counter-Terrorism Financing (AML/CFT) activities.

Decon was initially allocated under the Supervision Board umbrella. When BCB incorporated the responsibility of ensuring a competitive financial system in its institutional mission in 2019, it was transferred to the area created to deal with issues related to competitiveness[428]. The hierarchical segregation of the supervision

---

428. Since 2019, Decon is subordinated to the Deputy Governor for Institutional Rela-

area came to reinforce its independence and alignment with the 'Twin Peaks' model. Operationally, however, its work processes continue to maintain a strong link with the supervision area, especially monitoring, where the warnings received are essential inputs for the supervision of AML/CFT issues.

Supervision infrastructure also comprehends the Strategic Management and Specialized Supervision Department, responsible for the strategic management and planning of the supervision area.

Figure: Composition of the Board of Supervision

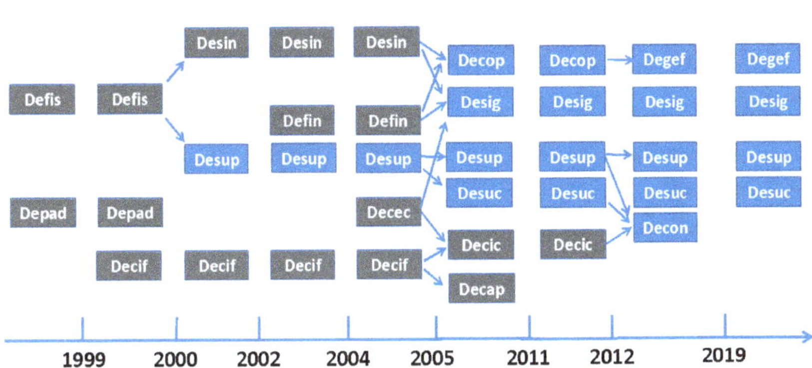

Current Departments:

Decon – Department of Conduct Supervision

Degef – Strategic Management and Specialized Supervision Department

Desig – Financial System Monitoring Department

Desuc – Credit Unions and Non-Banking Financial Institutions Supervision Department

Desup – Banking Supervision Department

Former Departments:

Decap – Department of Control and Analysis of Punitive Administrative Proceedings

Decec – Department of Foreign Capital and Foreign Exchange

---

tions, Citizenship and Conduct Supervision (Direc).

Decic – Department for Preventing Illicit Financial Activities and Responding to Demands for Information from the Financial System

Decif – Department for Combating Foreign Exchange and Financial Illicits

Decop – Department of Supervision Management and Planning

Defin – Financial System Information Management Department

Defis – Supervision Department

Depad – Department of Control of Administrative Proceedings and Special Regimes

Desin – Off-site Supervision Department

Source:Banco Central do Brasil

Figure: BCB Authorized Entities by Type

Type	Abbr.	2013 Dec	2014 Dec	2015 Dec	2016 Dec	2017 Dec	2018 Dec	2019 Dec	2020 Dec	2021 Dec	2022 Dec
Multiple Bank	BM	132	130	132	133	132	131	132	137	137	137
Commercial Bank[1]/	BC	23	22	21	21	21	20	20	20	20	19
Development Bank	BD	4	4	4	4	4	4	4	4	4	4
Savings Banks (State/Federal)	CE	1	1	1	1	1	1	1	1	1	1
Investment Bank	BI	14	14	13	14	13	12	11	10	10	10
Exchange Bank	B Camb	3	3	3	3	3	4	5	5	5	5
Consumer Finance Company	CFI	58	55	53	53	56	58	59	60	61	64
Platform Lending Company	SCD						1	11	41	64	98
Peer-to-peer Lending Company	SEP							4	9	10	11
Security Brokerage Company	CTVM	93	92	87	79	75	68	67	64	66	62
Exchange Brokerage Company	CC	62	66	63	63	61	63	55	53	54	55
Security Distribution Company	DTVM	116	108	102	101	95	94	94	96	99	102
Leasing Company	SAM	29	27	27	25	24	21	21	19	18	18
Real Estate Credit Company2/ and Savings and Loan Association	SCI e APE	11	9	8	4	3	3	3	3	2	2
Micro-financing Institution	SCM	38	40	40	38	38	36	33	31	30	26
Development Agency	AG FOM	16	16	16	16	16	16	16	16	16	16
Mortgage Company	CH	8	7	8	9	7	6	6	6	5	6
Payment Institution	IP				1	6	10	19	26	37	74
subtotal		**608**	**594**	**578**	**565**	**555**	**548**	**561**	**601**	**639**	**710**
Credit Union	COOP	1209	1163	1113	1078	1023	973	920	886	860	834
subtotal		**1817**	**1757**	**1691**	**1643**	**1578**	**1521**	**1481**	**1487**	**1499**	**1544**
Consortium Manager	CONS	199	186	172	166	156	152	148	144	142	141
Total		**2016**	**1943**	**1863**	**1809**	**1734**	**1673**	**1629**	**1631**	**1641**	**1685**

Source: Unicad

1/ It includes Foreign Banks Full Branches.
2/ It includes Societies of Home Loans that cannot raise funds from the public.

Source: Banco Central do Brasil - https://www.bcb.gov.br/content/statistics/annualreportsnfs/nfs202212-T1ES_Chart%2001%20-%20Quantity%20of%20authorized%20institutions%20by%20type.pdf

Figure: Geographic Distribution of Authorized Entities by Type

Position: 12.31.2022

State/Region		BM	BC	BD	CE	BI	B Camb	CFI	SCD	SEP	CTVM	CC	DTVM	SAM	SCI e APE	SCM	AG FOM	CH	COOP	CONS	IP	Total
Alagoas	AL															1	1		5			7
Bahia	BA	2							3		1	2					1		20	1		30
Ceará	CE	1							3			1				2			3	1	1	12
Maranhão	MA																		6			6
Paraíba	PB																		12	1		13
Pernambuco	PE								2		1	2				1	1		6			13
Piauí	PI							1									1		1		1	4
Rio Grande do Norte	RN											1					1		3	2		7
Sergipe	SE	1							1										1	1		4
Northeast Region		4						1	9		2	6				4	5		57	6	2	96
Acre	AC																		2			2
Amapá	AP																1					1
Amazonas	AM											1					1		2			4
Pará	PA	1	1						1			1				1			8	1		14
Rondônia	RO																		17		1	18
Roraima	RR		1														1		1			3
Tocantins	TO																1		1			2
North Region		1	2						1			2				1	4		31	1	1	44
Distrito Federal	DF	3			1			1	2	2			2	1	1				12	8		33
Goiás	GO								4				1				1		34	2		42
Mato Grosso	MT							1					1				1		18	1	1	23
Mato Grosso do Sul	MS								2							1			9		1	13
Midwest Region		3			1			2	8	2			4	1	1	1	2		73	11	2	111
Espírito Santo	ES	1		1				2					1						25	2		32
Minas Gerais	MG	7		1		1		4	10	1	6		3			3		1	170	12	7	226
Rio de Janeiro	RJ	9	3	1		1		2	4		9	5	19			2	1	1	40	5	3	105
São Paulo	SP	96	13			8	4	27	47	7	40	28	70	17		8	1	2	175	63	54	660
Southeast Region		113	16	3		10	4	35	61	8	55	33	93	17		13	2	4	410	82	64	1023
Paraná	PR	9	1				1	3	4			5	4			5	1	1	73	12	2	121
Rio Grande do Sul	RS	7		1				18	10	1	4	7			1	1	1	1	93	18	1	164
Santa Catarina	SC							5	5		1	2	1			1	1		97	11	2	126
South Region		16	1	1			1	26	19	1	5	14	5		1	7	3	2	263	41	5	411
Overall total		137	19	4	1	10	5	64	98	11	62	55	102	18	2	26	16	6	834	141	74	1685

Source:Banco Central do Brasil - https://www.bcb.gov.br/content/statistics/annualreportsnfs/nfs202212-T1ES_
Chart%2002%20-%20Quantity%20of%20authorized%20institutions%20by%20type%20and%20state.pdf

4. BCB'S ROLE TO ENSURE FINANCIAL STABILITY

The BCB is legally in charge of fostering a sound, efficient and competitive financial system. To accomplish the mission related to financial stability, the BCB regulates and supervises financial institutions. Additionally, the BCB represents Brazil at the Basel Committee on Banking Supervision (BCBS) and the Financial Stability Board (FSB).

As a full member of those fora since 2009, the BCB implements domestically the regulatory standards set by them. Brazilian prudential regulation (capital framework, liquidity indicators and large exposures limits) is deemed compliant with the Basel Committee's global standards and has received the highest of the four possible assessment grades. The BCB also engages in financial stability policy debates under the periodic rounds of the IMF's Financial Sector Assessment Program (FSAP).

The BCB's financial stability policy is defined by its Board of Governors. The related functions are performed on an on-going basis and more focused when the Board meets as the Financial Stability Committee (Comef) on a quarterly basis. Comef is responsible for defining strategies, guidelines, macro prudential measures[429] and instruments to preserve financial stability and mitigate systemic risk. It is composed by all 9 members of the BCB Board[430]. Communication of financial stability issues is regularly released through the BCB's semi-annual Financial Stability Reports (REF), as well as by the Communiqués and Minutes of the Comef's meetings[431].

The Deputy-Governor for Supervision is responsible for coordinating the organization of Comef meetings and REF's

---

429. Quarterly, Comef defines the level of the countercyclical capital buffer (CCyB).

430. The heads of departments with financial stability functions-related may attend the Comef's quarterly meetings, but with no voting right.

431. All decisions involving the CCYB (ACCPBrasil) are disclosed immediately after the Comef meetings. Moreover, the Comef's vision on the policy and measures to preserve financial stability is disclosed in the BCB's Financial Stability Report (REF), among other contents.

elaboration, as well. Operationally, the Financial System Monitoring Department is in charge of conducting REF's elaboration. The department must also present at each Comef meeting an overview of the SFN, the assessment of risks to financial stability and a prospective evaluation of credit.

Glossary

ABBC	Brazilian Association of Banks	Associação Brasileira de Bancos
ACC	Ongoing Conduct Monitoring	Acompanhamento Contínuo de Conduta
ACL Analytics	Audit Command Language Analytics	
ACT	Technical Cooperation Agreements	Acordos de Cooperação Técnica
ADAM	Machine Learning Sampling Selection	Amostragem Determinada por Aprendizado de Máquina
ADM	Administrative Organization Manual	Manual de Organização Administrativa
AI	Artificial Intelligence	
ALM	Assets and Liabilities Management	
AML	Anti-Money Laundry	
ANEF	Economic-Financial Assessment	Análise Econômico-Financeira
APE	Savings and Loans Association	Associação de Poupança e Empréstimos
APS	Automation of Supervision Processes	Automação dos Processos de Supervisão
ARC	Assessment of Risks and Controls	Avaliação dos Riscos e Controles
ASBA	Association of Banking Supervisors of the Americas	
[B]³	[Brazilian trade, settlement, and custody entity – securities, derivatives, stocks and FX markets]	Brasil, Bolsa, Balcão
Bafin	Bundesanstalt für Finanzdienstleistungsaufsicht	
BB	[Brazilian commercial bank]	Banco do Brasil

BCB	Central Bank of Brazil	Banco Central do Brasil
BCBS	Basel Committee for Banking Supervision	
BHC	Bank Holding Company	
BI	Business Intelligence	
BIS	Bank for International Settlement	
BM&F or BM&F-Bovespa	[former Brazilian trade, settlement, and custody entity - derivatives and FX markets]	Bolsa de Mercadorias e Futuros
BNCC	Credit Union National Bank	Banco Nacional de Crédito Cooperativo S.A.
C3	[Brazilian registry entity - securitization market]	C3 Registradora
CAMELS	Capital, Assets, Management, Earnings and Liquidity	
CBLC	[former Brazilian trade, settlement, and custody entity - stocks market]	Companhia Brasileira de Liquidação e Custódia
CCP	Central Counterparty	
CCyB	Countercyclical Capital Buffer	
CEMLA	Center for Latin America Monetary Studies	
CETIP	[former Brazilian trade, settlement, and custody entity - private securities market]	Central de Custódia e Liquidação de Títulos Privados
CFM	Capital Flow Measures	Capital Flow Measures
CFT	Combat for the Financing of Terrorism	
CGI	Information Governance Committee	Comitê de Governança da Informação
CGU	Comptroller General of the Union	Controladoria Geral da União
CH	Mortgage Company	Companhia Hipotecária
Cinsp	Training Course for Inspector	Curso de Formação de Inspetores
CIP	Interbank Payments Chamber	Câmara Interbancária de Pagamentos
CMN	National Monetary Council	Conselho Monetário Nacional
CNPC	National Council for Complementary Social Security	Conselho Nacional de Previdência Complementar
CNSP	National Council of Insurance	Conselho Nacional de Seguros Privados
Comef	Financial Stability Committee	Comitê de Estabolidade Financeira
COMPE	Clearing System for Checks and Other Bills	Sistema de Compensação de Cheques e Outros Papéis

Copad	Administrative Proceeding Committee	Comitê de Processo Administrativo
Copom	Monetary Policy Committee	Comitê de Política Monetária
Corec	Risk and Control Assessment Committee	Comitê de Avaliação de Riscos e Controles
Cosif	Standard Financial Statements Report	Plano Contábil das Instituições do Sistema Financeiro Nacional
CPI	Inquiry Parliament Commission	Comissão Parlamentar de Inquérito
Cr\$	[former Brazilian currency]	Cruzeiro
CR\$	[former Brazilian currency]	Cruzeiro Real
CRC	Credit Risk Center	Central de Risco de Crédito
CRD	System for the Control of Documents' Delivery	Controle de Remessa de Documentos
CSD	Central Securities Depository	
CTVM	Securities Broker	Corretora de Titulos e Valores Mobiliários
CVM	Securities and Exchange Commission	Comissão de Valores Mobiliários
Cz\$	[former Brazilian currency]	Cruzado
Decad	Department of Registry and Information	Departamento de Cadastro e Informações
Defis	Supervision Department	Departamento de Fiscalização
Depep	Research Department	Departamento de Pesquisa Econômica
Desin	Offsite Supervision Department	Departamento de Supervisão Indireta
Desuc	Credit Unions and Non-Banking Financial Institutions Supervision Department	Departamento de Supervisão de Cooperativas e de Instituições Não Bancárias
Difis	Supervisory Board	Diretoria de Supervisão
DNB	De Nederlandsche Bank	
DPGE	Time Deposit with Special Guarantee	Depósitos a Prazo com Garantia Especial
DRL	Report on Liquidity Risk Management	Demonstrativo de Risco de Liquidez
DRM	Report on Market Risk Management	Demonstrativo de Risco de Mercado
DTVM	Securities Dealer	Distribuidora de Titulos e Valores Mobiliários
EGI	Information Governance Office	Escritório de Governança da Informação
ES	Supervised Entity	Entidade Supervisionada

FATF-GAFI	Financial Action Task Force	
FED	Federal Reserve	
FGC	[Brazilian deposit insurance company]	Fundo Garantidor de Crédito
FFIEC	Federal Financial Institutions Examination Council	
FI	Financial Institution	
FinTech	Financial Technology	
FMI	Financial Market Infrastructure	
FSAP	Financial Sector Assessment Program	
FSB	Financial Stability Board	
FSI	Financial Sector Indicator	
FX	Foreign Exchange	
Gedoc	System for Reported Documents' Management	Sistema de Gestão de Documentos
GDP	Gross Domestic Product	
GFC	Great Financial Crisis	
GPS	Supervision Practices Guide	Guia de Práticas da Supervisão
I2M	Integration of Monitoring Information	Integração das Informações de Monitoramento
ICAAP	Internal Capital Adequacy Assessment Process	
IF.Data	Financial Institutions' Data	
IGC	Consolidated Global Inspection	Inspeção Geral Consolidada
IL	Liquidity Ratio	Índice de Liquidez
ILAAP	Internal Liquidity Adequacy Assessment Process	
IMF	International Monetary Fund	
Indcon	Accounting Indicators System	Sistema de Indicadores Contábeis
INSS	National Social Security Institute	Instituto Nacional de Seguro Social
IP	Payment Institution	Instituição de Pagamento
IREE	Institute for the Reform of State-Business Relations	Instituto para a Reforma das Relações entre Estado e Empresa
IT	Information Technology	
KSA	Knowledge, Skills, and Abilities	
LAI	Law on Access to Public Information	Lei de Acesso à Informação

LC	Complementary Law	Lei Complementar
LCR	Liquidity Coverage Ratio	
LFG	Guaranteed Financial Letter	Letra Financeira Garantida
LGD	Loss Given Default	
LIA	Analytical Intelligence Laboratory	Laboratório de inteligência Analítica
LIQ	[BCBS] Liquidity Group	
LTEL	Special Temporary Liquidity Facility	Linha Temporária Especial de Liquidez
M&S	Monitoring and Supervision	Monitoramento e Supervisão
MDIC	Ministry of Development, Industry, Foreign Trade and Services	Ministério do Desenvolvimento, Indústria, Comércio Exterior e Serviços
MEF	Financial Stability Map	Mapa de Estabilidade Financeira
MLAS	Machine Learning as a Service	
MPR	Routines and Procedures Manual	Manual de Procedimentos e Rotinas
MSU	Supervision Manual	Manual da Supervisão
NBFI	Non-Bank Financial Intermediary	
NCz$	[former Brazilian currency]	Cruzado Novo
NGFS	Network for Greening the Financial System	
NLP	Natural Language Processing	
NPL	Non-Performing Loan	
NSFR	Net Sable Funding Ratio	
OCC	Office of the Comptroller of the Currency	
OTC	Over the Counter	
PA	Administrative Proceeding	Processo Administrativo
PAS	Supervision Annual Program	Programa Anual de Supervisão
PD	Probability of Default	
PF	Natural Person	Pessoa Física
PGI	Information Governance Policy	Política de Governaça da Informação
PIER	Integrated Platform of Regulatory Entities	Plataforma Integradora de Entidades Reguladoras
PJ	Legal Entity	Pessoa Jurídica

PPC	Permanent Training Program	Programa Permanente de Capacitação
PRE	Required Reference Equity	Patrimônio de Referência Exigido
Previc	National Superintendency of Complementary Social Security	Superintendência Nacional de Previdência
PROER	Program to Stimulate the Restructuring and Strengthening of the National Financial System	Programa de Estímulo à Reestruturação e ao Fortalecimento do Sistema Financeiro Nacional
PROES	Incentive Program for the Reduction of Public Sector in Financial Activities	Programa de Incentivo à Redução da Presença do Setor Público na Atividade Financeira
PSF	Semiannual Inspection Program	Programa Semestral de Fiscalização
Q&A	Questions and Answers	
R$	[current Brazilian currency]	Real
RAIS	Social Information Annual Report	Relação Anual de Informações Sociais
REB	Banking Economy Report	Relatório de Economia Bancária
REBC	Banking Economy and Credit Report	Relatório de Economia Bancária e Crédito
REF	Financial Stability Report	Relatório de Estabilidade Financeira
RTEC	Interdepartmental Technical Networks	Rede Técnica Interdepartamental
SAM	Leasing Company	Sociedade de Arrendamento Mercantil
SAMOA	System for the Automatic Monitoring of Atypical Operations	Sistema Automático de Monitoramento de Operações Atípicas
SCAV	[FSB] Standing Committee on Assessment of Vulnerabilities	
SCD	Direct Credit Company	Sociedade de Crédito Direto
SCFI	Credit, Finance and Investment Companies	Sociedade de Crédito, Financiamento e Investimento
SCIG	System for the Monitoring of Costs and Management Information	Sistema de Custos e Informações Gerenciais
SCR	Credit Information System	Sistema de Informações de Crédito
SELIC	[Brazilian trade, settlement, and custody entity - government securities market]	Sistema Especial de Liquidação e de Custódia
SEP	Peer-to-Peer Loan Company	Sociedade de Empréstimo entre Pessoas
SFN	National Financial System	Sistema Financeiro Nacional

SGM	System for the Automatic Collection of Fines	Sistema Geral de Multas
SIM	Integrated Monitoring System	Sistema Integrado de Monitoramento
SISCAP	Capacitation Management System	Sistema de Gestão da Capacitação
SisCom	Integrated System for Supervision Support and Communication	Sistema Integrado de Suporte e Comunicação da Supervisão
SM	Monitored Issue	Situação Monitorada
SMM	System for the Monitoring of Liquidity and Market Risks	Sistema de Monitoramento de Mercado
SMQ	Monitored Quality Issues	Situação Monitorada de Qualidade
SPB	Brazilian Payment System	Sistema de Pagamentos Brasileiro
SQL	Structured Query Language	
SRC	System for the Assessment of Risks and Controls	Sistema de Avaliação de Riscos e Controles
Sumoc	Superintendence of Currency and Credit	Superintendência da Moeda e do Crédito
SupTech	Supervisory Technology	
Susep	Superintendence of Private Insurance	Superintendência de Seguros Privados
TCU	Federal Court of Auditors	Tribunal de Contas da União
TPF	Federal Government Securities	Títulos Públicos Federais
TR	Trade Repository	
UBPR	Uniform Bank Performance Report	
UNESCO	United Nations Educational, Scientific and Cultural Organization	
Unicad	Information on Entities of Interest of the BCB	Informações sobre Entidades de Interesse do Banco Central